LONG-TERM CARE FOR OLDER PEOPLE

LAW AND FINANCIAL PLANNING

LONG-TERM CARE
FOR OLDER PEOPLE
LAW AND FINANCIAL PLANNING

Margaret Richards

J O R D A N S
2001

Published by
Jordan Publishing Limited
21 St Thomas Street
Bristol BS1 6JS

British Library Cataloguing-in-Publication Data
A catalogue record for this book is available from the British Library.

ISBN 0 85308 571 4

Typeset by Mendip Communications Ltd, Frome, Somerset
Printed in Great Britain by MPG Books Ltd, Bodmin, Cornwall

PREFACE

Much has happened since *Community Care for Older People* was published in 1996. At that time 'community care' was a ubiquitous term which encapsulated the policy objectives of the White Paper on Community Care, published in 1989 and translated into law by Part III of the National Health Service and Community Care Act 1990. Many people never really understood how residential and 'community' care could be talked about in the same breath, and the epithet 'long-term', which is associated with the work of the Royal Commission during 1998 and 1999, seems better to reflect the fact that some older people continue to receive care at the end of their lives in a residential setting. Hence the new title to this second edition.

As far as the law is concerned, what was a relatively blank canvas in 1996 has been filled in by new legislation, case-law and guidance. The legal structure that I identified in 1996 is still in place, but there is more detail to consider, and the legal literature is more extensive than it was then. Recent legal monographs are listed in the bibliography, along with all the other sources of information that I have drawn on this time round.

Since 1996, legal practitioners have become aware of both the importance and the complexity of this field of practice. A new interest group, Solicitors for the Elderly, was set up a few years ago to encourage practice development and the share of skills and information between older client practitioners. Later this spring, Jordans will be launching a new journal, *Elder Law and Finance*, which will identify and address the know-how needs of practitioners in this and related areas. This book is intended to be a source of reference for all lawyers and others who advise older people, their relatives and carers. It attempts to provide an understanding of the policy framework around long-term care as well as an analysis of the legal rules themselves.

In many respects, this is much more than a second edition of an earlier work. The language has changed, policy has moved on, and a different perspective is required. I have elected to focus on financial issues, providing a detailed and, I hope, practical analysis of the public financing of long-term care. My own experience, gained from the cases which are referred to me, demonstrates that there is a particular need amongst practitioners, carers and older people themselves for accurate and intelligible information about funding, linked with the rights of the individual, and that the Royal Commission's criticisms of the complexity of the law and the funding process were well made. I have paid less attention to service provision, which is now well covered elsewhere, and have omitted previous chapters on housing and remedies for the same reason. At the time of writing, there is considerable speculation about, but little hard evidence of, the impact of the Human Rights Act 1998 on social care provision for older people. I have made reference in the text to possible human rights issues, where relevant. I do anticipate that the absence of a substantive right of appeal against local authority financial decisions will, sooner or later, provoke a challenge under Art 6 of the European Convention.

In recent weeks, there has been press comment about the effects of devolution on health and social care in different parts of the UK. A gap has already opened up between England and Scotland in relation to long-term care funding, and the parliamentary debates on the Health and Social Care Bill suggest that Wales too may adopt different policies on this issue. The legislation analysed in this book is that which applies in England and Wales. Scottish law is the same in some respects, and different in others. Given the developments referred to above, I have not specifically considered law, guidance or policy which relate specifically to Scotland or Wales. Diversity will increase complexity and, at present, I am confident only in my understanding of English law and practice.

This book sets out the law as at the end of February 2001. I have also tried to incorporate some details of the Health and Social Care Bill 2000, which presents the Government's response to the Report of the Royal Commission on Long Term Care. The raising of the capital thresholds for public funding of residential care to £18,500 and £11,500 was announced very late, although it takes effect from April 2001, and I have added references to this change at final proof stage. The calculations used throughout the book to demonstrate and exemplify the rules explained in the text are based on 2000/2001 benefit rates. Appendix 3 contains details of the 2001 updating.

As ever, I would like to thank Jordans, and my editor, Martin West, for their support and their patience with my slow progress in writing and my inability to meet deadlines. I would also like to acknowledge once again my personal debt to St Anne's Shelter and Housing Action in Leeds, a provider of long-term care for many vulnerable people, my association with which has been a source of insight and inspiration. Final thanks are due to my husband, John, for his loving support and encouragement.

I dedicate this book to my mother, who received long-term care at the end of her life, and who was loved by all who knew her.

The opinions expressed, errors and omissions in this book are mine alone.

Margaret Richards
Leeds
February 2001

ABOUT THE AUTHOR

Margaret Richards is a solicitor specialising in social welfare law and finance. She is a frequent writer and speaker on all aspects of long-term care and edits Jordans' new journal *Elder Law and Finance*. She is a chairman of disability tribunals and of a NHS continuing care review panel. She is also chair of St Anne's Shelter and Housing Action, a major not-for-profit provider of long-term care for people with learning difficulties and mental health problems.

CONTENTS

TABLE OF CASES

References are to page numbers of the Introduction and paragraph numbers of the narrative.

TABLE OF STATUTES

References are to page numbers of the Introduction and paragraph numbers of the narrative and Appendix numbers.

TABLE OF STATUTORY INSTRUMENTS

References are to page numbers of Introduction and paragraph numbers of narrative.

TABLE OF INTERNATIONAL CONVENTIONS

References are to paragraph numbers.

TABLE OF DIRECTIONS, GUIDANCE AND DECISIONS

References are to page numbers of the Introduction and paragraph numbers of the narrative.

General Guidance

Commissioners' Decisions

TABLE OF ABBREVIATIONS

AA Regs 1991	Social Security (Attendance Allowance) Regulations 1991
AOG	*Adjudication Officer's Guide to Income Support* (replaced by the *Decision Makers Guide* (DMG)
BUPA	British United Provident Association
CC(RA)A 1998	Community Care (Residential Accommodation) Act 1998
CDCA 2000	Carers and Disabled Children Act 2000
CRAG	*Charging for Residential Accommodation Guide* (DoH Circular LAC (99) 9)
CRSA 1995	Carers (Recognition and Services) Act 1995
CSA 2000	Care Standards Act 2000
CRASSCH	Continuing Random Sample Survey of Care Homes
CSDPA 1970	Chronically Sick and Disabled Persons Act 1970
DoH	Department of Health
DLA	disability living allowance
DMG	*Decision Makers Guide* (which replaced the AOG)
DPSCRA 1986	Disabled Persons (Services, Consultation and Representation) Act 1986
DSS	Department of Social Security
EL	executive letter
EPA	enduring power of attorney
GP	general practitioner
HASSASSAA 1983	Health and Social Services and Social Security Adjudications Act 1983
HIMP	health improvement programme
HSG	Health Service guidelines
HSPHA 1968	Health Services and Public Health Act 1968
ISG Regs 1987	Income Support (General) Regulations 1987
LAC	local authority circular
LASSA 1970	Local Authority and Social Services Act 1970
LPA 1925	Law of Property Act 1925
MHA 1983	Mental Health Act 1983
NAA 1948	National Assistance Act 1948
NA(AR) Regs 1992	National Assistance (Assessment of Resources) Regulations 1992
NHS	National Health Service
NHSA 1977	National Health Service Act 1977
NHSCCA 1990	National Health Service and Community Care Act 1990

NICE	National Institute for Clinical Excellence
NOP	National Opinion Poll
PCG	primary care group
PCT	primary care trust
RHA 1984	Registered Homes Act 1984
SSA	standard spending assessment
SSCBA 1992	Social Security Contributions and Benefits Act 1992
SSI	Social Security Inspectorate
STG	special transitional grant

GLOSSARY OF TERMS

Care management The process of co-ordinating and arranging services for an individual person.

Care manager A person who carries out community care assessments, prepares the care plan, and co-ordinates and monitors service provision. The care manager has budgetary responsibility, but is not usually involved in providing particular services.

Carer A person, usually a family member, who provides care and support for someone without being employed to do so.

Commission To contract for services which are to be provided for older people. Health authorities and PCTs commission 'health' services. Local authorities commission 'social' services. Possible providers are specified by statute.

Community Health Council Patients' Watchdog which has a statutory duty to monitor the NHS and to recommend improvements in services. This will be abolished in 2001.

Complaints procedure The process set up by all social services departments to deal with complaints.

Day care Non-residential care provided at centres within the community usually by the local authority or by voluntary organisations. Workers may be paid or unpaid.

Directions (and approvals) Delegated legislation by which central government targets the general statutory responsibilities of public authorities.

Domiciliary care Services provided in people's own homes, usually by the local authority, but increasingly by voluntary or commercial organisations.

Health Service Commissioner The Health Service Ombudsman.

Independent sector Voluntary, charitable, not-for-profit and commercial organisations.

Local authority	Used to emphasise corporate responsibility within local government for, in particular, social services functions. Social services departments/authorities derive their responsibilities from LASSA 1970.
Provider	Agency or individual outside the local authority from whom the local authority purchases services.
Residential accommodation	Used as a generic term referring to residential care homes and/or nursing homes. On implementation of the Care Standards Act 2000, the new generic term will be 'care home'.
Respite care	Short-term periods of care which relieve the immediate family carer; usually involves residential care, but may be organised at home. Both the NHS and social services authorities have statutory responsibilities.
User	An older client in respect of whom services are provided or commissioned by a local authority, an NHS body, or a voluntary or commercial organisation.

INTRODUCTION

This book is about legal rights and duties to receive or provide care and the costs of care. The perspective is that of the older client and his or her legal adviser. The main focus is an area of public law, the scope and content of which is largely unfamiliar to many practitioners.

Working with older clients requires wide-ranging skills, both legal and personal, making this a particularly challenging area for practice and for practice development.

The skills are as follows.

(i) *Legal*
    Knowledge and understanding of relevant areas of public and private law and public finance.

(ii) *Know-how*
    An understanding of how long-term care is provided; how decisions are made in public authorities, and by whom; local priorities and policies in respect of local services. Throughout this book, there is emphasis on the fact that policy and practice in almost every area are determined locally rather than nationally. Advisers need to build up a database of local services and local ways of doing things.

(iii) *Interpersonal*
    Communicating effectively with this client group and offering appropriate client care; ethical practice, which is nevertheless holistic and creative, negotiation and dispute resolution with public authorities.

This introductory chapter summarises the most important and useful know-how and know-how sources in this field of practice.

1 PRIMARY LEGISLATION

The most important pieces of primary legislation are listed below.

National Assistance Act 1948 – residential and nursing home care; other community services

Health Services and Public Health Act 1968 – welfare of elderly people

Chronically Sick and Disabled Persons Act 1970 – domiciliary services; duty to identify local needs and to provide information about services

Local Authority Social Services Act 1970 – social services functions (eg complaints) and provision for 'directions' and 'guidance' from the Secretary of State

National Health Services Act 1977 – the duty to provide a comprehensive health service; some limited social services functions

Health and Social Services and Social Security Adjudications Act 1983 – charges for non-residential services

Mental Health Act 1983 – compulsory treatment for mental disorder; after-care services; guardianship; jurisdiction of the Court of Protection

Registered Homes Act 1984 – registration and inspection of residential accommodation

Housing Act 1985 – duty on housing authorities to consider housing needs plus power to repair/improve their own stock

Disabled Persons (Services, Consultation and Representation) Act 1986 – assessment of disabled people; disabled school-leavers

National Health Service and Community Care Act 1990 – duty to assess need for community care services; community care plans; NHS internal market

Social Security Contributions and Benefits Act 1992 – entitlement to most welfare benefits

Carers (Recognition and Services) Act 1995 – duty to assess, on request, and during an assessment of the needs of the person cared for, the ability of an informal carer to provide care

Housing Act 1996 – housing associations become registered social landlords; provision for homelessness; housing allocation

Housing Grants, Construction and Regeneration Act 1996 – home repair assistance; disabled facilities grants

Community Care (Direct Payments) Act 1996 – direct payments to enable certain groups (not older people at present) to buy community care services

Data Protection Act 1998 – right of access to personal information, whether stored manually or electronically

Health Act 1999 – sets up primary care groups; ends GP fund-holding; pooled budgets between health and social service authorities

Carers and Disabled Children Act 2000 – freestanding carers' assessments; power to provide services for carers

Care Standards Act 2000 – regulation of long-term care in residential or domiciliary settings

2 REGULATIONS

Social Security (Invalid Care Allowance) Regulations 1976, SI 1976/ 409 – entitlement to invalid care allowance

Residential Care Homes Regulations 1984, SI 1984/1345; Nursing Homes and Mental Nursing Homes Regulations 1984, SI 1984/1578 – quality assurance

Income Support (General) Regulations 1987, SI 1987/1967 – income support means test

Social Security (Attendance Allowance) Regulations 1991, SI 1991/ 2740 – entitlement to the attendance allowance for people over 65

National Assistance (Assessment of Resources) Regulations 1992 – the residential care means test

NHS (General Medical Services) Regulations 1992, SI 1992/635 – responsibilities of GPs

Residential Accommodation (Relevant Premises, Ordinary Residence and Exemptions) Regulations 1993, SI 1993/477 – local authority powers to make arrangements for people with preserved rights

Community Care (Direct Payments) Regulations 1997, SI 1997/734 – detailed provision for direct payments by local authorities to enable those needing community care to purchase their own services (not available for residential care); over-65s may now receive direct payments

National Assistance (Sums for Personal Requirements) Regulations 2000, SI 2000/798 – annual personal allowance for residential care

3 DIRECTIONS AND GUIDANCE

Reference is made to directions and guidance throughout this book. Their legal significance is as follows.

Directions have legislative force, but do not require parliamentary approval. The Secretary of State for Health has express powers under much social welfare legislation to make directions or give approval in respect of the exercise of general powers contained in the primary legislation. In addition, s 7A of the Local Authority Social Services Act 1970 (LASSA 1970) states that every local authority is to exercise its social services functions in accordance with general or specific written directions which 'may' be given by the Secretary of State.

As far as guidance is concernced, s 7(1) of the LASSA 1970 provides that local authorities 'shall' act under the general guidance of the Secretary of State. This is often referred to as 'statutory guidance', since the courts have now indicated that failure to follow it is likely to be unlawful. In *R v London Borough of Islington, ex parte Rixon*,[1] for example, where a care plan which did not conform to s 7 guidance was held to be unlawful.

Much *policy* guidance is issued under s 7; *practice* guidance is not, and consequently carries less weight, although local authorities are expected to at least 'have regard to' such guidance.

Section 7 does not apply directly to NHS guidance, but it is clear that at least some of this will be regarded as equivalent to s 7 guidance.[2]

Most guidance to local authorities is in the form of circulars, but general guidance has also been issued under s 7 of the LASSA 1970, and executive letters (ELs) are issued from time to time by the Department of Health or the Social Services Inspectorate.

Some of the most important directions and circulars are listed below. Guidance can be obtained, free of charge, from The Department of Health, PO Box 777, London SE1 6XH. Fax: 01623 724 524. It can also be downloaded from the internet, at www.doh.gov.uk/coinh.htm.

Relevant guidance on long-term care funding issues

(Section 7 guidance is asterisked)

LAC (92) 24 (HSG (92) 50)	Local Authority Contracts for Residential and Nursing Home Care: NHS Related Aspects
LAC (92) 17	Health Authority Payments in Respect of Social Services Functions
LAC (92) 27 (LAC (93) 18)	The National Assistance Act 1948 (Choice of Accommodation) Directions 1992
★LAC (93) 6	Local Authorities' Powers to Make Arrangements for People who are in Independent Sector Residential Care and Nursing Homes on 31 March 1993
LAC (93) 7	Ordinary Residence
January 1994	Discretionary Charges for Adult Social Services: Advice Note for Use by Social Services Inspectorate
LAC (95) 5 (HSG (95) 8)	NHS Responsibilities for Meeting Continuing Health Care Needs
LAC (95) 17 (HSG (95) 39)	Discharge from NHS In-Patient Care of People with Continuing Health or Social Care Needs

---

1   (1998) 1 CCL Rep 119.
2   *R v North Derbyshire HA ex parte Fisher* (1998) 1 CCL Rep 150.

HSG (95) 45   Arrangements between Health Authorities and NHS Trusts and Private and Voluntary Sector Organisations for the Provision of Community Care Services

★LAC (96) 7   Carers Recognition and Services Act 1995: Policy Guidance

★LAC (98) 19   Community Care (Residential Accommodation) Act 1998

★LAC (99) 9   Charging for Residential Accommodation Guide (CRAG)

Useful general know-how

The Bibliography refers to a number of general legal texts as well as to more specialist source material. There is still a conspicuous lack of detailed, analytical material on many of the legal and financial issues which are relevant to long-term care. The following distillation of accessible and current sources of know-how may be helpful.

(a)   Age Concern offers a comprehensive information service on many issues relevant to older clients, and a subscription is very cost-effective. In particular, there is a fact sheet service, with titles ranging from 'Legal Arrangements for Managing Financial Affairs', through 'Raising Income or Capital from your Home' to 'Local Authority Charging Procedures for Residential and Nursing Home Care' (Astral House, 1268 London Road, London SW16 4ER, tel: 0181 765 7200).

(b)   Briefings by other charities, for example, Alzheimers Society, Counsel and Care for the Elderly, Help The Aged, Carers' National Association.

(c)   The Community Care Practitioners Group. This a special-interest group which meets regularly in London to share know-how. Material is circulated, even if members are unable to attend meetings (c/o Professional Briefings, 120 Wilton Road, London SW1V 1JZ).

(d)   The Department of Health website: www.doh.gov.uk.

(e)   *Community Care Law Reports* (published by Legal Action).

(f)   *Elder Law and Finance*. A new bi-monthly journal, published by Jordans, which focuses on older client issues, including long-term care.

There is a list of useful sources of information specifically on financial issues at the end of Chapter 7.

Chapter 1

LONG-TERM CARE: THE POLICY FRAMEWORK

'Seeing old age as a "problem" is of relevance not just to the provision of long-term care. It applies to the provision of income in old age, health care, housing, transport, the facilities for daily life which everyone takes for granted in their youth and middle years . . . The whole approach to long-term care should be to view the management of older people's needs as a set of positive actions over time which help people to lead the kind of fulfilling lives they want to lead – and to be able to continue to contribute to society in a positive way – both economically and intellectually – and not as a management of decline.'[1]

1.1 WHO NEEDS LONG-TERM CARE?

The demographic evidence presented to the Royal Commission on Long Term Care[2] confirmed that the number of people aged 65 or over is projected to rise by almost 57 per cent between 1995 and 2031, and that the over-85 age group will increase more rapidly, by about 79 per cent. By 2050, there will be nearly three times as many people over the age of 85 as there are today. That should not be surprising when today's young people have an average life expectancy of well over 80.

In the constant debate over who should pay for long-term care, it is often forgotten that increasing longevity is one of the greatest achievements of the twentieth century.[3] The Royal Commission has challenged the assumption that old age is a 'problem',[4] saying that it should be seen as a natural part of life, which presents new opportunities, rather than as a burden, and that society as a whole should begin to recognise the value inherent in older people, dismissing the assumption that they are simply passive recipients of other people's goodwill or are inevitably 'incapacitated, befuddled or redundant'.[5]

It is, of course, dependency, rather than old age alone, which gives rise to the need for long-term care. Although the Royal Commission took an optimistic view about improvements in the health and material well-being of older people, there is a clear and dramatic association between advancing years and the incidence of disability. A recent longitudinal study[6] which set out to ascertain numbers of cognitively impaired and physically disabled older people in England and Wales came to the following conclusions.

---

1   Royal Commission on Long Term Care *With Respect to Old Age*, Cm 4192-I (Stationery Office, 1999), para 1.2.
2   Ibid.
3   Audit Commission *The Coming of Age* (1997), para 2.
4   *With Respect to Old Age*, para 1.11.
5   Ibid, para 1.14.
6   See *Age Concern Information Bulletin*, July 1999.

- 11% of men and 19% of women aged 65 and over (1.3m people) are disabled.
- 38% of disabled people are aged 85 or over, and a similar percentage are cognitively impaired.
- More than 80% of older disabled people need help on at least a daily basis.

For many older people, disability or incapacity is likely to be prolonged. It may involve physical or mental illness or impairment, and is frequently characterised by loss of mobility; impairment in sight or hearing; general physical frailty; confusion or dementia.

People who are temporarily incapacitated may need hospital treatment and/or recuperative care at home before they can resume their normal lives. Where incapacity or disability is prolonged, there are likely to be day-to-day needs for support and help. Apart from intensive medical treatment, these might include:

- the provision of day care;
- domestic assistance;
- personal and/or nursing care in the community;
- equipment or adaptations;
- access to transport; and
- in some cases, sheltered accommodation or even full-time care given in a residential establishment.

Prior to 1983, most publicly funded care was provided by the public sector. The National Health Service (NHS) provided acute care, community health services and long-term care beds. Social services departments of local authorities provided residential, day and homecare services, and housing authorities provided housing support.[1] During the 1980s, a number of factors came together in an arbitrary way and altered, quite radically, the way in which long-term care is both funded and delivered. This chapter will outline those changes and their consequences.

1.2   WHO IS RESPONSIBLE FOR LONG-TERM CARE?

The post-war legislation of the 1940s determined the structure of long-term care services. Local authorities and the new National Health Service (NHS) were then allocated statutory responsibilities which were, and have remained, partly complementary and partly overlapping. There has never been a clear-cut distinction between health care and social care, and this is problematic for two reasons.

(1) Traditionally, the agencies concerned have found it difficult to work together in order to deliver a 'seamless' service. The reasons are mainly cultural and bureaucratic, but have proved very difficult to overcome.

---

1   *The Coming of Age*, op cit, para 10.

(2) Since 1948, social care services have had to be paid for, at least in part, by service users. Services provided by the NHS have, from the outset, been free at the point of delivery, and funded through general taxation.

There have been countless governmental and managerial initiatives over the years to promote 'working together'.[1] Until recently, however, the research and policy literature has largely ignored the question of payment for care, and there has been little public debate about why, for example, older people should have had to pay for care in nursing homes, or why people suffering from cancer have received NHS care whereas people with Alzheimer's disease have not.[2]

The Royal Commission on Long Term Care was set up in 1997 to address, for the first time, the way in which the costs of such care should be apportioned between the State and individuals. Its main recommendation offered an ethical and radical solution to a problem which has dogged social policy for many years. However, the Government has opted not to accept the recommendation because of its potential cost to the taxpayer:

> 'Actioning the proposal would absorb huge and increasing sums of money without using any of it to increase the range and quality of care available to older people.'[3]

As is explained in the next chapter,[4] that decision seems likely to exacerbate the inequities and inconsistencies in the present system and may also lead to an increase in litigation, often at public expense.

1.3 HEALTH CARE OR SOCIAL CARE?

The history of social policy has been characterised by a failure to recognise older people as a priority for health and welfare expenditure.[5] The 'health' perspective has been that illness in old age is chronic, inevitable and barely treatable. The social services approach has been to give older people lower priority for services than other client groups (eg children) and to encourage informal caring.

The NHS was engrafted on to a system in which both financial support and long-term care for people of modest means had been provided by local authorities under the Poor Law. The emphasis was always on institutional care, since statutory non-accommodation services did not exist before 1948.

---

1   See, most recently, ch 7 of the Government's response to the Royal Commission on Long Term Care *The NHS Plan 2000*, Cm 4818-I.

2   *With Respect to Old Age*, op cit, para 3.7.

3   *The NHS Plan 2000*, op cit, para 15.20.

4   See **2.4.10**.

5   Means, R and Smith, R *From Poor Law to Community Care: The Development of Welfare Services for Elderly People, 1939–1971* 2nd edn (Policy Press, 1998) at p 3. The writer is much indebted to this seminal account of the development of welfare services for older people and of the health and social care interface.

Institutional provision for the majority of older people needing long-term care was made in the public assistance institutions, run by local authorities.[1]

The National Health Service Act 1946 set up a 'comprehensive' service which was divided into three separate parts:

(1) the hospital sector;
(2) the Executive Council sector, which ran GP services;
(3) the local health authorities (local authorities) which ran what we now describe as 'public health services', plus midwifery, health visitor, district nurse and domestic help services.

The hospital sector was always dominant; the local authority sector always under-resourced.

Policy in respect of long-term care at that time was based on the assumption that it was possible to make a distinction, in terms of provision, between the frail, who are in need of care and attention, and the sick who are in need of medical and nursing support. The NHS was expected to concern itself with the sick and the National Assistance Act 1948 (NAA 1948) was to establish a system of local authority residential care for those in need of care and attention, not being constant medical and nursing attention. This wording was eventually incorporated into s 21 of the NAA 1948. It was intended that residents in local authority homes should pay for their accommodation and maintenance out of their pensions.

There was concern in the late 1940s that coordination between health care and local authorities would be a problem area, and a case was made for medical control through the geriatric units in the NHS. The NAA 1948 prevented this from happening, however, and geriatric medicine became, and remained, a 'Cinderella' service within the NHS.

As time went by, it was perceived that it was in fact impossible to distinguish between being in need of care and attention and being in need of medical treatment or, as commentators put it, between being 'partly sick' and 'partly well'.[2] It also became clear that local authority residential homes were accepting elderly people with greater degrees of disability than was intended, mainly because there was a shortage of hospital beds for people who would ordinarily be regarded as sick, and because independent or voluntary sector provision was almost non-existent. Local authority residential homes were not intended for people suffering from incontinence, serious loss of mobility or dementia but, soon enough, many such people were being cared for by local authorities.

In 1954, where to draw the line between the two sectors was described as 'perhaps the most baffling problem in the whole of the NHS'.[3] One suggested

1   Means and Smith, op cit, p 16.
2   Ibid, p 160.
3   Ibid.

solution to the problem was to restore hospitals to local authority control, but with the underlying assumption that all care would then be means tested. In the event, there was little support for such a course of action outside local authorities. In 1957, however, a ministerial circular[1] was issued, which purported to lay down detailed guidelines about the respective responsibilities of local authorities and hospital authorities. This circular was partially updated in 1965, but remained in operation throughout the 1960s. Further circulars followed, most recently in 1995.[2] Comparing the 1957 and 1995 circulars, it is quite clear that the boundary between NHS and local authority care has shifted substantially towards including increasing numbers of frail and sick older people within the 'care and attention' provision of the NAA 1948. In 1957, for instance, hospital authorities were responsible for 'care of the chronic bedfast who may need little or no medical treatment but do require prolonged nursing care over months or years'. The present position, recently explored by the Court of Appeal in *R v North and East Devon Health Authority ex parte Coughlan*[3] is much more equivocal. The reasons behind this most recent policy shift are set out at **2.4**.

Throughout the period under review, the cost of long-term care to the individual appears to have been little discussed. As noted already, the principle of means testing was incorporated into the NAA 1948. It does appear, however, that local authorities, by and large, did not collect charges for non-accommodation services[4] until quite recently. In the immediate post-war period, the vast majority of older people receiving residential care had very modest resources. They were required to contribute their pensions towards the cost of local authority residential accommodation, but most had little else. In hospital, then as now, their pensions would be reduced. They were provided for, one way or another, out of the public purse. In the late twentieth century, however, owner-occupation has become 'the dominant tenure of later life'[5] and the inheritance of home equity a major source of wealth for subsequent generations. Inevitably, therefore, charging has become a major issue. This development coincides with the shift described above, whereby long-term care has largely ceased to be a free service provided by the NHS and has become a service for which older people are required to pay, out of capital as well as income.

---

1   DoH Circular 14/57, *Local Authority Services for the Chronic Sick and Infirm*; HM (57) 86, *Geriatric Services and the Care of the Chronic Sick*.

2   DoH Circular HSG (95) 8; LAC (95) 5, *NHS Responsibilities for Meeting Continuing Health Care Needs*.

3   (1999) 2 CCL Rep 285.

4   Means and Smith, op cit, p 327.

5   Ibid, p 328.

1.4   THE DEVELOPMENT OF LOCAL AUTHORITY NON-RESIDENTIAL SERVICES

The NAA 1948 gave local authorities power to provide a variety of services for adult disabled people. Over the years, further responsibilities were added, but it was not until 1968 that the Health Services and Public Health Act (HSPHA 1968) gave them a general responsibility for promoting the welfare of older people resident in their area, and a specific duty to introduce a home help service. Only in the 1970s were local authorities empowered to provide more extensive domiciliary services for the elderly, although a few authorities had previously derived powers from local Acts of Parliament. In 1970, the Local Authority Social Services Act (LASSA 1970) created new social services departments, which carried clear statutory responsibilities for the welfare of four client groups:

- elderly people;
- disabled people;
- children and their families;
- people with mental disorder.

The LASSA 1970 was intended to improve social services provision, but also to assist and encourage families, and the community itself, to promote 'welfare through community'. At the same time, the home nursing service and some other services for which local authorities had previously been responsible were transferred to the NHS.

1970 also saw the first major piece of legislation requiring local authorities to provide services for older and disabled people.[1] The Chronically Sick and Disabled Persons Act 1970 (CSDPA 1970) was considered to be a landmark in social provision. Generally speaking, however, before April 1993, social services departments saw themselves essentially as providers of services rather than, for example, as commissioners and planners of services provided by other agencies. This was partly because the legislation itself was so framed, but also because, for political and historical reasons, that mantle had always fitted the local authorities. In April 1993, a major cultural change was initiated which required social services departments to take stock of their existing philosophies of care and revise their previous attitudes towards effective service provision.

1.5   THE ADVENT OF 'COMMUNITY CARE'

Community care is often understood as the antithesis of institutional care, which was a hallmark of nineteenth-century social policy. In the twentieth century, particularly after the Second World War, home-based care came to be

---

1   Many of the provisions in the CSDPA 1970 were inchoate, however, and were taken further by the Disabled Persons (Services Consultation and Representation) Act 1986, which is still only partially implemented.

seen as preferable to placing people in institutions, and research evidence of institutional abuse and malpractice has supported this approach. The child care service, which was set up in 1948, led policy in this respect. Then, in 1957, the Royal Commission on the Law Relating to Mental Illness recommended a shift from hospital to community care for the mentally ill, and a massive closure programme was instituted in respect of the long-stay mental hospitals.

As regards older people, there was no real impetus towards community care until much more recently. Historically, the 'problem' of the elderly was poverty, and for many years the provision and resourcing of retirement pensions dominated the policy agenda. As noted at **2.2**, there was institutional provision in hospitals or residential homes but the care needs of older people who wanted and were able to live in the community were largely ignored. This was partly because there was, and always had been, a network of informal care provided within families or by voluntary organisations. Only when research began to highlight the implications of the 'demographic time bomb', and the plight of older people living alone without family support and without services, did governments begin to address the care issues.

Translating general policy into clear objectives and eventual action took 20 years. Between 1970 and 1974, expenditure on personal social services rose by 12 per cent each year, but the 1974 economic crises reversed this trend and since then the policy of successive governments has been largely directed towards capping public expenditure and pushing back the frontiers of the State. In this financial climate, care in the community was seen as a highly desirable objective. In 1991, a White Paper[1] indicated that community care really meant care *by* the community and that the primary sources of support which enable older people to live independently should be informal and voluntary. Public services were seen as sustaining, developing, but never displacing 'the community'. The White Paper advocated strengthening primary health care and social services in tandem with neighbourhood and voluntary support, whilst maintaining adequate NHS provision for acute care, together with residential care facilities for a minority of older people.

What happened was rather different. By the mid-1980s, it was apparent that a reduction in the numbers of older people in hospital geriatric wards had taken place, but that this had been more than offset by substantial growth in the residential homes sector. The reasons for this change are explained in the following section.

---

1   *Growing Older* (1991).

1.6　THE 'PERVERSE INCENTIVE' TOWARDS RESIDENTIAL CARE

An Audit Commission Report published in 1986[1] observed that the effect of the community care policies first developed in the 1950s had largely been to shift people, and expenditure, from hospitals to residential homes. The Audit Commission concluded that the 'perverse incentive' exerted by the then government's social security policies was mainly to blame for this.[2] From the early 1980s, means-tested supplementary benefit (and from 1988, income support) was available to meet the full fees of residential care homes or nursing homes[3] for people on low incomes and with limited capital assets. Individuals were permitted to arrange their own placements, without an assessment of need, on the understanding that benefits would be available if their own resources were, or became, insufficient.

Between 1981 and 1996, there was a 29 per cent increase in the number of older people in residential accommodation, far in excess of the overall increase in the number of over 65-year-olds in the population as a whole. The system was open to financial opportunism; the guaranteed subsidy from the DSS encouraged entrepreneurs to set up residential establishments and pushed up the level of fees. At length, in 1986, the Conservative Government imposed a statutory ceiling on benefit payments for residential care. From then on, home fees slowly rose above benefit levels, particularly in the south of England, and 'topping-up' payments made by residents' families became an essential part of the financial arrangements. There was still, however, no test of need for residential care. The Audit Commission commented:

> 'In short the more residential the care, the easier it is to obtain benefits, and the greater the size of the payment . . . very large sums of public money are being paid to people living in private homes without there being any mechanism (other than means-tested income) for ensuring that the benefits are appropriate . . . perversely, money is available for some of the high cost institutional options, while the low-cost options are starved of finance.'[4]

1.7　THE NEW FRAMEWORK FOR SOCIAL CARE

Following the Audit Commission's highly critical report, Sir Roy Griffiths (then deputy chairman of Sainsbury's and the government's adviser on health services) was asked to review the use of public funds in implementing community care policies, and to advise on how resources might be more effectively deployed.

1　Audit Commission *Making a Reality of Community Care* (1986).
2　Ibid, para 87.
3　But not fees for services delivered at home.
4　*Making a Reality of Community Care*, op cit, paras 89 and 96.

His conclusions[1] were taken up in the White Paper which followed in 1989,[2] with the significant exception of his strongly expressed view that resources for community care should be 'ring-fenced' and thus protected from competing claims from other interest groups. Griffiths highlighted, in particular, the need to allocate more specifically both responsibility and accountability for the provision of community care; he saw clarification of the respective roles of health and social services authorities as essential.

The proposals put forward in the White Paper were to involve a number of changes in the funding, organisation and delivery of community care. Some of these changes would require legislation. The original intention was to introduce new legislation on community care in tandem with provisions creating a new infrastructure for the NHS, and the National Health Service and Community Care Bill went through Parliament in 1990. Parts I and II reconstructed the NHS; Part III addressed care in the community. Parts I and II were brought into force in 1991 but, for political reasons, Part III was phased in more gradually, with the most important changes taking effect from April 1993. Equally, if not more important, were the operational changes which were outlined in the White Paper and described in more detail in the accompanying Policy Guidance.

1.8 THE KEY CHANGES IN 1993

1.8.1 Service development

On 1 April 1993, local authorities became both facilitators and gatekeepers of community care policies. Part III of the National Health Service and Community Care Act 1990 (NHSCCA 1990) created a 'market' in social care, as in health. In the new marketplace, the local authority's role is to purchase or commission services, rather than to provide its own services. In NHS parlance, the purchaser and provider functions in the social care field are now largely split. In theory, the effect of this change was to allow 'enabling' local authorities to unlock the enterprise of the independent sector and so encourage the development of more imaginative and effective community care services.

The Government also passed over to local authorities the major financial responsibility for community care services. The huge commitment of DSS funds to residential care, via the benefits system, ceased from April 1993 and local authorities now have equivalent transferred funding available to them to enable them to implement their community care programmes.[3]

This very significant cultural and financial shift has not occasioned much new law. There was, on the whole, no need to give local authorities added

---

1   *Community Care: Agenda for Action* (1986).
2   *Caring for People*, Cmnd 849 (1989).
3   See **1.10**.

responsibilities to provide services, or to enable them to commission services from others, as comprehensive powers and duties were already in existence.[1] On the whole, Part III of the NHSCCA 1990 is concerned with the execution of those existing responsibilities.

The one exception is s 42, which amends the NAA 1948 by extending the local authority's obligation to provide residential accommodation for elderly or infirm adults to include a duty to make nursing home placements for people who are sick.[2] This amendment led directly to the 1995 guidance on NHS responsibilities for continuing care[3] which endorsed the reduction of continuing in-patient provision for most older people and effectively transferred responsibility for providing non-acute nursing care to social services departments.[4]

One major problem for local authorities is to allocate their limited resources in the target areas identified by the White Paper, namely home-based services for those in greatest need. Substantial guidance has been issued by central government to assist them with service planning and prioritisation.[5] Section 46 of the NHSCCA 1990 requires them to prepare and publish annual community care plans, in consultation with all major providers of care services, service users and carers. These plans should state objectives and priorities for community care and the local authority's targets for meeting them. They should also be used to 'manage the market' by giving information about the kinds of services the local authority wishes to purchase.[6]

1.8.2 Community care assessments

Section 47 of the NHSCCA 1990 requires local authorities to assess people who may be in need of community care services and to determine whether assessed needs call for the provision by them of such services. It builds on a narrower duty to assess disabled people under the Disabled Persons (Services, Consultation and Representation) Act 1986 (DPSCRA 1986). Assessment and service provision are discussed in more detail in Chapter 5.

Section 47 of the NHSCCA 1990 reflects the concerns expressed by the Audit Commission in 1986, and by Sir Roy Griffiths in 1988, that public spending was being geared towards residential care placements, made without assessment of need, and that more cost-effective home-based services were being starved of investment.

Assessment is now the cornerstone of the community care reforms because it unlocks service provision. The assessment process raises many questions for

---

1   See Chapter 4.
2   NAA 1948, ss 21 and 26.
3   See **2.4.3**.
4   See Chapter 2.
5   See *Care Management and Assessment – A Practitioner's Guide* (HMSO, 1991).
6   DoH Circular EL (93) 119 *Community Care*.

local authorities, both practical and philosophical. In particular, who defines 'need' and what happens where 'needs' exceed resources?

1.8.3   The mixed economy of care

Local authorities are now expected to be arrangers and purchasers of care services, rather than monopolistic providers.[1] This posits a fundamental change in social services culture and ethos. The 'helping' role of social services is subordinated to the 'case-management' approach, which requires managers to contract for, monitor and evaluate services which are to be delivered largely by others.

As noted, before April 1993, most independent sector activity was concentrated on residential care. Home-based services were provided almost exclusively by local authorities themselves. The expectation now is that a case-management approach on the part of local authorities will stimulate competition and encourage diversification in the independent and voluntary sectors. Every year, between 1993 and 1997 local authorities were required to spend 85 per cent of the new resources made available to them by central government on commissioning services in the independent sector.[2]

1.9   COMMUNITY CARE: AN APPRAISAL

The community care philosophies put forward in the 1989 White Paper on Community Care have great resonance, especially when matched with the culture of the 1990s. All of us can sign up to the key goals of promoting choice and independence by providing the right support, at the right time and in the right setting. However, the White Paper also makes it quite apparent that the major changes in the delivery of public social services, which were being proposed, were, to a very large extent, financially driven.

As has been observed, both the strategic and operational roles of social services departments altered dramatically as a result of the White Paper. The vehicles for change were Part III of the NHSCCA 1990 and substantial contemporaneous policy guidance. However, it is clear that the additional funding made available to local authorities to implement the changes has not matched the expectations created by the White Paper of a needs-led, choice-driven, independence-facilitating system of long-term care. Social services departments have made progress in implementing the White Paper, but constant publicity about cuts in social services along with the proliferation of legal challenges since 1993 have highlighted the fact that, more than ever before, local authorities are engaged in the management of rationing, a role which sits uneasily alongside the creative, facilitative, market-oriented image put forward in the White Paper. Obviously

---

1   White Paper *Caring for People* (1989) para 3.1.3.
2   See **1.11**.

the public needs to receive value for money, and many local authorities are still learning how to deliver best value. The recent case-law emphasises only poor practice and/or the apparent inadequacy of public resources to provide what many people would regard as very basic levels of care.

One outcome of the 1993 changes, and the subsequent case-law, has been the development of service eligibility criteria[1] which prioritise between client groups, and have the effect of targeting support on those in high-risk categories. As a result, many people with low-level support needs are denied services, notwithstanding the evidence that good preventive services are the best way of sustaining independent living and of keeping costs down.[2] A further outcome has been a development of another 'perverse incentive'; costs of residential placements are now so keen, that residential care is a cheaper option than an intensive package of services delivered at home. There is now considerable evidence of local authorities effectively forcing older people into residential care by capping the value of domiciliary packages.

1.10   THE CONTINUING DEBATE OVER NURSING CARE

Between 1983 and 1996, there was a 38 per cent reduction in long-stay beds for older people (a loss of 21,300 beds), and the number of private nursing home places increased by 900 per cent (an increase of 141,000 beds). Only 8 per cent of the additional private nursing home places have been funded by the NHS. In effect, the NHS has increasingly narrowed its role to that of a provider of acute care.[3] The Royal Commission commented:

> '... there remains a lingering suspicion that, in order to concentrate its resources on acute care, the NHS has become increasingly reluctant to provide long-term care for older people'.[4]

Commentators have observed that the White Paper on Community Care[5] signally failed to address what was happening in the NHS or to predict what was to come. As noted already, the White Paper was concerned to delineate the boundary between personal social services and the social security system, in line with the previous Audit Commission recommendations. It made no proposals for altering the statutory responsibilities of the NHS and the grey area between health and social care remained unclarified. Indeed, the new emphasis on the role of local authorities, plus the amendments to the NAA 1948, gave health authorities a further incentive to withdraw from the provision of nursing care.

---

1   See Chapter 5.
2   Watson, L *High Hopes: Making Housing and Community Care Work* (Joseph Rowntree Foundation, 1997).
3   *The Coming of Age*, op cit, para 15.
4   *With Respect to Old Age*, op cit, para 4.8.
5   Wistow, G *Options for Long Term Care* (HMSO, 1996).

1.11 HOW IS LONG-TERM CARE FUNDED?

Local authority services for children, older people, the disabled and the mentally ill are funded principally through the revenue support grant, which is made available by central government from general taxation. Allocation of the grant between authorities is based on the government's 'standard spending assessment' (SSA), which is matched to demographic factors in each area. This funding is topped up with council tax, raised locally, and with fees charged by local authorities for some services.

There is far less direct central government control over the detailed allocation of local authority expenditure than with the NHS. Social services departments are high spenders within local authorities, but the division of resources between different client groups is always a difficult exercise, informed ultimately by the political agenda of the day. Most authorities spend at or above the SSA for social services as a whole (9 per cent above, on average) but spend *less* than the SSA on services for older people, while spending more on younger disabled people and on children.[1]

NHS funds for hospital and community health services are devolved from central government through the purchasing budgets of health authorities and, increasingly, primary care groups (PCGs) and the new primary care trusts (PCTs). The money comes from general taxation, with a small amount being top-sliced from the national insurance scheme to reflect the 'NHS' element in national insurance contributions.

Most services provided by the NHS are free at the point of use, although a few peripheral charges (for example prescription fees) are specifically authorised and produce a significant revenue stream. Local authorities, on the other hand, have statutory powers or duties to charge for services which affect older people.[2] Many such charges have increased massively since April 1993.

As previously noted, the creation of a new funding structure for long-term care was fundamental to the Griffiths reforms and to the 1989 White Paper. The imperative was to curtail the 'perverse' effects of funding residential care through the DSS by:

(1) transferring from central government to local authorities resources equivalent to the enhanced benefit provision previously allocated by the DSS for people in residential care homes and nursing homes; and
(2) requiring local authorities to act as the guardians of this public expenditure.

Griffiths called for a large degree of ring-fencing of community care funding to avoid the danger that other imperatives might dominate the allocation of resources within local authorities. This never materialised at the level suggested

---

1   *With Respect to Old Age*, op cit, para 4.21.
2   See Chapter 7.

by Griffiths although, until 1997/8, there was a small degree of protection through the special transitional grant (STG) which was intended to facilitate transition to the new system. The bulk of this funding, known as the 'transfer element' represented what the DSS calculated it would have spent on supporting residential placements under the old system. The STG is now incorporated within the general SSA for each local authority, so that the additional resources built into the system since 1993 are now subject to the annual local authority spending round where, for example, education will compete with social services for a share of the money available.

Notwithstanding the transfer arrangements, benefit funding by central government remains an often problematic element in the funding of long-term care. Consequently, good benefits advice is of the greatest importance for most people who receive care services.

At present, 600,000 people over the age of 65 receive non-residential services from local authorities. About 450,000 people (1 in 20) are in residential care homes or nursing homes, and about 34,000 are in hospital. Of these, approximately 320,000 are publicly financed, and 126,000 privately financed.

The Royal Commission estimated that the total cost of long-term care in the UK in 1995 was £11.1bn, of which an estimated £7.1bn comes from public funds via the NHS and social services. About £4bn is contributed by older people themselves. However, the living expenditure and rent of people living in ordinary or sheltered housing are not included in these figures. Most importantly, the figures do not include the social security expenditure attributable to people with long-term care needs, which is estimated to be about £6bn a year. This is a distorting factor because a good deal of benefit money will be used by older people to pay for long-term care, and is inseparable from expenditure which they make from their 'private' resources.

The Commission criticised the fact that so much uncertainty exists as to the actual overall expenditure on long-term care, and recommended that further research be commissioned. In its recent response to the Commission's report, the Government acknowledged the need for greater transparency in the system, but maintained that it would be 'meaningless' to differentiate between interventions delivered to people receiving long-term care and other interventions, and that any division between acute and long-term healthcare spending would be somewhat arbitrary.[1]

1.11.1 Partnership arrangements

It is now accepted that the organisational divide between health and social services creates structural, legal and financial barriers which prevent professionals from working well together and from developing flexible, seamless

---

1   *The NHS Plan 2000* op cit.

services.[1] There is a perception that there can be no hard and fast distinction between health and social care, and that it is illogical to maintain boundaries. However, the status quo is firmly entrenched, and the task of breaking down boundaries a formidable one.

The ability to pool resources and delegate functions is obviously important if public authorities are to work together. Since they are entirely creatures of statute, the legal position is all important, and may be summarised as follows.

– Section 31 of the Health Act 1999 permits 'partnership arrangements' between health authorities (working with PCGs), NHS trusts, primary care trusts, and local authorities. Partners will agree on the functions to be fulfilled by a partnership, which is not limited as to size or number of partners. Most health-related functions,[2] such as social services, housing, education, community health services and acute health services may be provided by partnerships.
– Partnership arrangements include pooled funding, lead commissioning,[3] and integrated provision, whereby different professionals work within one management structure.

1.11.2 Joint funding and pooled budgets

The Health Act 1999 has extended previous powers for health and social services authorities to combine forces, resources-wise for the sake of providing better coordinated services. The current position is as follows.

(a) Health authorities have power under s 28A of the National Health Services Act 1977 (NHSA 1977) to make capital or revenue payments to local social services authorities towards expenditure 'incurred or to be incurred by them in connection with any function which … is to be performed through their social services committees'. Payments may also be made to registered social landlords (housing associations) in connection with the provision of housing accommodation.
(b) Health (and local) authorities may make grants to voluntary organisations under ss 64 and 65 of the HSPHA 1968. Organisations providing services which statutory agencies are either required or empowered to provide are eligible for such funding.
(c) Section 28A payments are frequently made in pursuance of the reprovisioning of services formerly provided in long-stay hospitals. They are currently used, for example, to fund supported living schemes in the community. However, the section is wide enough to permit s 28A money to be used to fund residential care for older people. In these circumstances the funds must be used for social care purposes (which local authorities are

---

1   House of Commons Select Committee on Health, 1st report (1999).
2   NAA 1948, s 22 (the charging provision) is excluded from s 31 arrangements.
3   Where one agency takes on the commissioning of the services delegated to it by all the partner agencies.

empowered to provide) and will bear the NAA imprint. Consequently, residents who have the benefit of such funding will be means tested.

(d) Section 30 of the Health Act 1999 now permits local authorities to make payments to NHS bodies towards expenditure incurred, or to be incurred, in connection with healthcare.[1] These are the converse of s 28A payments. The Secretary of State has now signed directions with regard to both s 28A and s 28BB payments.[2] In each case the body making the payment must be satisfied that the payment is 'likely to secure a more effective use of public funds that the deployment of an equivalent amount' on the provision of local authority or NHS services respectively.

Once pooled, resources lose their discrete identity, although managers will still need to demonstrate that the respective statutory responsibilities are being discharged, and the pooled funds are subject to a separate annual audit return which will be based on contributions and total expenditure.

As regards charges to individual service users, the new arrangements are far from transparent. Guidance on s 31 partnership arrangements states:

> 'NHS services are free at the point of delivery and nothing in the Health Act has changed this. Local authorities have a *requirement* to charge for some services, such as the provision of residential care, and the discretion to charge for other services such as … non-residential social care. In agreeing partnership arrangements agencies will have to consider how best to manage charging (where local authorities charge for services) and how to clarify the difference between charged-for and non-charged for services. … Partners will need to bear in mind that, where charging is retained, the arrangements will need to be carefully explained to users of services, to avoid any misunderstanding that NHS services are being charged for, especially when an NHS trust is providing a service, part of which is being charged for.'

The powers and duties of local authorities to charge for services are discussed fully in Chapters 7, 8 and 9 of this book. It is easy to see the difficulty involved in calculating what element of a particular partnership arrangement is provided by the NHS, and so may not be charged for. In the past, the DoH has taken the view that where non–residential services are provided under s 28A arrange-ments, it will be 'permissible for the local authority to recover from service users the full cost of the social care service, even though a health authority has met some or all of the cost of the social care service'.[3]

When it comes to residential services, the decision in *R v North and East Devon Health Authority ex parte Coughlan*[4] underlines the point that where an older

---

1   A new s 28BB is inserted into the NHSA 1977.
2   Directions as to the conditions governing payments by health authorities to local authorities and other bodies under NHSA 1977, s 28A. Directions as to the conditions governing payments by local authorities to health authorities and other bodies under NHSA 1977, s 28BB. Both sets of directions took effect on 1 April 2000.
3   Advice Note for use by the SSI, January 1994.
4   (1999) 2 CCL Rep 285.

person has a primary need for long-term nursing care, that is to be funded by the NHS. However, NHS managers may consider that their funds are better deployed by assisting social services authorities to make residential placements, in order to prevent the blocking of hospital beds. The legal position is discussed in some detail in Chapter 2, and readers will notice the likely impact of the Government's new proposals in relation to the funding of nursing care.

Chapter 2

NHS RESPONSIBILITIES FOR LONG-TERM CARE

'. . . there remains a lingering suspicion that in order to concentrate its reserves on acute care, the NHS has become increasingly reluctant to provide long-term care for older people.'

'The Commission is clear about the strong lack of trust in the current system. There are pronounced feelings that Government was meant to underwrite the system in some universal sense through taxation, and it has not done so. People are not clear as to what they should expect. There is a linked feeling that the Health Service is abnegating its responsibility for care and making people rely on their own resources.'[1]

2.1 THE LEGAL DUTY TO PROVIDE A COMPREHENSIVE HEALTH SERVICE

The only statement of the responsibilities of a 'comprehensive' national health service is to be found in s 3(1) of the NHSA 1977:

'It is the Secretary of State's duty to provide throughout England and Wales, to such extent as he considers necessary to meet all reasonable requirements—

(a) hospital accommodation;

(b) other accommodation for the purpose of any service provided under this Act;

(c) medical, dental, nursing and ambulance services;

(d) such other facilities for the care of expectant and nursing mothers and young children as he considers are appropriate as part of the health service;

(e) such facilities for the prevention of illness, the care of persons suffering from illness and the after-care of persons who have suffered from illness as he considers are appropriate as part of the health service;

(f) such other services as are required for the diagnosis and treatment of illness.'

It is clear that s 3 of the NHSA 1977 imposes on the Secretary of State a 'target' duty, rather than a duty owed to individuals; therefore he must exercise judgement about how to use available resources in the interests of the community at large.

The NHSA 1977 allowed many statutory functions to be delegated to what are now health authorities.[2] In addition, the new organisational model created by Parts I and II of the NHSCCA 1990 gave health authorities overall

---

1   Royal Commission on Long Term Care *With Respect to Old Age*, Cm 4192-I (Stationery Office, 1999), paras 4.3 and 4.3.4.

2   From 1 April 1996, health authorities combined the responsibilities of the former district health authorities and family health service authorities.

responsibility for assessing the health needs of their populations, for allocating resources, and for commissioning appropriate services within the NHS internal market.

At the time of writing, the NHS is going through a further process of change.[1] In particular, the Health Act 1999 abolishes GP fund-holding, which was a creation of the 1990 Act, and establishes primary care groups (PCGs).[2] There is also a growing emphasis on the importance of joint working between health and social services, on health improvement programmes (HIMPs) and on high-quality, evidence-based practice.[3]

2.2   ACUTE SERVICES

Acute care services are usually delivered in hospital. In the past, patients entered hospital for surgery or treatment of acute conditions and generally would expect to remain there for the immediate post-operative/recuperative period before returning home or, if necessary, moving to a residential establishment for a more extended period of convalescence.

Over the past 20 years, pressure on acute care has been growing, partly because of an increase in emergency admissions, and older people have been using hospital services more. At the same time, however, hospitals have been encouraged to reduce lengths of stay and increase throughput. Between 1989 and 1994, for example, the average length of stay in the geriatric specialty fell by 45 per cent.[4]

Shorter stays in hospital make discharge planning more difficult. In addition, it seems that the ready availability of private residential care beds may have encouraged a reduction in rehabilitation services. The obvious need for 'intermediate' care, to break the cycle of early discharge from hospital, lack of appropriate support/rehabilitation facilities, and readmission to acute care is now being addressed. In particular, *The NHS Plan 2000*[5] will provide additional resources for the NHS to develop intermediate care facilities. In the past, acute hospitals have looked to social services to provide such resources.

At present, advisers are likely to see NHS practice as forcing the discharge of older clients from hospital before the social care and financial implications have been fully grasped, and there is a need for advocacy services or even legal intervention on behalf of such clients. This issue is discussed more fully in

---

1   See the White Paper, *The New NHS,* published in December 1997.
2   See **2.3**.
3   The National Institute for Clinical Excellence (NICE) was recently set up. Its brief is to produce clinical guidelines based on 'relevant evidence of clinical and cost effectiveness'. Commentators and user groups have already pointed out that this brief inevitably involves a consideration of the 'fair' rationing of NHS resources.
4   Audit Commission *The Coming of Age* (1997), para 67.
5   Cm 4818–I, July 2000.

Chapter 3. It remains to be seen whether or when the new initiatives referred to above will bring about an improvement in the situation.

2.3 PRIMARY CARE SERVICES

Within the NHS, primary care services meet the health care needs of people living at home, or in residential care homes or nursing homes, who do not require the centralised services of hospitals. The main users are children, older people and people with physical disabilities, learning disabilities or mental health problems. One-third of all NHS expenditure is deployed in the community.

After the NHS internal market was set up in 1991, funds were devolved to the combined health authorities to commission community health services and, in many areas, community health trusts were set up to coordinate the provider function. Fund-holding GPs also had a purchaser role, alongside health authorities, and were able to commission services for their patients from community health or hospital trusts. Not all GPs were fund-holders, however, and the government perceived inequities in the system.[1] The Health Act 1999 abolishes the internal market and GP fund-holding,[2] and establishes PCGs, which are groups of local GPs, primary care teams, and community nurses who are expected to work together with other health professionals and social services to commission services for the local population. PCGs have devolved budgetary responsibility for managing health care budgets in their areas, and should operate as committees of their health authority. There is also a statutory option for PCGs to become autonomous commissioning bodies, with added responsibility for the provision of community care services, when they are known as primary care trusts (PCTs). It is intended that, over time, health authorities will relinquish direct commissioning functions to PCTs and will assume an advisory/monitoring role, with particular reference to the development of HIMPs and the involvement of users, carers and voluntary organisations in decisions about local health provision.

Primary care services include:

- GP services;
- dental services;
- optical services;
- pharmaceutical services;
- community nursing and health visiting services;
- mental health and learning disability services; and

---

1   *The New NHS*, op cit, para 1.5.
2   Section 1. The Health Act 1999 came into force in April 2000. A flowchart illustrating the responsibilities of the different organisations within the NHS is set out in Appendix 2.

      —   special therapeutic or para-medical services, such as occupational therapy, physiotherapy, speech therapy and chiropody.[1]

GPs must provide 'appropriate personal medical services'.[2] All GP practices belong to a PCG, but there is no formal contractual relationship, and GPs remain independent contractors. However, it is envisaged that peer pressure generated by PCGs will encourage GPs to improve their services.

As regards all patients aged 75 or over, there is a specific duty for a GP to hold at least an annual consultation, and to offer to make a home visit in order to assess whether there is a need for 'personal medical services'. Such services include 'giving advice, as appropriate, to enable patients to avail themselves of services by a local social services authority'.[3] Recent research evidence reveals that few GPs have more than a basic understanding of their patients' needs for social services, or of what services may be available to them.[4]

Although it regulates the role of the GP, the law does not purport to define 'primary care' or 'community' services or to specify in detail what the range of such services might be. Section 3 of the NHSA 1977 refers only generally to 'medical' and 'nursing' services, and implicitly leaves health authorities to set priorities and allocate resources. The section does not, for example, make any reference to nursing specialisms, therapeutic services or para-medical services which, in practice, are an important part of community provision.

There are many 'grey areas' of provision where 'health' and 'social care' seem to overlap and where either health authorities or social services departments, or both agencies, may have responsibilities. Such services include washing, dressing, bathing, lifting, incontinence care, laundry and mobility rehabilitation. Overlapping responsibilities may appear to offer benefits for patients. In fact, however, the opposite is true. Recent evidence suggests that the inability to attribute clear and exclusive responsibility for service provision leads to buck-passing between agencies and sometimes to a failure to deliver services at all. In addition, serious financial implications for older people arise out of the fact that health services are free of charge, whereas social care services must be charged out to users.

A report by Age Concern cites two examples of 'grey' areas, leading to gaps in services:

> 'Mr A cares for his mother who has mental health problems and is incontinent. He was told that his mother does not require a medical bath and that, as social services do not do bathing, he would have to find private help.'

---

1   *A Rough Guide to the New NHS* (Alzheimer's Society Resource Pack, 2000).

2   National Health Service (General Medical Services) Regulations 1992, SI 1992/635.

3   Ibid, Sch 1, para 12(ii).

4   DoH, *The Role of the GP and Primary Health Care Team* (1994); Leeds Community Health Council, *Getting the Message Across* (1995).

'Mrs B, who has had a stroke, can wash herself, but cannot manage a bath without assistance. She is sometimes incontinent and would like an occasional bath. Her husband is in poor health and cannot help her and she is not considered in need of a medical bath. She, therefore, cannot be bathed at all.'[1]

2.4   CONTINUING IN-PATIENT CARE

In 1948, when the Welfare State was set up, it was intended that 'sick persons who needed treatment in hospital' were to be the responsibility of the NHS, whilst the new local authorities were to provide 'comfortable' accommodation for 'older' people who could not 'wholly' look after themselves.[2] For many years after that, hospitals provided psychogeriatric beds for victims of strokes, dementia sufferers, or for frail elderly people with no one to care for them.

Section 3(1) of the NHSA 1977 lays on the Secretary of State for Health a clear, albeit qualified responsibility to provide medical and nursing services, and facilities for the care and after-care of persons suffering from illness. Section 23 enables health authorities to arrange for health care to be provided in private or voluntary sector nursing homes. Before 1993, many independent providers of nursing care were the beneficiaries of block contracts with health authorities, and the White Paper on Community Care emphasised the continuing role of the NHS:

> 'Health authorities will need to ensure that their plans allow for the provision of continuing residential health care for those highly dependent people who need it.'[3]

Nevertheless, it is well known that few hospital or nursing home beds are now available for chronically sick, frail or mentally impaired patients, and that health authorities are generally reluctant to allocate resources to this kind of in-patient care. As noted earlier, amendments made by Part III of the NHSCCA 1990 to the statutory responsibilities of local authorities to provide residential care have enabled health authorities to shift responsibility on to social services departments.[4]

The effective withdrawal of the NHS from in-patient care came about for a number of reasons, which may be summarised as follows.

(i)   During the 1980s, the Government, apparently without a discernible general strategy, opened up demand-led DSS funding of residential care.[5] Benefits were made available, initially without limit, and without evidence of need (other than financial) to meet care fees. The market responded very

---

1   Age Concern, *The Next Steps, Lessons for the Future of Community Care* (1994).

2   Means, R and Smith, R *From Poor Law to Community Care: the Development of Welfare Services for Elderly People, 1939–1971* 2nd edn (Policy Press, 1998), ch 5.

3   Cm 849, 1989, para 24.

4   See **1.8.1**.

5   See **1.6**.

quickly to the injection of resources and, between 1981 and 1996, there was a 29 per cent increase in the numbers of older people in residential care, far in excess of the overall increase in the numbers of over 65-year-olds in the population as a whole.

(ii) At the same time, the NHS, driven by technological change and governmental demands for 'efficiency' was beginning to re-focus its services more obviously on acute care. Between 1983 and 1996, there was a 38 per cent reduction in beds designated for older people.

(iii) It seems clear that the availability of DSS funding did, in fact, facilitate an 'opportunistic shifting of costs from NHS to social security budgets'.[1] However, other policy initiatives during the 1980s turned attention away from the NHS, and the developments described above went largely unremarked.

(iv) In particular, the White Paper on Community Care made no proposals for clarifying or altering NHS responsibilities, concentrating instead on the Audit Commission's criticisms of the 'perverse incentive' towards residential care which was being created by unrestricted benefit funding.[2]

(v) Implementation in April 1993 of Part III of the NHSCCA 1990 underwrote the shift in provision away from the NHS which had already taken place. Local authorities, with their 'modernised' purchasing/commissioning role, became lead agencies for the coordination and delivery of 'community care services' which, significantly, included an enhanced responsibility to purchase long-term care in nursing homes as well as residential care homes.[3]

2.4.1 The 1992 Guidance: local authority contracts for residential and nursing home care

In 1992, a circular was published,[4] which purported to identify local authority and NHS responsibilities for funding *community health services* for people in residential care after April 1993. It took for granted the fact that the White Paper on Community Care intended local authorities to 'have responsibilities for purchasing nursing home care for the great majority of people who need it and who require to be publicly supported.'[5]

The circular refers to contractual arrangements made under s 23 of the NHSA 1997[6] between health authorities and nursing homes, in respect of patients whose needs are 'primarily for health care',[7] and where the NHS carries full

---

1   Wistow, G *Options for Long-Term Care* (HMSO, 1996).
2   See **1.6–1.9**.
3   NHSCCA 1990, s 42(1), amending NAA 1948, ss 21 and 26. See **1.8.1**.
4   DoH Circular LAC (92) 24; HSG (92) 50: *Local Authority Contracts for Residential and Nursing Home Care: NHS related aspects.*
5   Ibid, para 3.
6   See **2.4**.
7   These words were emphasised by the Court of Appeal in the *Coughlan* case. See **2.4.3**.

funding responsibility. It makes clear, however, that in most cases, local authorities will have responsibility for purchasing services to meet 'general nursing care needs'. These will include the cost of incontinence services (eg laundry) and those incontinence and nursing supplies which are not available on NHS prescription.[1] Health authorities remain responsible for purchasing physiotherapy, chiropody and speech and language therapy, with appropriate equipment, and for the provision of *specialist* nursing advice such as continence advice and stoma care, plus advice to homes about the management of incontinence, maintenance of mobility and management of behavioural disorders.

The circular guidance requires local authorities to ensure that, under their contracts with nursing homes,[2] general nursing care services are fully provided and that there are agreements with the NHS in respect of the supply of *specialist* nursing care and other community health services – for example, physiotherapy. There is also a reference to the possibility that there will be joint local authority/health authority service contracts with nursing homes.

HSG (92) 50 envisages:

(a) that some nursing care will be provided and funded in full by the NHS. Eligibility will be determined by whether or not there is a 'primary need for health care';

(b) that, in most cases, local authorities will arrange 'general' nursing care under the NAA 1948, and that this will be means tested;

(c) that, where patients need 'specialist' nursing, or other provision such as physiotherapy, in addition to general nurisng, this will again be an NHS responsibility, and will not be charged for.

One of the obvious difficulties raised by the circular guidance is how to distinguish between what are effectively three levels of nursing care.[3]

2.4.2 The *Leeds* Case

In a highly publicised report on the failure of the NHS to offer continuing care to the victim of a catastrophic stroke, the Health Service Commissioner found that the health authority under investigation neither provided continuing hospital care for people with neurological conditions, nor made contractual arrangements with nursing homes in the independent sector. It was, apparently, the health authority's policy to spend 'no' resources on patients in this category. The Commissioner ordered the authority to refund to the patient's relatives the substantial sums which they had been obliged to spend on private nursing home fees.[4] He stated:

---

1   DoH Circular LAC (92) 24; HSG (92) 50, para 3.
2   Referring to contracts made under NAA 1948, s 26 with private nursing homes; see Chapter 6.
3   These were clearly exposed in the *Coughlan* case; see **2.4.3**.
4   HSC, *Failure to Provide Long-term NHS Care for a Brain-damaged Patient*, (HMSO, 1994).

'This patient was a highly dependent patient . . . and yet when he no longer needed care in an acute ward, but manifestly still needed what the NHS is there to provide, they regarded themselves as having no scope for continuing to discharge their responsibilities to him because their policy was to make no provision for continuing care. The policy had the effect of excluding an option whereby he might have the cost of his continuing care met by the NHS. In my opinion the failure to make available long-term care within the NHS for this patient was unreasonable and constitutes a failure in the service provided by the health authority.'

2.4.3 The Guidance on *NHS Responsibilities for Meeting Continuing Health Care Needs*

Publication of the Health Service Commissioner's highly critical report caused the NHS Executive to seek to clarify the statutory responsibility for meeting continuing care needs. After an extended period of consultation, circular guidance entitled *NHS Responsibilities for Meeting Continuing Health Care Needs* was published in February 1995.[1] It emphasised that the NHS remains responsible for arranging and funding a range of services to meet the continuing physical and mental health needs of older people and others. However, health authorities and local authorities share responsibilities for 'arranging and funding services to meet people's needs for continuing care'.[2]

Paragraph 10 identified the range of services for which the NHS is, or may be, responsible. These are:

- specialist medical and nursing assessment;
- rehabilitation and recovery;
- palliative health care;
- continuing in-patient care under specialist supervision in hospital or in a nursing home;
- respite health care;
- specialist health care support to people in nursing homes or residential care homes or the community;
- community health services to people at home or in residential care homes;
- primary health care; and
- specialist transport services.

There was, however, no unequivocal commitment to any particular level of provision. Instead, there were many references to local planning and local eligibility criteria, based on the needs of local populations and demographic trends.

---

1 DoH Circular HSG (95) 8; LAC (95) 5. This was not s 7 guidance, but it was accepted that it must carry significant weight, especially as it was also issued to social services authorities. See *R v North Derbyshire Health Authority ex parte Fisher* (1998) 1 CCL Rep 150.

2 DoH Circular HSG (95) 8; LAC (95) 5, para 2.

2.4.4   NHS-funded in-patient care

'All health authorities and GP fund-holders should arrange and fund an adequate level of service to meet the needs of people who because of the nature, complexity or intensity of their health care needs will require continuing in-patient care arranged and funded by the NHS in hospital or in a nursing home.'[1]

HSG (95) 8 set out four eligibility criteria for NHS-funded care, *viz*:

(1)   where the complexity or intensity of patients' medical, nursing care or other clinical care or the need for frequent not easily predictable interventions requires the regular supervision of a consultant, specialist nurse or other NHS member of the multi-disciplinary team (in most cases, interventions might be weekly or more frequent);

(2)   where patients require routinely the use of specialist health care equipment or treatments which must be supervised by specialist NHS staff;

(3)   where patients have a rapidly degenerating or unstable condition which means that they will soon require specialist medical or nursing supervision; and

(4)   where patients have finished acute treatment or in-patient palliative care, but their prognosis suggests that they are likely to die in the very near future. These patients should be able to choose between remaining in NHS-funded accommodation or returning home with appropriate support.

Health authorities, in collaboration with local authorities, were required to produce local eligibility criteria for continuing health care which reflected the particular needs of their local population. Implicitly, local criteria were to elaborate on the conditions set out above, or possibly to extend them. As the stated responsibilities were meant to be an integral part of NHS provision, it would not have been appropriate for local policies to restrict them further. Such policies were expected to state how continuing in-patient care would be purchased, and give details of arrangements for contracting beds in the independent sector.

All new health authorities were told to have their local policies and eligibility criteria in place by 1 April 1996. Health authorities were expected to report annually to the NHS Executive on their planned and achieved levels of spending and activity on continuing health care.[2]

The guidance also laid down new procedures for the discharge of patients from hospital which were explored in more detail in later guidance.[3] These are reviewed, in some detail, in Chapter 3.

---

1   DoH Circular HSG (95) 8; LAC (95) 5, Annex A, para E.

2   Ibid, paras 38 and 39.

3   DoH Circular HSG (95) 39; LAC (95) 17: *Discharge from NHS In-Patient Care of People with Continuing Health or Social Care Needs*; see para 3.2.

Two things are now clear.

(1) The setting of local priorities for continuing care means that 'entitlement' varies up and down the country. In one area, a chronically ill elderly patient may receive long-term in-patient care in an NHS-funded unit, while in another area a patient with similar needs may be placed by social services in a nursing home and will have to meet part or all of the cost of the placement.

(2) Some of the local eligibility criteria have been, throughout, more restrictive than the original guidance, placing too much emphasis on the need for patients to meet multiple criteria in order to qualify for NHS-funded care. Some time ago, the NHS Executive warned that there should not be 'an over-reliance on the needs of the patient for specialist medical supervision in determining eligibility for continuing in-patient care'.[1]

Both these issues were addressed recently by the Court of Appeal in *R v North and East Devon Health Authoritiy ex parte Coughlan*,[2] an important judicial review, which is likely to generate a flurry of litigation and which, at the least, will require all health authorities to review their existing eligibility criteria.

2.4.5   The decision in *R v North and East Devon Health Authority ex parte Coughlan*

The Court of Appeal identified the critical issues in this case as:

(a) whether nursing care for a chronically ill patient may lawfully be provided by a local authority as a social service, which must be charged for, or whether it is required by law to be provided free of charge as part of the NHS; and

(b) if social services may lawfully provide such care, what eligibility criteria the NHS may lawfully lay down in order to define its sphere of responsibility.

Ms Coughlan has been cared for by the NHS since she suffered devastating injuries in a road traffic accident almost 30 years ago. Since 1993, she has lived at Mardon House, an NHS purpose-built specialist unit which cares for people with severe physical disabilities and also provides rehabilitation services. The decision, made on economic grounds, to close Mardon House and reprovision the services, triggered the judicial review. The North and East Devon Health Authority originally proposed that Ms Coughlan's care needs should be met by the Devon Social Services Authority after the closure of Mardon House. This would have meant that Ms Coughlan would have been required to pay for her own care – either in full or according to her means.

---

1   DoH Circular EL (96) 8.
2   (1999) 2 CCL Rep 285.

In the Divisional Court, Hidden J ruled in Ms Coughlan's favour on a number of grounds, stating very firmly that *all* nursing care is the sole responsibility of the NHS, and is consequently to be funded by the taxpayer.

The main points in the Court of Appeal's ruling may be summarised as follows.

(1) The NHS does not have an absolute duty to provide nursing care or any other 'health service'.[1] The current legislation is qualified in its terms, implying that the Secretary of State for Health must exercise judgment in the prioritisation of resources.

(2) Local authority social services departments have a responsibility under Part III of the NAA 1948 to provide or arrange residential accommodation, and s 21(5) empowers them to provide nursing services in connection with such accommodation. Section 21(8) enables local authorities to provide, as *social care*, such nursing services as the Secretary of State for Health has legitimately decided not to provide under s 3 of the NHSA 1977.

(3) The fact that social care services are means tested whereas health care is free of charge does not prevent the Secretary of State for Health from declining to provide some nursing services.

(4) The distinction between nursing services which can and cannot be provided by a local authority is one of fact and degree. In general, if nursing services are merely 'incidental or ancillary' to the provision of accommodation and are 'of a nature' that a local authority, whose primary responsibility is to provide social care, can expect to provide, then they fall within the scope of the NAA 1948. However, where the primary need is a health need, the NHS is required to meet it.

(5) It is lawful and appropriate for health authorities to use criteria which determine an individual's eligibility for NHS nursing care. These criteria will be based on the formal guidance[2] issued by the Department of Health, but it is not essential that all criteria should be the same. There may be legitimate variations between the services provided by the NHS in different areas.

(6) However, the criteria operated by the North and East Devon Health Authority (and, it seems, by many other health authorities) were unlawful, because they purported to place a responsibility on Devon Social Services which went beyond the NAA 1948 and was properly within the domain of the NHS. Notwithstanding local variations there is, it seems, an irreducible minimum level of responsibility which all health authorities must accept.

---

1   NHSA 1977, s 3.
2   DoH Circular HSG (95) 8; LAC (95) 5.

Ms Coughlan is paralysed from the waist down. She is doubly incontinent and needs frequent catheterisation. She needs assistance with feeding, and she has breathing difficulties. She can use an electric wheelchair, but has to be transferred from bed to chair. Notwithstanding her severe difficulties, Ms Coughlan did not meet the eligibility criteria set by the Health Authority. Given that, in the judgment of the Court of Appeal, her disabilities are of a scale which goes beyond the scope of local authority services, it follows that the Health Authority placed excessively rigorous limits on its definition of NHS services.

The discussion in Chapter 1 emphasises that the Court of Appeal's decision marks one further step in an ongoing demarcation dispute between health and local authorities as to what is truly 'health' care. Lord Woolf MR (who gave the only judgment) was clearly well aware of the enormous public expenditure implications of the incautious ruling by the Divisional Court. As was to be expected, he accepted that HSG (95) 8 did not alter NHS responsibilities in respect of continuing in-patient care, and underlined the fact that (as the guidance states) nursing services may be NHS services either because of their nature or quality, or because the need for them is continuous and intense.

Local criteria which purport to limit the scope of the guidance will be unlawful. Ms Coughlan, for example, has needs which go well beyond the 'care and attention' to be provided under the NAA 1948 and the criteria which excluded her from NHS provision were, therefore, unlawful.

2.4.6 General and specialist nursing care

There was some discussion in the Court of Appeal about the distinction to be drawn between 'general' and 'specialist' nursing care. As noted at **2.4.1**, this distinction is built into circular HSG (92) 50 which identifies the community health provision to be made for people in residential care homes or nursing homes. Permanent long-term nursing care is not a community health responsibility, although nurses do deliver discrete care for patients at home, or in residential accommodation. Where an elderly person is in a nursing home which is supposed to be delivering 'nursing for persons suffering from any sickness, injury or infirmity',[1] unless it is accepted (which clearly is not and never has been the case) that the NHS has sole responsibility for funding, then a line has to be drawn between the ongoing, day-to-day care provided by the home, and additional, or 'special' nursing needs. Both the 1992 and the 1995 guidance placed the emphasis on 'specialist' care as being the hallmark of NHS-funded care.

The Court of Appeal, whilst accepting that the distinction between 'specialist' and 'general' can provide an indicator of NHS responsibility in some circumstances, was not inclined to treat it as the sole distinguishing factor

---

1   Registered Homes Act 1984, s 21(1).

between health and social care. 'The expressions should not be regarded as giving anything more than the most general indication of what is and is not health care which the NHS should provide'.[1]

North and East Devon's Health Authority's own definition of specialist nursing was said to be 'idiosyncratic' and the Court of Appeal was manifestly concerned at the fact that its eligibility criteria purported to rely on a recommendation by the NHS Executive (which subsequently could not be traced) that specified services in nursing homes were to be regarded as standard, and so not 'specialist'. These included general physical and mental nursing care, artificial feeding, continuous oxygen therapy, wound care, pain control, administration of drugs and medication, catheter care, bladder wash-outs, tracheotomy care and tissue viability. In North and East Devon, therefore, patients requiring such services were not eligible criteria for NHS continuing care. Ms Coughlan was one of these.

The Court of Appeal indicated that it would be preferable to define 'specialist' by reference to qualification rather than to employment or task, so that services provided by district nurses, health visitors, community psychiatric nurses, community mental handicap nurses and midwives, for example, might justifiably be regarded as 'specialist services'.

It must be accepted that the Court of Appeal did not purport to offer a definition of 'specialist', although its decision suggests that eligibility criteria which turn exclusively on the general/specialist distinction may be unlawful. It also affirmed that both HSG (92) 50 and HSG (95) 8 constitute lawful guidance on NHS responsibilities, notwithstanding the references in both pieces of guidance to 'specialist' care. It made clear, however, that eligibility criteria must also cover a situation where the demand for nursing care is 'continuing and intense', and where the care which the patient needs may still exceed what can be properly provided by social services. Reference was made to para 21 of HSG (95) 8 which does refer, among other things, to the 'complexity, nature or intensity of the patient's medical, nursing or other clinical needs'.

2.4.7   The '*Coughlan* test'

To summarise the current legal position, the Court of Appeal has laid down two principles against which local eligibility criteria have to be measured, and has made clear that Pamela Coughlan is to be the benchmark, in the sense that criteria which exclude patients with her level of need from NHS care will be unlawful.

This means, in effect, that the NHS *must* fund nursing care for patients who:

(a) need 'specialist' care, as explained, although not clearly defined by the Court of Appeal; and/or

---

1   *R v North and East Devon Health Authority ex parte Coughlan* (1999) 2 CCL Rep 285 at 301.

(b) need care which is 'continuous and intense' and so exceeds what may
     properly be provided by social services.

Lord Woolf suggested that criteria ought to address both 'specialist' and
'continuous' care needs. However, despite disapproving of the North and East
Devon criteria, he did not lay down an exact marker as to exactly what level of
need for specialist and/or continuous nursing care can *only* be met by the NHS.
For some older clients this may well be the crucial issue.

2.4.8   The response to *Coughlan*

A study of the eligibility criteria operated by 25 health authorities across
England and Wales was published by the Royal College of Nursing in
December 1999.[1] It concluded that 90% of the criteria, in what was a small
sample, were 'likely' or 'highly likely' to be unlawful. The researchers worked
on the assumption that criteria must incorporate both a 'quality' and a 'quantity'
test, but the study does not make clear where it purports to draw the line, in
respect of criteria which are not identical to those used in Devon.

In fact, criteria are very diverse, and where they do differ from those considered
in *Coughlan*, the grey areas in the Court of Appeal's decision become apparent as
soon as they come under review. The RCN report has to be viewed with some
scepticism because its methodology in these cases is uncertain.

Circular HSG (95) 8 expired at the end of February 2000 and a revised version
was expected in the autumn of 2000.[2] However, interim guidance was issued
on 11 August 1999,[3] summarising the DoH's view of *Coughlan*. It identified the
following areas for action:

(a) health and local authorities, in consultation with each other and, where
     appropriate, with PCGs, should satisfy themselves that their continuing
     and community care policies, eligibility criteria and other relevant
     proceedings are in line with both *Coughlan* and the 1995 guidance;
(b) further legal advice should be taken where necesssary;
(c) where eligibility criteria are revised, health and local authorities should
     further consider what action they need to take to reassess service users
     against the revised criteria.

The interim guidance does not mention possible claims for reimbursement of
care fees, but the legal principles involved are likely to be explored through

---

1   *Rationing by Stealth* (RCN, 1999).
2   That deadline now appears to have slipped back to March or April 2001.
3   DoH Circular HSG (99) 180; LAC (99) 30; *Ex parte Coughlan: Follow-up Action.*

further test cases.[1] It does state, however, that all eligibility criteria should identify at least *two* categories of patients in nursing homes who are entitled to receive NHS-funded care. These are:

— those who, because of the nature of their needs, cannot properly be regarded as a social services responsibility at all, and whose care is therefore solely the responsibility of the NHS;[2]
— those who have some needs which fall outside the responsibility of social services, and in respect of which the NHS must provide additional funding.

As noted in **2.3.1**, this classification is implicit in HSG (92) 50, but it raises further problems in that criteria will seemingly be required to specify two levels of cut-off from NHS provision. In *Coughlan*, the Health Authority's chief executive stated her opinion that it would be very difficult, if not impossible, to distinguish between different types of nursing care, or between 'nursing' care and 'social' care, given the context in which 'nursing' generally is carried out, whether in a hospital or in a nursing home.

This raises a further issue in that Lord Woolf indicated in *Coughlan* that, where it is impossible to draw the line between basic 'social services' nursing care and additional NHS care, then the NHS must take the entire financial responsibility. However, he did not find it inherently unlawful to charge patients in nursing homes for some 'nursing' services and not others. As will be seen, the Government's most recent proposals in respect of long-term care funding reflect this position.[3]

2.4.9 New guidance

In the summer of 1999, a continuing care review was set up by the DoH. Its terms of reference were: 'to consider existing continuing care policy and guidance in the context of the Government's modernisation agenda for health and social services'.

It appears that the review revisited the Executive Letter issued to health authorities by the NHS Executive in 1996,[4] which seemed to anticipate the

---

1   At the time of writing, more than a year has passed since the Court of Appeal handed down its decision in *Coughlan*. Within that time there has been surprisingly little legal activity. However, a more recent decision of the Court of Appeal in *R v Richmond LBC ex parte Watson* (2000) 3 CCL Rep 276, CA to local authorities' power to charge for services provided under the Mental Health Act 1983 also raises the possibility of restitution, and an appeal is now likely to go to the House of Lords. See **4.2.4**.

2   Further guidance, DoH Circular HSG (95) 45: *Arrangements between health authorities or NHS trusts and private and voluntary sector organisations for the provision of community care services* emphasises that once a patient has been *assessed as requiring continuing NHS in-patient care* and the health authority has determined to arrange such care in an independent nursing home, the service must be provided free of charge.

3   See **2.4.10**.

4   EL (96) 8.

possibility of a judicial review, such as *Coughlan*. It emphasised that eligibility criteria need to be sensitive to the complexity *or* intensity *or* unpredictability of a patient's needs, and that patients should not be required to meet multiple criteria in order to qualify for NHS-funded care.

EL (96) 8 was not considered in *Coughlan*. Given, however, that it represents the NHS Executive's opinion as to the scope of the 1995 guidance, and given that it is also consistent with the *Coughlan* ruling, it may be anticipated that the forthcoming new guidance, which is now expected in October 2000, will draw the health/social care boundary more explicitly, perhaps, but essentially in the same place as before. However, forthcoming new legislation, discussed in the next paragraph, raises some further uncertainties.

2.4.10   *The NHS Plan 2000*

In July 2000 the Government published *The NHS Plan 2000*, which purports to 'reshape' the health service. It was accompanied by the Government's response to the recommendations made by the Royal Commission on Long Term Care.[1] The Government has already acted on one of the key recommendations – to establish a National Care Commission[2] – and has adopted many of the secondary recommendations.[3] However, the main task of the Royal Commission was to address the central policy issue of how the costs of long-term care should be apportioned between public funds and individuals. Its conclusion on this issue is well known: that the costs of long-term care should be split between living costs, housing costs and personal care. Personal care should be available after an assessment, according to need and paid for from general taxation: the rest should be paid for by individuals, according to their means.[4]

In its response to the Royal Commission, the Government commented: 'making personal care free for everyone carries a very substantial cost, both now and in the future. It would consume most of the additional resources we plan to make available for older people through *The NHS Plan 2000* . . . we have not followed this recommendation because we believe our alternative proposals to improve standards of care and their access to services will generate more important benefits of health and independence for older people, now and in the future'.[5]

The Government's counter-proposal, which is to be implemented in October 2001, is to make 'nursing care' available free of charge under the NHS to everyone in a 'care' home who needs it. The NHS will meet the costs of

---

1   *With Respect to Old Age*, op cit.
2   The Care Standards Act 2000 (which will come into force in April 2002) establishes a National Care Standards Commission.
3   These are incorporated in the text, but there is a summary of all the Government's proposals in Appendix 1.
4   *With Respect to Old Age*, op cit, ch 6.
5   *The NHS Plan 2000*, the Government's response to the Royal Commission on Long Term Care, para 2.6 (available from www.nhs.uk/nhsplan/ltcindex.htm).

'registered nurse' time spent on 'providing, delegating or supervising care in any setting ... therefore people identified as needing nursing home care will no longer have to meet any of the costs for the registered nurses involved in their care, or for the specialist equipment used by these nurses'.[1]

Considering that it is negating the considered views of a Royal Commission, which spent a year receiving evidence on this issue, the brevity of the governmental response, and its lack of clarity, are astonishing. Reading between the lines, however, it appears that the new proposal in relation to nursing care is lifted from the Note of Dissent to the Royal Commission which, whilst opposing the main recommendation, drew attention to the 'glaring anomaly' that nursing care provided in a hospital, residential home or community setting is free, but has to be paid for by people who live in nursing homes, and put forward the option of making nursing care free in nursing homes.[2] The dissenters made it very clear that theirs was a minimum cost proposal, based on a strict definition of 'nursing care' as 'care which requires the specific knowledge and skill which only registered nurses can provide. Such nursing care would, for example, include the assessment of health needs and specific interventions which require technical competence and knowledge of disease states in such matters as tissue and skin care, administration of drugs, complex medication, incontinence, stoma care and parenteral nutrition'.[3]

In its recent statement, the Government draws attention to the fact that its proposed definition of 'nursing care' is wider than that proposed in the Note of Dissent, presumably because of the reference to 'delegating and supervising care'. However, the indications are that nursing care itself is to be defined in terms of specialism, and that the Government, like the dissenters, is envisaging that such care will be provided free of charge as a component of care packages tailored to the assessed needs of individual older people. This would raise a number of obvious difficulties.

First, neither the Government, nor the Note of Dissent, makes any reference to the *Coughlan* ruling that basic, non-specialist nursing care which is continuous or intensive is to be considered 'health' care. A great deal of the care provided in hospitals falls into this category, and to use the term adopted in the Note of Dissent, it would be 'anomalous' if such care were not considered to be an NHS responsibility in a nursing home setting. However, the present indication is that the anomaly is intended to remain, and that the Government will adopt a narrow definition of nursing care. There will need to be primary legislation to override *Coughlan* and also to clarify the extent of local authority responsibilities under the NAA 1948 for arranging care in nursing homes.

In addition, assuming that nursing care is indeed intended to be provided as a 'component' of individual care packages, the financial implications, and the

---

1   *The NHS Plan 2000*, op cit, paras 2.8–2.10.
2   *With Respect to Old Age*, op cit, 'Note of Dissent', ch 4.
3   Ibid, para 65.

scope for disputes appear to be potentially endless. In many respects, clients who have assets in excess of £16,000 (£18,500 from April 2001[1]) will be most affected. The Government estimates that its introduction of 'free' nursing care will benefit around 35,000 people at any one time, and that they could save 'up to around £5,000 for a year's stay in a nursing home'.[2] Given the amount of money potentially at stake, there will inevitably be battles over assessments and the stated 'NHS component' in care plans. In addition, there may be major disputes over the basic eligibility criteria for care in a nursing home as opposed to a residential care home.

The Government thinks that the introduction of free nursing care will provide the 'right incentives to the NHS and social services to work together', and will encourage the provision of rehabilitation services, which would include the intermediate care provision which is proposed in the NHS Plan.[3] The 'perverse incentive' to discharge patients from hospital into social services funded residential care as quickly as possible will be removed. All of these outcomes are indeed highly desirable, but practicalities, and past experience, suggest that creating a seamless structure without demarcations to fight over and where there is, in fact, consistency of approach across the board, will be very difficult.[4]

2.4.11 Free nursing care in nursing homes

Clause 48 of the Health and Social Care Bill, published in December 2000, introduces the proposed new definition of 'nursing care' which is to be funded by the NHS.

When this provision is implemented, which is expected to be in October 2001, local authorities will cease to be 'authorised or required' to provide or arrange, for any person, 'nursing care by a registered nurse'. Since local authorities' present responsibilities in this area relate only to nursing homes, residential care homes will not be affected.[5]

'Nursing care by a registered nurse' means services which are provided by a registered nurse and involve either direct, hands–on care, or the planning, supervision or delegation of such care. However, it does not include services which do not *need* to be provided by a registered nurse, even if he or she is actually providing them.[6]

---

1   See Appendix 1.
2   *The NHS Plan 2000*, para 2.11.
3   Ibid, para 15.14.
4   Clause 48 of the Health and Social Care Bill, published in December 2000, incorporates the proposed new definition of nursing care which is to be funded by the NHS. Given the complexity of the issues raised, this clause is analysed separately at Appendix 3.
5   However, once the Care Standards Act 2000 comes into force in April 2002, nursing homes and residential care homes will be replaced by generic 'care homes'.
6   Health and Social Care Bill 2000, cl 48(2).

At the time of writing, clause 48 had passed through most of the parliamentary process without amendment. Tentative observations are as follows.

(1) It may be inferred that the Government's intention is for the NHS to pay the salaries of registered nurses who are employed in nursing homes. However, clause 48 does not *require* the NHS to make such provision,[1] although it will become unlawful for local authorities to do so. This gap in responsibility is bound to cause problems in individual cases.

(2) Clause 48 implicitly anticipates the publication of guidance as to what exactly a registered nurse is expected to do. As noted earlier,[2] the formulation of a suitable job description is unlikely to be straightforward, especially given the proviso to clause 48(2).

(3) In *The NHS Plan 2000*, the Government suggested that 'nursing care' needs will be the subject of individual assessments and announced the introduction of a single assessment process for health and social care needs from April 2002. If nursing care 'relief' on fees is to be calculated on the basis of individual needs assessments, there will be scope for endless disputes, particularly where a resident is otherwise self-funding.

(5) Changes in funding will require changes in the mechanics of contracting for nursing home beds. The Government has emphasised the importance of the 'flexibilities' and pooled budgets provided for in the Health Act 1999, but local authorities will not have power to contract for the nursing care element of nursing home placements. Inevitably, contracts will proliferate as health authorities become involved, and there will be added complexity with, quite possibly, cash flow problems for care providers. If it is assumed that health authorities will contract with providers to cover the employment costs of registered nursing staff, then it is difficult to envisage how relief on fees can be delivered to individual residents, according to their needs, without problems arising along the way. What will happen, for instance, if there are staff shortages, and registered nurse posts go unfilled for any length of time?

(5) Finally, it is clear from the parliamentary debates, that the *Coughlan* principle, that a person whose primary need is for nursing care should be fully funded by the NHS, is intended to remain intact. Clients will still require advice as to their eligibility for continuing NHS care, as well as (or instead of) advice as to the amount of nursing care relief that they may expect to receive under the new measures.

---

1   Section 3 of the NHSA 1977 gives the Secretary of State for Health only a qualified duty to provide nursing care.
2   See **2.4.10**.

Chapter 3

DISCHARGE FROM HOSPITAL

'Health and social services authorities also need to ensure that procedures are carried out to a high standard. In busy hospitals and in the community, staff need periodic reminders of the importance and relevance of particular processes and procedures.' [1]

An elderly person is admitted to an NHS trust hospital following a stroke. Given the unrelenting pressure on acute care beds, it is highly likely that discharge of this patient will be considered as soon as her condition has stabilised, and almost certainly while she still needs continuing care and support. There are various options. The patient may be discharged into residential care either for a period of rehabilitation[2] or on a permanent basis. Alternatively, she may be discharged home, with support from social services and from the community health service. Hopefully, informal care will be available from a partner or other relative. If not, it will be important that the support services are on hand immediately to prevent deterioration in the patient's condition, and subsequent re-admission to hospital.

3.1   INTRODUCTION

Hospital discharge is a critical interface between the systems of health and social care. Although the White Paper on Community Care commented that 'health authorities will need to ensure that their plans allow for the provision of continuous residential health care for those highly dependent people who need it', in fact provision of continuing care and psychogeriatric beds in hospitals has been cut by 38 per cent since 1983, whilst the number of private nursing home places has increased by 900 per cent.[3] Health authorities have also been cutting back on contractual arrangements made under s 23 of the NHSA 1977 to fund nursing home beds; only 8 per cent of the additional places are currently funded by health authorities, the rest are paid for by local authorities or individual patients.[4]

However, the health/social services interface is, and always has been, built on shifting sand. A year ago the patient in the above example would probably have

---

1   *The Coming of Age: Improving Care Services for Older People*, Audit Commission (1977), para 32.

2   *The NHS Plan 2000* will provide an additional £900 million by 2003/04 for investment in new intermediate care services for older people. See *The NHS Plan 2000*, op cit, para 7.4.

3   *With Respect to Old Age*, op cit, para 4.7.

4   The impact of the new partnership arrangements (including pooled budgets) between health and social services authorities, initiated by the Health Act 1999, remains to be assessed. See **1.11.1** and **1.11.2**.

been advised not to expect to have the option of a long-stay hospital bed or nursing home place funded by the NHS. Since then, the Court of Appeal's decision in *R v North and East Devon Health Authority ex parte Coughlan* has re-opened the debate as to the extent of the legal responsibility on the NHS to provide long-term care (quite apart from the recommendation of the Royal Commission) and it is now clear that the 'entitlement' of older people to NHS provision will be extended.

Given this context, it is of crucial importance that patients have access to good legal advice *before* they are discharged from hospital. This chapter will address the following issues:

(1) the decisions that have to be made;
(2) hospital discharge procedures – the practice guidance and what clients and their advisers should expect; and
(3) reviewing decisions as to eligibility for NHS continuing care – strategies and tactics.

3.2 ARRANGEMENTS FOR DISCHARGE

Guidance to health authorities and local authorities on the management of hospital discharges has always emphasised the importance of maintaining effective procedures to ensure that patients do not leave hospital without adequate arrangements being made for their support in the community. The key to successful discharge is said to be 'good joint planning at all stages'.

The Patients' Charter includes hospital discharge as one of its national standards, stating:

'The Charter Standard is that before you are discharged from hospital a decision should be made about any continuing health or social care needs you may have. Your hospital will agree arrangements for meeting these needs with agencies such as community nursing services and local authority social services departments before you are discharged. You, and with your agreement, your carers, will be consulted and informed at all stages.'

The guidance will be of considerable importance when advising clients and their families about hospital discharge, and about the options for long-term care which may be available to them. At the time of writing, guidance issued in 1995 on NHS responsibilities for meeting continuing health care needs[1] has expired, and replacement guidance is awaited. Among other things, this guidance outlined the procedures which are to be adopted when patients are discharged from hospital. Subsequent guidance, issued in the same year, explained these

---

1   DoH Circular HSG (95) 8; LAC (95) 5. This guidance is examined, in detail, in Chapter 2. It was considered by the Court of Appeal in *R v North and East Devon Health Authority ex parte Coughlan*.

procedures in more detail.[1] There is no reason to anticipate that new guidance will alter the procedures described in this chapter.

Hospital consultants carry the ultimate responsibility for deciding when a patient no longer needs acute hospital care. Where a patient is likely to need intensive long-term support, a decision about discharge should be taken only after an 'appropriate multidisciplinary assessment' of his or her needs has been carried out. This should normally involve referral to a consultant with specialist responsibility for continuing care (for example, a geriatrician or psychogeriatrician) and input from nursing staff, occupational therapists, hospital social workers and, in some cases, from physiotherapists and speech therapists. The patient's GP should be consulted, and the assessment should take into account the views and wishes of the patient, his or her family and carers. Where the patient has no accommodation or where the patient's housing is no longer suitable for his or her needs, housing authorities and housing providers should also be involved in the assessment.[2]

The guidance makes no reference to any statutory basis for the multidisciplinary assessment. Whilst best practice clearly dictates an assessment, the only legal responsibility is in s 47 of the NHSCCA 1990, which requires local authority social services departments to assess actual or potential needs for 'community care services', including residential care and after-care for patients discharged from mental hospitals.[3]

Section 47(3) requires a local authority to notify the patient's health authority, and invite it to assist in any assessment where it appears that there may be a need for services under the NHSA 1977. This is an awkward provision, given the purchaser/provider split in the NHS. Health authorities (and, in the future, PCTs) are purchasers; trust hospitals are providers of health care. Consequently, where NHS in-patient care or health services delivered in the community are at issue, a representative of the health authority, quite apart from all the hospital staff, should be involved in the assessment process.

More fundamentally, the guidance makes clear that the 'multidisciplinary assessment' is intended to enable a decision to be taken as to whether the patient qualifies for NHS-funded or joint-funded continuing care. This is not a 'community care service', as referred to in s 47.

There was some discussion of the nature of the assessment on hospital discharge in *R v North and East Devon Health Authority ex parte Coughlan*,[4] both in the Divisional Court and in the Court of Appeal. However, no clear ruling has

---

1   *Discharge from NHS In-Patient Care of People with Continuing Health or Social Care Needs*; *Arrangements for Reviewing Decisions on Eligibility for NHS Continuing In-Patient Care*, DoH Circular HSG (95) 39; LAC (95) 17.
2   DoH Circular HSG (95) 8, para 19.
3   See Chapter 5.
4   See **2.4.5**.

emerged, and the practical expectation must be that one multidisciplinary assessment will be carried out, subsuming the functions laid down in s 47 and in the NHS guidance. Legal advisers need to be alive to the nature and extent of the decisions which are likely to result from the multidisciplinary assessment, and must be prepared to act as advocates for their clients throughout the process. When the assessment has been completed, the NHS consultant, in consultation with the 'multidisciplinary team', must decide whether:

–   the patient qualifies for continuing in-patient care arranged and funded by the NHS;
–   the patient needs a period of rehabilitation arranged and funded by the NHS;
–   the patient can be discharged from hospital into a nursing home or residential care home, funded by social services and/or by the patient; or
–   whether the patient can be discharged home or to other accommodation (for example sheltered housing) with a suitable package of social and health care support.[1]

In making this decision, the consultant must consider whether the patient meets the local eligibility criteria for continuing NHS in-patient care. These are discussed in Chapter 2. As each health authority sets its own criteria, consultants in large trust hospitals, whose patients may be drawn from several health authority areas, must be familiar with various sets of eligibility criteria and apply them. This means that patients with similar needs may be treated differently.

3.3   CONSULTATION WITH THE PATIENT

All the published guidance on s 47 assessments emphasises the importance of consulting with patients or carers, and their right to express choices. HSG (95) 8 insists that patients, their families and their carers should be given adequate information to enable them to understand the discharge process and to take sensible decisions about continuing care.

In particular, it allocates responsibility to social services staff to provide written information about the likely cost to a patient of any option which he or she is asked to consider and, where appropriate, details of social security benefits which may be available in those circumstances. It is clear, however, that patient choice does not enter directly into the decision as to whether NHS care should continue or whether responsibility for making continuing care arrangements, and for funding those arrangements, is to pass to social services and the patient's family. The guidance states only that 'the assessment should take account of the views and wishes of the patient, his or her family and any carer'.[2]

---

1   DoH Circular HSG (95) 8, para 21.
2   Ibid, para 19.

3.4 DUE PROCESS

The guidance emphasises that discharge from acute care must be subject to procedural safeguards for patients, and that all decisions must be recorded. Advisers must insist that there is a written assessment; a written care plan and written evidence of whether and how the local eligibility criteria for continuing NHS care have been applied. If, as frequently happens, the written assessment is not sufficiently comprehensive; or the views of relevant people (such as the patient, family members and prospective carers) are not recorded; or if the care plan does not appear to meet the assessed needs; or if there is no record of the decision on the eligibility criteria, it may not be appropriate to accept discharge. Once the patient is out of hospital, then leverage regarding the nature of the care arrangements or the financial package is considerably diminished.

3.5 CARERS

Under the Carers (Recognition and Services) Act 1995,[1] where a person is the subject of an assessment under s 47 of the NHSCCA 1990, an individual who provides or intends to provide a substantial amount of care for that person on a regular, non-professional basis, has the right to ask the local authority to assess his or her ability to provide such care. The local authority must carry out an assessment and must take the outcome into account when determining what the care package should be. Guidance made under the NHSCCA 1990 states that hospital discharge procedures must reflect this statutory duty, and that the needs of carers or prospective carers must be taken into consideration from the outset.

The Carers and Disabled Children Act 2000[2] will require local authorities to consider whether carers themselves have support needs which, if met, would help them to provide care, and whether or not to provide appropriate support services directly to carers, or indirectly, to the individuals being cared for. When the Act comes into force, this enhanced right for carers or prospective carers to have access to services *for themselves* will also have to be incorporated into the discharge process.

3.6 FINANCIAL IMPLICATIONS

HSG (95) 8 states that social services staff should provide written details of the likely cost to the patient of any discharge option which is being put forward. Information about social security benefits available to the patient should be included. Advisers should ensure that this requirement is met, and that any financial package is thoroughly checked. If a residential care financial

---

1   Discussed at **5.9**.
2   See **5.9**.

assessment is undertaken at this stage, the adviser should always expect to liaise with the finance department of the local authority and to advocate on the client's behalf over difficult issues.

3.7　IMPLICATIONS OF THE *COUGHLAN* DECISION

The decision by the Court of Appeal is examined in some detail in Chapter 2. As noted, new guidance is expected as to the extent of the legal responsibility on the NHS to provide nursing care, following *Coughlan*. It seems clear that many local eligibility criteria are challengeable, and some have already been reviewed. Advisers acting for clients with advanced dementia or with severe physical disabilities consequent upon, for example, a stroke, Parkinson's disease, motor neurone disease or multiple sclerosis, particularly where the condition is degenerative, should always vigorously pursue the possibility of NHS funding, whether in a nursing home or special unit.

In addition, from October 2001, when clause 48 of the Health and Social Care Bill 2000 is expected to be implemented, nursing care which is delivered or supervised by a registered nurse in a nursing home setting will have to be funded by the NHS, so that fees payable by all nursing home residents (whether or not subject to a means test) should decrease. It is likely that advisers will have to establish what proportion of an individual client's care is attributable to a registered nurse and ensure that the changes made reflect this.[1]

3.8　REVIEWING DISCHARGE DECISIONS

Before a discharge plan is finally implemented the patient and/or his or her family or carers may ask the health authority in which the patient is normally resident to review the decision on eligibility for NHS continuing in-patient care. HSG (95) 8 required that the health authority should deal with such a request as a matter of urgency, and should respond, in writing, within two weeks.

HSG(95)39 contains more details of the review procedure.[2] Once the written care plan has been circulated, a patient may initially discuss his or her concerns informally with a 'named person', who is usually a member of the multi-disciplinary team. If no resolution is possible, the patient must be given information about the formal review procedure, and, on request, will be put in touch with the advocacy services. The patient or carer may then ask a designated officer in the health authority to initiate the review. At that point, the two-week period referred to above starts to run, and the patient may not be discharged pending the outcome of the review. The time-limit, which will be

---

1　　See **2.4.11**.
2　　See the flowchart at **3.12**.

very difficult to achieve in practice, is clearly intended to reduce bed blocking. The hospital, therefore, has an incentive to facilitate the review. For the patient, on the other hand, the process buys time, even if it does not alter the outcome.

The guidance limits the scope of any review to two functions:

–   to check that proper procedures have been followed in reaching decisions about the need for NHS continuing in-patient care; and
–   to ensure that the health authority's eligibility criteria for NHS continuing in-patient care have been properly and consistently applied.

The designated officer must carry out preliminary investigations, and must then decide whether or not to refer the matter to a review panel, which consists of an 'independent' chairman and single representatives of the health authority and local authority. There is discretion not to convene a panel, for instance, where the designated officer concludes that the patient falls well outside the relevant eligibility criteria or where the review is being used to raise issues such as the content of the care package or the substance of the eligibility criteria, which are outside its scope.

Once convened, a review panel has access to all existing documentation on the case, including the patient's record of assessment. Panels may also require access to independent clinical advice in order to explain and interpret the original clinical judgments and their relationship with the health authority's eligibility criteria, but not, however, to provide a second opinion on clinical diagnosis, management or prognosis for the patient.

The guidance appears to rule out a hearing as such. Those seeking review are encouraged to put their views in writing or to request an interview with the designated officer. The designated officer is expected to attend review panel meetings and to communicate information gleaned from his or her investigations. There is no provision for written representations to be made directly to the panel, but advisers should still be prepared to make the case in writing, albeit channelled through the designated officer. The two-week review period allows little time for the adviser to obtain a clinical opinion on the patient's continuing care needs, and speed will be of the essence. Ultimately, the role of the review panel is advisory, although the expectation is that its recommendations will be accepted in all but very exceptional circumstances.[1] The health authority must communicate the outcome of a review to the patient, in writing, and with reasons.

---

1   See the flowchart at **3.12**. The guidance gives no hint as to what those circumstances might be, but it is reasonable to infer that financial considerations would determine a health authority's rejection of a panel recommendation. Following *Coughlan*, the Department of Health is reconsidering the role of review panels as part of its Continuing Care Review.

3.9   BED BLOCKING

Every winter there are press reports of acute hospital beds being blocked by elderly patients requiring discharge to community care. A major contributory factor is social services authorities' chronic lack of resources for community care.

HSG (95) 8 states that, where patients have been assessed as not requiring NHS continuing in-patient care, they do not have the right to occupy indefinitely an NHS bed. It remains to be tested whether a hospital would be acting unlawfully if it were to discharge an actively protesting patient, although in the aftermath of *Coughlan*, and given the general responsibilities of the Secretary of State for Health laid down in s 3 of the NHSA 1977, the proposition in the guidance may not be legally sustainable.

The guidance goes on to state that any patient who is not sectioned under Part III of the Mental Health Act 1983 (MHA 1983) may refuse to be discharged into residential care. In such circumstances, social workers, in conjunction with hospital and community-based staff and with the patient, his family and carers must explore 'alternative options'. If these are not acceptable, it may be necessary to discharge the patient home with a package of health and social care – for which the social services department may make a charge. In fact, it is difficult to see what 'alternative option' there might be, apart from discharge to the patient's own home or to the home of a carer. There is no suggestion, for example, that the hospital consultant would at this point reconsider a decision not to authorise NHS continuing care. The guidance also does not confront the possibility that a home-based package may be more costly than a residential placement. The implication of the reference to the social services' charge is that, once the hospital bed has been freed, the local authority, not the NHS, will have to deal with funding problems.

The vaguely threatening tones of para 27 of HSG (95) 8 seem to carry a warning for the patient, or his or her advisers, who might otherwise consider blocking beds in an effort to extract a commitment from the NHS to fund nursing home placements. Given the importance of throughput times for NHS performance targets, as has already been observed, a refusal to accept a discharge may be a useful means of putting pressure on a health authority. Whether it is appropriate or ethical to use such a tactic on behalf of frail, possibly confused elderly clients, is another matter.

Manifestly, however, patients who are unaware of their rights, and for whom there is no properly coordinated care package, are discharged home every day. As a result, re-admission rates give cause for concern. It may be noted that, where the patient lacks mental capacity, there is no legal power to accept discharge on his or her behalf, as neither an attorney nor a receiver has the power to make decisions about personal care. This means that the 'best-interests' test laid down in *F v West Berkshire Health Authority*[1] provides the only authority for discharging a patient who is unable to give consent. It is difficult to see how this test can be satisfied unless the discharge fully meets the procedural requirements laid down in both sets of guidance.

3.10   PRACTICE POINTS

(a)   For some clients, the discharge from hospital has crucial long-term financial implications which may also affect the quality of care that they receive. Well-informed legal advice at this stage is invaluable. Practitioners may wish to consider educating their clients in this respect.

(b)   The role of the legal adviser will be first of all to ensure that his or her client has understood the terms on which he or she is to be discharged from hospital and that the financial implications of discharge have been explained and digested by the client and his or her family. If a client is unhappy about the arrangements being put forward, then other steps may need to be considered.

(c)   A client may instruct his or her legal adviser to make representations to the person named in the written care plan. If, for example, the appropriate procedures have not been followed, or if the decision has not been properly explained, the plan may be challenged. Crucially, however, HSG (95) 39 does not suggest what the possible outcomes might be. It refers to the possibility of 'agreement', but it is difficult to envisage a health authority reversing a decision not to fund a continuing care placement because, for example, the patient was not fully aware of the relevant eligibility criteria. It may be predicted, therefore, that any agreement may be peripheral to the client's main concern.

(d)   The client may want to ask the health authority to review the decision. The independent panel must meet and make its recommendation within a fortnight of the request, so the legal adviser must prepare the case quickly and effectively. The adviser must be thoroughly familiar with the local community care plan and with the local eligibility criteria for NHS continuing in-patient care. Information about the culture and previous practice of the independent panel will be helpful.

(e)   There will be no right of appeal against a decision made by a health authority on the recommendation of the review panel. However, the *Coughlan* decision has now shown that eligibility criteria may themselves be susceptible to judicial review if they are unduly restrictive, and the hospital discharge process, including the reviews, may also be challenged if it is not seen as operating fairly.

---

1   [1989] 2 All ER 545.

3.11   ISSUES TO CONSIDER ON A DISCHARGE

The following might serve as a checklist.

–   Has there been a multidisciplinary assessment of the patient's needs?

–   Have the patient, relatives and carers been involved in the assessment?

–   Has the patient seen the written assessment?

–   Has the multidisciplinary team applied the local criteria for NHS continuing in-patient care and has its determination been recorded?

–   Is there a written care plan?

–   Does it reflect the assessment?

–   Is it realistic?

–   What are the cost implications of the care plan?

–   Have they been communicated and explained?

Where the patient is to be discharged into residential care, the following checklist is applicable.

–   If the patient is to be discharged into residential care under NAA 1948 arrangements, could/should the patient or relatives/carers seek a review of the decision that the patient is not entitled to NHS continuing care?

–   After October 2001, are the patient's needs for nursing care, delivered or supervised by a registered nurse in a nursing home setting, explictly recorded and reflected in the fees charged?

–   Has the patient or his or her family been given the opportunity to visit possible homes?

–   Has the patient been permitted to put forward his or her choice of home, as opposed to establishments on social services' lists?[1]

–   Where the patient needs nursing home care, has his or her health authority given consent to the arrangements under s 26(1C) of the NAA 1948?

–   Has funding been considered?

–   Has a financial assessment been carried out by the local authority?

–   Has advice been given about the implications of the charging regulations?

---

1   Note the Directions on Choice (DoH Circular LAC (92) 2) which are intended to ensure that prospective residents have a genuine choice as to where they should live. The local authority may argue against a preferred placement because it is too expensive by reference to other, equally suitable placements, but the directions allow for topping-arrangements, see **6.6**.

- If the patient has sufficient resources for a self-funding option to be available, would there be advantages or disadvantages in the patient purchasing his or her own residential care?

- Has the local authority suggested this course of action to the patient?[1]

Where the patient is to be discharged home with a care package, the checklist is as follows.

- Is the care package sufficiently detailed?

- Does it spell out the input which is to be made by the community health services?

- Have times and frequency of service delivery been specified?

- Has the care manager been identified and has the programme been discussed with him or her?

- Has there been an assessment of a potential carer's needs under the Carers (Recognition and Services) Act 1995 (CRSA 1995)? Does the care plan reflect that assessment? Does the carer have support needs which may be met under the Carers and Disabled Children Act 2000 (CDCA 2000)?

- Has respite care been considered? Would the health authority be prepared to provide some respite care for this patient?

- Has detailed consideration been given to the patient's possible entitlement to welfare benefits such as income support, attendance allowance or disability living allowance? Has any carer been advised about his or her entitlement to invalid care allowance?

- Have any necessary aids or adaptations to the patient's home been put in place? How far should discharge be made conditional upon the work being done in advance?

- Will the NHS provide essential equipment, for example pressure mattresses or wheelchairs? If any high-tech health care is to be delivered at home, is it clear that the community health team has had an input into the discharge plan?

---

1   See **6.10** for a discussion on the contractual aspects of private residential care arrangements.

3.12   FLOWCHART OF THE REVIEW PROCEDURE[1]

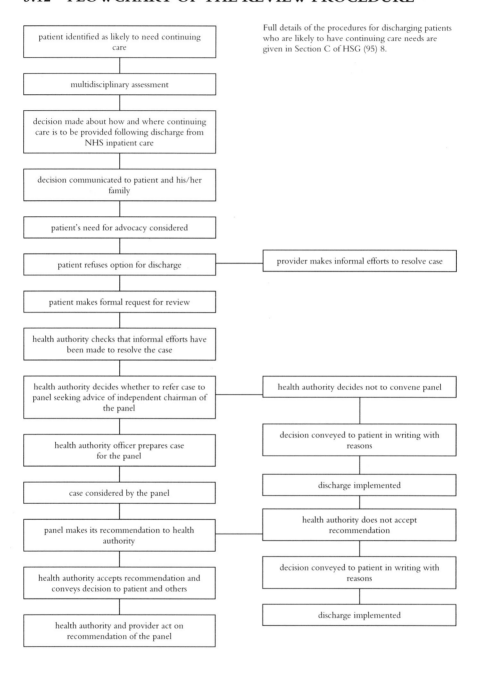

Full details of the procedures for discharging patients who are likely to have continuing care needs are given in Section C of HSG (95) 8.

---

1   Taken from DoH Circular HSG (95) 39; LAC (95) 17, *Discharge from NHS In-patient Care of People with Continuing Health and Social Care Needs; Arrangements for Reviewing Decisions on Eligibility for NHS Continuing In-patient Care.*

Chapter 4

LOCAL AUTHORITY SERVICES FOR OLDER PEOPLE

'Community care is still seen as about organising and rationing "practical" help ... The argument for the retention of social services as the lead agency in community care may be being undermined on the grounds that they now have much more in common with primary healthcare.'[1]

4.1 INTRODUCTION

As stated in Chapter 1, the policy objectives set out in the White Paper on Community Care centred on the creation of a coherent framework for the provision of services for adults within the context of a new market philosophy for social care. The legislative changes introduced in Part III of the NHSCCA 1990 overlaid the existing legislation referred to in Chapter 1, purporting to modernise and harmonise legal responsibilities for service planning and delivery by the addition of a few key provisions.

Of these, the most important was s 47, which imposes a duty on local social services authorities to assess the needs for community care services of people whom they have power to assist and who may be in need of such services. The content of the duty to assess and the assessment process itself are discussed in Chapter 5. 'Community care services' are defined in s 46(3) as services which local authorities may provide or arrange under any of the following legislation:

- Part III of the NAA 1948;
- s 45 of the HSPHA 1968;
- s 21 of and Sch 8 to the NHSA 1977; and
- s 117 of the MHA 1983.

Apart from assessing need, social services authorities have a duty under s 47 of NHSCCA 1990 to decide whether or not to provide community care services. Patently, therefore, NHSCCA 1990 is concerned with reinforcing statutory powers and duties which already exist. The framework is comprehensive. It emanates from the NAA 1948, one of the foundations of the Beveridge Welfare State, which abolished the nineteenth-century Poor Law and made new provision for income maintenance and social care services for disabled, sick and elderly people. Only Part III of the NAA 1948 remains in force, but it underpins all subsequent legislation in creating statutory powers and duties for (the then new) local authorities.

---

1   Means, R and Smith, R *From Poor Law to Community Care*, (Policy Press, 1998) p 323.

Most of this legislation is characterised by the creation of powers or qualified[1] duties to be exercised by local authority social services departments. Qualified duties have always been regarded as subject to available resources and implicitly leave local authorities to allocate priorities appropriately. Some duties (for example the duty created by s 117 of the MHA 1983 in respect of people suffering from a mental disorder) are legally sharper and appear to be more susceptible to enforcement by individuals, irrespective of resources. Recent case-law has shown, however, that there is, in general, no absolute right to service provision.[2] This theme is discussed more fully in Chapter 5.

The primary responsibilities laid down by the various pieces of community care legislation are extensively written subject to a requirement for local authorities to act under directions made or approval given by the Secretary of State. The right to issue directions means that central government, through the Secretary of State, has the final say over which, out of a range of general responsibilities, a local authority will be obliged[3] to carry out. Approvals are weaker; they simply identify areas of service provision to which local authorities should attach some priority.

4.2 COMMUNITY CARE SERVICES

4.2.1 Part III of the NAA 1948

Section 21

Section 21 of the NAA 1948, which was amended by s 42 of NHSCCA 1990, requires local authorities to arrange residential accommodation for 'persons aged eighteen or over who by reason of age, illness, disability or any other circumstances are in need of care or attention which is not otherwise available to them' (s 21(1)).

The client group covered by s 21 is very broad indeed. The 'illness' criterion was introduced in 1993[4] and, as far as the Department of Health was concerned, it signalled local authority responsibility for purchasing nursing home care for the 'great majority of people who need it, and who require to be publicly supported'.[5] Illness is not defined in the NAA 1948, but it must be taken to

---

1   In the 1990s, such duties have come to be known as 'target' duties (see Woolf LJ in *R v ILEA ex parte Ali* [1990] 2 All ER 822, 828). Sedley J (as he then was) recently commented: 'the metaphor recognises that the statute requires the relevant public authority to aim to make the prescribed provision but does not regard failure to achieve it without more as a breach' (in *R v London Borough of Islington ex parte Rixon* [1997] ELR 66, 69).

2   *R v Gloucestershire County Council ex parte Barry* (1997) 1 CCL Rep 40, HL.

3   Often subject to available resources; see Chapter 5.

4   NHSCCA 1990, s 42(1)(a).

5   DoH Circular LAC (92) 24, *Local Authority Contracts for Residential Nursing Home Care: NHS-related Aspects*, para 3. Note the discussion of the Circular and of the Court of Appeal's decision in *R v North and East Devon Health Authority ex parte Coughlan* in Chapter 2.

include mental disorder and physical disability. Age itself, without more, may give rise to a need for care and attention. As regards 'other circumstances', the Court of Appeal has now held that asylum seekers, without financial resources, without accommodation and without the opportunity to work are to be regarded as in need of care and attention where their cumulative difficulties create a risk of illness or disability.[1] The same will be true of older people who are homeless or destitute.

Section 21(5) provides that 'accommodation' includes 'board and other services, amenities and requisites provided in connection with the accommodation except where in the opinion of the authority managing the premises their provision is unnecessary'. Although the conventional model of s 21 care is the residential care home or nursing home, this subsection makes it clear that other types of residential accommodation arrangements may be made under s 21. In *R v Bristol City Council ex parte Penfold*,[2] for example, it was held that 'normal' housing can be provided under s 21, in circumstances where there is a need for care and attention, which would otherwise have to be met by other community care services.

The operation of s 21 is subject to the approval of and directions made by the Secretary of State. Various directions have been issued over the years, and were consolidated in 1993.[3] In particular:

(1) the Secretary of State now directs that the s 21(1) duty is owed to those who are ordinarily resident in the local authority's area.[4] It also extends to providing temporary accommodation for other people not directly referred to in s 21(1) but who are in urgent need of care in unforeseen circumstances. By contrast, the Secretary of State merely approves and empowers the making of residential arrangements for people with no settled residence;

(2) the Secretary of State further directs local authorities to make arrangements for the care and after-care of people with a mental disorder, whether or not they have settled residence in a particular local authority area;

(3) there is, finally, an approval of arrangements by local authorities to provide accommodation which will meet needs in respect of the prevention, care and after-care of illness.

Section 29

The responsibility covered here is the provision of a variety of services for disabled people. Section 29(1) defines the client group as people aged 18 or over who are blind, deaf or dumb or who suffer from a mental disorder of any description, and other adults who are substantially and permanently handi-

---

1   *R v Westminster City Council and Others ex parte M* (1997) 1 CCL Rep 85.
2   (1998) 1 CCL Rep 315.
3   DoH Circular LAC (93) 10, App 2.
4   See **6.4**.

capped by illness, injury, congenital deformity or such other disabilities as may be prescribed by the Secretary of State. Circular LAC (93) 10 extends this definition to people who are partially sighted or hard of hearing. 'Mental disorder' means mental illness, arrested or incomplete development of mind, psychopathic disorder and any other disorder or disability of mind.[1]

Section 29(4) sets out a non-exhaustive list of services which fall within the scope of the local authority's general responsibility. As with s 21, the Secretary of State must decide which particular services must or may be provided. LAC (93) 10 directs local authorities to make the following arrangements for people who are 'ordinarily resident'[2] in their areas:

- to provide a social work service and 'such advice[3] and support as may be needed for people in their own homes or elsewhere';
- to provide facilities for social rehabilitation and adjustment to disability;
- to compile and maintain registers of disabled people[4]; and
- to provide facilities for occupational, social, cultural and recreational activities; including setting up workshops providing employment for particular client groups (for example, people with learning disabilities).

The Secretary of State has also approved, and so empowered local authorities to provide:

- holiday homes;
- travel concessions;
- assistance in finding accommodation which will enable service users to take advantage of arrangements made under s 29(1);
- warden services for occupiers of private housing, and contributions towards the cost of employing wardens on 'welfare functions' in warden-assisted housing schemes; and
- hostel accommodation for people for whom workshop or other occupational activities are being provided.[5]

Section 30 of the NAA 1948 empowers local authorities to employ voluntary or commercial organisations as their agents in arranging any services under s 29. Social services authorities may, for instance, fund housing officers employed by

---

1 MHA 1983, s 1.

2 Considered at **6.4**.

3 Appendix 2, para (1)(a). Welfare benefits advice is clearly included in 'such advice'. Various complaints to the Local Government Ombudsman (for instance 94/B/2128) have demonstrated that a direct advice service need not be provided but, if provided, must be staffed by appropriately trained people. Inaccurate benefits advice constitutes maladministration.

4 These provide a useful source of information about the extent of disability and the need for services, which feeds into the local community care plan.

5 The same charging rules (made under of the NAA 1948, s 22) apply here as for residential accommodation.

registered social landlords[1] to deliver advice and support services ancillary to their housing management function.

4.2.2 Section 45 of the Health Services and Public Health Act 1968

Section 45 of the HSPHA 1968 enables local authorities, subject again to directions or approval from the Secretary of State, to make arrangements for promoting the welfare of old people. The client group is intended to include people whose needs arise out of frailty rather than disability, who are not substantially and permanently handicapped, and who could benefit from services which might help to postpone personal or social deterioration or breakdown.[2] The Secretary of State has chosen only to approve provision rather than to issue directions, which means that this section is inherently weaker than ss 21 and 29 of the NAA 1948. Approval exists in respect of arrangements for domiciliary services, such as:

- meals and recreation in the home and elsewhere (which could include day-centre provision);
- identifying old people in need of services and giving information about services available;
- advice and social work support;
- practical assistance in the home, for example, home help or laundry services, together with other facilities 'designed to secure the greater safety, comfort or convenience' of the service user; and
- providing warden services for the occupiers of private housing, and contributing towards the cost of employing a warden on welfare functions in warden-assisted housing schemes.

The guidance on service development for older people places considerable emphasis on the role of voluntary organisations and voluntary workers on account of the 'scarcity of manpower, both skilled and unskilled'. There is more than a suggestion that services for older people had been, and would continue to be, 'Cinderella' services, run on a shoestring.[3] The fact that no directions have been made under s 45 supports that perspective.

As with s 29 of the NAA 1948, there is power to employ voluntary agencies as agents to deliver services and s 65 of the HSPHA 1968 adds permission to provide grant aid. The NHSCCA 1990 now permits the delegation of all these functions to private sector providers.

---

1   Better known as 'housing associations'; the new term was introduced by the Housing Act 1996. The new rules in respect of 'partnership' funding are discussed at **1.11.1**.
2   DHSS Circular (71) 19.
3   See **1.3**.

4.2.3 Section 21 of and Sch 8 to the National Health Service Act 1977

The NHSA 1977 deals principally with health service provision. However, Sch 8 contains a list of responsibilities in respect of adults who are 'ill', rather than disabled or elderly, which s 21 specifically attributes to social services authorities. These consist of powers to make arrangements for the care of expectant and nursing mothers; for the prevention of illness; and for the care or after-care of people suffering from illness. As usual, they are subject to the Secretary of State's approval or directions.

There is a clear overlap between these provisions and the social care responsibilities of local authorities under the enactments discussed earlier, and for this reason neither s 45(4) of the HSPHA 1968 nor s 29(6) of the NAA 1948 authorises or requires provision which could be made under Sch 8 to the NHSA 1977. It is possible to read ss 45(4) and 29(6) as indicating that any overlapping services which the NHSA 1977 makes the responsibility of the Secretary of State for Health are to be delivered by the NHS rather than by social services departments.[1] A more cautious interpretation would be that services required to be provided by *social services authorities* under the NHSA 1977 are excluded from ss 29 and 45.

The Secretary of State has directed local authorities to make arrangements under para 2(1) of Sch 8 for the purposes of preventing mental disorder, and of providing after-care facilities, including domiciliary services.[2] Approval has also been given for the following general preventative and after-care services:

- meals on wheels for house-bound people, where not provided under other legislation, for example s 45 of the HSPHA 1968;
- night-sitter services;
- recuperative holidays;
- facilities for social and recreational activities;
- advice and support for the purposes of preventing the impairment of physical or mental health of adults in families where such impairment is likely, and for the purpose of facilitating family rehabilitation; and
- services specifically for people who are alcoholic or drug-dependent.

Before April 1993, local authorities could discharge their general responsibility under para 2 by making residential accommodation arrangements on behalf of the prescribed client group. This power is now repealed by s 66 of the

---

1   See *R v Gloucestershire County Council ex parte Mahfood and Barry* (1997) 1 CCL Rep 7, p 17; services provided by the NHS are, of course, free of charge at the point of delivery, and there is a clear, albeit general duty for the Secretary of State for Health to provide after-care services under NHSA 1977, s 3(1)(c). In *R v North and East Devon Health Authority ex parte Coughlan*, the Court of Appeal suggested that, where it is impossible to draw a clear line between health and social services responsibilities, the NHS must provide the service (see Chapter 2).

2   DoH Circular LAC (93) 10, App 3.

NHSCCA 1990, and replaced by the new, extended powers in s 21 of the NAA 1948.[1]

Paragraph 3 of Sch 8 imposes a clear duty on social services authorities to provide home-help services for *households* where a person is ill, aged, or handicapped as a result of illness or by congenital deformity. The duty, which is not subject to directions by the Secretary of State, is linked with a power to provide laundry facilities for such households. In this instance, services are not restricted to adults.

Local authorities must provide services 'on such a scale as is adequate for the needs of their area'. The generality of the language used indicates that this is a target duty, rather than a specific duty owed to particular individuals. In practice, the priorities and eligibility criteria set by a local authority may reflect the language in para 3, but would-be service users will not necessarily take priority over people who need other community care services.[2]

When exercising any responsibilities under Sch 8, local authorities must co-operate with health authorities 'in order to advance the health and welfare of the people of England and Wales'.[3]

4.2.4   Section 117 of the Mental Health Act 1983

This section applies to certain categories of mentally disordered patients who have ceased to be compulsorily detained[4] in hospital under the MHA 1983, and who have been discharged into the community. It imposes a *joint duty* on health and social services authorities to provide after-care services for such patients, in co-operation with voluntary agencies. There is some overlap with the provisions of the NHSA 1977 described above, but s 117(2) is more focused than Sch 8, and does require the responsible authorities to consider the needs of the individuals to whom the section applies. It is, therefore, more susceptible to enforcement by individuals. The new Mental Health Act Code of Practice (1999) emphasises the importance of identifying patients who are subject to s 117 and of establishing an after-care plan in consultation with the patient, informal carers and, where appropriate, the nearest relatives. The plan is to be recorded in writing and the patient's key worker is to arrange reviews 'until it is agreed that it is no longer necessary'.[5]

The Code of Practice does not point out that the ultimate decision as to whether after-care services are still required is to be made jointly by the health and social services authorities. This was made clear in *R v Ealing District Health*

---

1   See Chapter 6.
2   See *R v Gloucestershire County Council ex parte Mahfood and Barry* (1997) 1 CCL Rep 7, p 40.
3   Section 22 of the NHSA 1977.
4   Under ss 3, 37, 45, 47 or 48 of the MHA 1983.
5   Mental Health Act Code of Practice, para 27.11.

Authority ex parte Fox,[1] where Otton J held that statutory authorities must jointly provide after-care services under s 117, and will act unlawfully if they fail to make practical arrangements for these before a patient is discharged from hospital. The responsibility continues until both authorities concerned are satisfied that the former patient is no longer in need of after-care services.

The range of possible services which may be provided under s 117 is not circumscribed. Obvious examples are social work advice; counselling and support services; day-centre and drop-in provision; and domiciliary care. Residential services are not ruled out.

Social services authorities have no power to charge for s 117 services.[2] Given, therefore, the substantial overlap between statutory responsibilities in respect of people with mental disorder, it is important for authorities to identify which powers are being used, so as to avoid charges being levied ultra vires. This applies particularly where a patient is discharged into residential accommodation. Consequently, the position of elderly people suffering from dementia who become psychiatric in-patients and are subsequently discharged into residential accommodation must be considered carefully, because the financial implications are considerable.

It is now clear that, where the starting point was compulsory detention, s 117 will apply.[3] It has always been arguable that s 21 of the NAA 1948 cannot apply where residential accommodation is 'otherwise available' under s 117, but a recent decision by the Divisional Court on judicial review has further clarified the legal position and the scope of s 117. In *Ex parte Watson*,[4] Sullivan J held that the section creates a free-standing duty to provide after-care services for a group of seriously ill patients. Each patient's needs must be assessed individually, but the judge commented that it was difficult to see how a patient with dementia could fall outside s 117. Where such a patient needs residential care, only s 117 applies. Section 21 of the NAA 1948 is excluded because it prevents local authorities from making any residential provision 'authorised or required to be made ... by or under any enactment not contained in this part of this Act',[5] ie s 117. In consequence, residential care provided in these circumstances cannot be charged for.

---

1   [1993] 3 All ER 70.

2   See Chapter 8.

3   This is one respect in which 'sectioning' under the MHA 1983 offers greater protection than voluntary admission. One issue in relation to dementia patients is whether they 'can' be subject to voluntary admission.

4   *R v London Borough of Richmond ex parte Watson; R v Redcar and Cleveland ex parte Armstrong* [2000] 3 WLR 1127; *R v Manchester City Council ex parte Stenett; R v London Borough of Harrow ex parte Cobham* (1999) 2 CCL Rep 402. See Thompson, P 'Charging for Section 117 of the Mental Health After-care Services' ECA, vol 4, 6 p 10.

5   NAA 1948, s 21(8).

In July 2000 the Court of Appeal[1] affirmed the decision in *Re Watson*, emphasising that the duty to provide after-care services stands alone and is not merely a gateway to other service provision, which permits charging. In the past, some local authorities have charged for all s 117 services; about 50 per cent have purported to charge (under s 22 of the NAA 1948) for residential services, which are part of an after-care package. Claims for restitution are now being actively pursued[2] and local authorities are obviously very concerned about this further drain on their budgets.

Apart from seeking refunds of fees which have been paid, advisers will need to ensure, in future, that after-care arrangements are not prematurely terminated for reasons of financial expediency, rather than changed needs. *Ex parte Watson*[3] provides a helpful analysis of how decisions should be made.

4.3 THE CHRONICALLY SICK AND DISABLED PERSONS ACT 1970 AND THE DISABLED PERSONS (SERVICES CONSULTATION AND REPRESENTATION) ACT 1986

The statutory services discussed so far are unequivocally identified as 'community care services' by s 46 of the NHSCCA 1990. However, it has consistently been the view of the Department of Health that services provided under the Chronically Sick and Disabled Persons Act 1970 (CSDPA 1970) are also 'community care services' because they are provided in exercise of a local authority's functions under s 29 of the NAA 1948 (s 1 of the CSDPA 1970). This is important because the CSDPA 1970 and its 'partner' the DPSCRA 1986 are, in legislative terms, powerful measures, and the statutory framework of social care responsibilities would be considerably weakened if they were omitted from the scope of the NHSCCA 1990. The Department of Health has always linked the CSDPA 1970 with Part III of the NAA 1948, both on a straightforward interpretation of ss 1 and 2 of the CSDPA 1970, and because s 47 of the NHSCCA 1990 also explicitly ties both the CSDPA 1970 and the DPSCRA 1986 to the assessment of need for community care services.

A recent ruling by the Court of Appeal in *R v Powys County Council ex parte Hambidge*[4] has clarified this issue. The applicant, a severely disabled woman, challenged her local authority's decision to charge her for community care services provided under s 2 of the CSDPA 1970 on the basis that it had no

---

1   LTL, 27 July 2000.
2   The Local Government Ombudsman recently awarded substantial compensation against a local authority which charged for residential care provided under s 117, after being advised that this was unlawful; 98/B/0341; see a discussion of the case by Thompson, P, ECA, vol 5, no 2, p 23.
3   Op cit.
4   (1998) 1 CCL Rep 458.

power to do so because s 17[1] of the Health and Social Services and Social Security Adjudications Act 1983 (HASSASSAA 1983) only gives power to charge for services provided under (among others) s 29 of the NAA 1948. The court accepted the local authority's argument that the s 2 services were in fact provided pursuant to arrangements made in the exercise of its functions under s 29. Consequently, the charges were lawful.

4.3.1   The Chronically Sick and Disabled Persons Act 1970

Section 2 of the CSDPA 1970 creates a duty in respect of disabled or chronically sick people who are ordinarily resident within a local authority's area. This is, broadly, the client group already defined by s 29 of the NAA 1948, but it also includes children. The local authority must arrange such of the services specified in s 2 as it is satisfied are necessary to meet the needs of a disabled person. As with s 117 of the MHA 1983, therefore, duties are apparently owed to individuals who, it seems, may seek to challenge shortcomings in the provision of services.

The specified services are:

– provision of 'practical assistance' within the home, which might include either home maintenance services, such as cleaning or decorating, or personal care;
– provision of, or assistance in obtaining, wireless, television, library or similar recreational facilities;
– provision of lectures, games, outings or other recreational facilities outside the home, or assistance in taking advantage of educational facilities that are available;
– provision of transport to and from home to enable disabled people to participate in services (for example day centres) provided by the local authority under s 29 of the NAA 1948;
– assistance in arranging for adaptations to the home to be carried out or for additional facilities for disabled people (such as handrails, hoists, or alarm systems) to be provided;[2]
– facilitating the taking of holidays by disabled persons;
– provision of meals at home or elsewhere; and
– provision of, or assistance in, getting a telephone or any special equipment necessary to use a telephone.

Under s 1, local authorities must gather information about disabled people and publicise services available. Then they must plan services in the light of the perceived needs of their population, and determine their own priorities within that framework. Section 2 is made subject to the general guidance of the Secretary of State, who has said that local authorities must 'assess the

---

1   See Chapter 8.
2   This responsibility may overlap with the duty of a housing authority to provide disabled facilities grants, under the Housing Grants, Construction and Regeneration Act 1996.

requirements of the individuals determined by them to be substantially and permanently handicapped as to their need; if they are satisfied that an individual is in need ... they are to make arrangements that are appropriate in his or her case'.[1]

Notwithstanding the guidance, however, the CSDPA 1970 is defective in that s 2 does not expressly require an assessment but merely requires that the local authority 'satisfies' itself as to the existence of need. This has been held to mean that the authority must 'make up its mind in each specific case'.[2] The duty to 'make arrangements' applies only where the local authority has made up its mind that services are needed and there is nothing in the section which directly requires the authority to do this.[3]

4.3.2   The Disabled Persons (Services, Consultation and Representation) Act 1986

The *raison d'être* of this legislation is to reinforce the duties imposed by the CSDPA 1970. In particular, under s 4, a local authority, when requested, must decide whether the needs of a disabled person call for the provision by it of any welfare services authorised by s 2 of the CSDPA 1970. The request may be made by an individual disabled person or by his or her carer, or by an 'authorised representative' who may be appointed by or on behalf of the disabled person under s 1 of this Act. The authorised representative may be the nearest relative or guardian where the disabled person is mentally disordered. Otherwise, friends or voluntary workers are likely to take on this role. Some voluntary agencies (for example, Age Concern) provide advocacy services for disabled people (see below). Authorised representatives may not be paid out of public funds.

Section 4 of the DPSCRA 1986 is more focused than s 2 of the CSDPA 1970 in imposing a duty on the local authority to respond to a direct request for services by making a decision one way or the other. That necessitates an assessment, although the term is not used in s 4. As will be seen, s 47 of the NHSCCA 1990 extends the duty still further. Moreover, the draftsman has indicated quite clearly that if an assessment is carried out and results in the conclusion that services under the CSDPA 1970 are required, then those services must be provided.[4]

Section 3 has never been brought into force because of its resource implications. It requires the local authority, when carrying out an assessment of need, to provide an opportunity for the disabled person or his or her authorised representative, to make representations as to that person's perceptions of his or

---

1   DHSS Circular (70) 12.
2   *Blyth v Blyth (No 2)* [1966] 2 WLR 634.
3   See, now, the discussion of NHSCCA 1990, s 47 in Chapter 5 and the House of Lords' decision in *R v Gloucestershire County Council ex parte Barry* [1997] 2 WLR 459.
4   However, see **5.15.**

her needs for services. Section 3 presupposes the availability of advocacy services for elderly and disabled people, which are given considerable emphasis in all the guidance on the NHSCCA 1990. There is a further duty to provide, on request, written details of the assessment.

4.3.3 Enforcement of service provision for disabled people

In the early 1970s the introduction of new services and new welfare benefits for the disabled was high on the political agenda following extensive research on the incidence and effects of disability carried out during the late 1960s. MPs who sponsored the CSDPA 1970 expected that the legislation would fill a serious gap in provision for disabled people and that services under s 2 would be available as of right.

Case-law never unequivocally supported this expectation. The courts were always extremely reluctant to allow private law remedies such as negligence or breach of statutory duty to lie against local authorities that failed to provide services. Before 1995, public law proceedings had yielded only indirect authority that the duty in s 2 of the CSDPA 1970 is enforceable by an individual service user.[1]

The underlying question, which is fundamental to decision-making in respect of all public law responsibilities, is how far may a local authority defend its failure to provide services for which there is an assessed need on the grounds that its resources are insufficient? Until June 1995, however, this point had never been confronted directly in proceedings to enforce service provision under s 2 of the CSDPA 1970, although there was some authority to suggest that the s 2 duty could not be qualified in this way.[2]

Now, following the decision of the House of Lords in *R v Gloucestershire County Council ex parte Barry*,[3] it appears that there will be few 'absolute' duties within this area of public law, and that service provision will generally be resource-led. The decision and its implications are discussed more fully in Chapter 5. It remains to be seen how for the effective 'rationing' of public services will be affected by the implementation of the Human Rights Act 1998 on 2 October 2000.[4]

---

1   See, for example, *R v Ealing Borough Council ex parte Leaman* (1984) *The Times*, 10 February.
2   See *R v Hereford and Worcester County Council ex parte Chandler* (CO/1759/91).
3   (1997) 1 CCL Rep 40.
4   It is possible, for instance, that Article 3 of the European Convention on Human Rights (the right to liberty) may be invoked to challenge funding decisions which effectively force older people into residential care.

4.4 PRACTICE POINTS

(a) Services of particular importance to clients may be as follows:

— *Home helps/home care assistants*

The statutory responsibilities are in s 2 of the CSDPA 1970 and Sch 8 to the NHSA 1977. Persons eligible under the NSHA 1977 specifically include 'the aged'. Those eligible under the CSDPA 1970 must be disabled, but may of course also be elderly. Neither statute places any ceiling on the type of help which may be provided. 'Cut backs' restricting the amount or type of housework undertaken by the home care services, without reference to need, remain challengeable.[1]

— *Day centres*

Provision is made by s 29 of the NAA 1948 and by s 2 of the CSDPA 1970 (see also LAC (93) 10).

— *Respite care*

Provision is made by s 21 of the NAA 1948. The NHS also has a responsibility for providing respite care (s 3 of the NHSA 1977), which is further defined by guidance.[2]

(b) There is no requirement that older people should be registered as disabled in order to be eligible for services. Under the CSDPA 1970, local authorities must keep a register of those covered by the definition of 'disabled' in s 29 of the NAA 1948. Registers, however, are intended only to facilitate the gathering of information and to assist in the planning of services.[3]

(c) Clients who want services should be advised as follows.

— They should initially get in touch with the social services department directly, or through their GP.

— The local authority has a qualified duty to assess their needs under s 47 of the NHSCCA 1990.[4]

— The local authority must decide whether certain needs call for the provision of any services. The eligibility criteria set out in the community care plan should indicate what provision clients may expect, and it will be important to match the assessed needs against such criteria. All clients should insist on receiving a full written record of their assessments and a copy of any care plan.

---

1   *R v Gloucestershire County Council ex parte Mahfood and Barry* (1997) 1 CCL Rep 7. See also **5.15**.
2   See Chapter 2.
3   DoH Circular LAC (93) 10.
4   See **5.2**.

–   Where clients are disabled, the local authority is only likely to provide services (if at all) under the CSDPA 1970. It will always be sensible to ask the local authority to clarify *which* statutory responsibility it is utilising in a particular case.

(d) Advisers should be aware of how to operate the local authority's complaints procedure. In general, a dispute over community care services should be taken through the complaints system before referral to the Local Government Ombudsman or judicial review are contemplated. The first step in challenging the local authority will be to obtain a copy of the client's social services file.

(e) Services will generally have to be paid for. There is evidence that charges for services provided at home are rising steadily and that there is no automatic exemption for people living on income support. Increasingly, clients may have problems in affording charges. Advisers should be aware of the provision in s 17 of the HASSASSAA 1983 that such charges must be 'reasonable'.[1]

4.5   CHECKLIST OF COMMUNITY CARE SERVICES FOR OLDER PEOPLE

Service	Client group	Duty/power	Statutory source
Residential accommodation	Older and/or disabled people who are in need of care and attention not otherwise available to them	Duty	Section 21 of the NAA 1948; LAC (93) 10
Day centres and activities	Older *and* disabled	Duty	Section 29 of the NAA 1948; LAC (93) 10
Meals at home or elsewhere	Older *and* disabled	Duty	Section 2 of the CSDPA 1970
	Older	Power	Section 45 of the HSPHA 1968
Home-help services	Older *and* disabled	Duty	Section 2 of the CSDPA 1970
	Older	Duty	Schedule 8, para 3 to the NHSA 1977
Personal care at home (including home respite)	Older *and* disabled	Duty	Section 2 of the CSDPA 1970
	Older	Duty	Schedule 8, para 3 to the NHSA 1977
	Older	Power	Section 45 of the HSPHA 1948

---

1   See Chapter 8.

Service	Client group	Duty/power	Statutory source
Aids, equipment and home adaptations	Older *and* disabled	Duty	Section 2 of the CSDPA 1970
	Older	Power	Section 45 of the HSPHA 1968; DHSS Circular (71)19
Social work support	Older *and* disabled	Power	Section 29 of the NAA 1948
	Older	Power	Section 45 of the HSPHA 1968
Respite care (away from home)	General: eligibility criteria relate to those with, for example, complex or intense health care needs	Duty	Section 3 of the NHSA 1977; HSG (95) 8; LAC (95) 5
	As for residential accommodation	Duty	Section 21 of the NAA 1948; LAC (93) 10
Holidays/breaks	Older *and* disabled	Duty	Section 2 of the CSDPA 1970
Assessment of need	Older *and* disabled	Duty	Section 4 of the DPSCRA 1986
	Older	Duty	Section 47 of the NHSCCA 1990
Information about services	Older *and* disabled	Duty	Section 1 of the CSDPA 1970
	Older	Power	Section 45 of the HSPHA 1968
Assessment of carer's needs	Informal carers	Duty	CRSA 1995
Incontinence services	Older *and* disabled	Qualified duty	Section 3 of the NHSA 1977; EL (91) 28
Assessment of carers' needs	Informal carers	Duty	CDCA 2000
Carers' services[1]	Informal carers	Power	CDCA 2000

---

1   See **5.9** and **5.14**.

Chapter 5

THE ASSESSMENT OF NEEDS AND THE PROVISION OF SERVICES

'Authorities must define what they consider to constitute a need for services, in such a way that the most disadvantaged are included but which still allows for the Authority to balance its budget. Furthermore they must do so in a way that allows local flexibility and adjustment to tailor services to the particular needs of individuals as part of the assessment process. To do all of this will be no mean feat.'[1]

5.1 THE RELATIONSHIP BETWEEN ASSESSMENT AND SERVICE PROVISION: AN OVERVIEW

The legislative framework outlined in Chapter 4 allows local authorities to exercise considerable discretion as to what services they actually provide. Since 1993, the thrust of community care policies and new funding arrangements has been the development of more user-friendly and better targeted services within existing powers. There is a clear expectation that local authorities will prioritise their expenditure by reference to need in their areas, and community care plans are now the vehicles for communicating and explaining what these priorities are.[2]

In relation to assessment, the expression of policy is to be found in s 47 of the NHSCCA 1990, one of the few legislative outcomes of the White Paper on Community Care. It contains a duty to assess individual needs for community care services, and a duty to determine whether or not to provide services to meet those needs. Nothing in s 47 is suggestive of a duty to provide services consequent upon an assessment of need. The requirements are, quite simply, to assess and then to consider. Recent case-law[3] has now indicated that s 47 is only the starting point of the decision-making process for a local authority. When a local authority determines whether or not to provide services for a person whose needs it has assessed, it must also be mindful of the precise terms of the particular statute or statutes under which it is empowered to provide the community care services which are identified by the assessment. Whether the local authority has an absolute duty, a qualified duty or simply a power to make provision is determined by the statute in question, not by s 47. The decision in *R v Gloucestershire County Council ex parte Barry*[4] now has to be read in this context.

---

1   Audit Commission *Taking Care* (1993).
2   See **1.8.1**.
3   *R v Kensington and Chelsea Royal London Borough Council ex parte Kujtim* (1999) 2 CCL Rep 340, CA.
4   (1997) 1 CCL Rep 40.

Therefore, it is important for clients to understand that assessments of need unlock the door to services, but do not necessarily push it open. Despite the needs-led approach advocated by the White Paper on Community Care, it cannot now be assumed that an assessment will always lead to the provision of services. Some needs will not be met. At present, the inference is that a need for residential care is more likely to be met than a need for assistance at home. Tight budgets have led to a situation where priority in terms of expenditure is given to cases which are perceived to be high risk, and resources are not being directed towards the low level support which is essential if an older person's independence within the community is to be maintained.

In many respects, developments since 1993 have highlighted the vulnerability of the community care policies outlined above and in Chapter 1, and few people would now argue with the view that there has been a failure to deliver what service users were led to expect.

5.2   THE 'RIGHT' TO AN ASSESSMENT

Section 47 of the NHSCCA 1990 makes assessment a necessary but not sufficient qualification for the provision of community care services. It creates a duty to assess need, and categorises assessment itself as a preliminary service, which may or may not constitute a threshold for further services.[1] There is no duty under the NHSCCA 1990 to provide community care services for every person who is assessed as having a need for services.

Section 47(1) states:

> 'Where it appears to a local authority that any person for whom they may provide or arrange for the provision of community care services may be in need of any such services, the authority –
>
> (a)   shall carry out an assessment of his needs for those services; and
> (b)   having regard to the results of that assessment, shall then decide whether his needs call for the provision by them of any such services.'

Paragraph (a) contains what appears to be an unequivocal duty to assess the need for community care services, which is owed to individuals. This breaks new ground. The preamble, however, limits the duty to assess to cases where the local authority has come to the conclusion that:

–   there is an apparent need for community care services; and
–   there are statutory powers (or duties) to provide services.

---

1   The same conceptual distinction between a general duty to assess need and a more targeted duty to determine provision is to be found in the sections of the Education Act 1996 which impose responsibilities on local education authorities in respect of children with special educational needs.

Therefore, the duty is not absolute, although, as will be seen, the threshold test is very low.

5.2.1 Apparent need

The duty to assess is triggered where a local authority perceives that an individual 'may' be in need of community care services. The apparent need does not have to be urgent or immediate, and it is also irrelevant whether or not there is any ultimate prospect that a particular need will be met.[1] 'Even if there is no hope that resources will be available to meet any needs identified in the assessment, the assessment may still serve a useful purpose in identifying for the local authority unmet needs which will help it to plan for the future'.[2] There is neither a requirement that a request for assessment be made,[3] nor a duty to assess on request, although approaches by service users will provide the local authority with one means of identifying possible need. The Policy Guidance requires local authorities to publish information about assessment, prepared in conjunction with other service providers, including health and housing authorities.[4]

5.2.2 Is the local authority permitted to provide services for an individual?

The duty to assess is also made subject to vires; s 47(1) of the NHSCCA 1990 refers to services which a local authority 'may' provide. When, therefore, will the local authority lack the power to provide community care services, so that it must decline to carry out an assessment? Practically speaking, rarely. The only readily foreseeable limitation on a local authority's powers is the general restriction of its responsibility, throughout the legislation, to service users who are ordinarily resident in its area. The duty to provide residential accommodation for vulnerable people under s 21 of the NAA 1948, for example, is so restricted.[5] Even then, however, s 24(3) of the NAA 1948 gives the added power to dispense with the residence qualification, so that accommodation may be provided for non-residents who are in urgent need, and, it would not be legitimate to refuse an assessment in such cases.

5.3 THE PROCESS OF ASSESSMENT

Section 47(4) of the NHSCCA 1990 states that the Secretary of State may give directions about how an assessment is to be carried out. Failing directions, and without prejudice to s 3 of the DPSCRA 1986, an assessment 'shall be carried

---

1   *R v Bristol City Council ex parte Penfold* (1998) 1 CCL Rep 315.
2   Ibid, at 322H.
3   In *R v Gloucestershire County Council ex parte RADAR* [1996] COD 253, Carnwath J held: 'The obligation to make an assessment for community care services does not depend on a request, but on the "appearance of need" '.
4   DoH Circular LAC (96) 7, para 5.5.2.
5   For further discussion on the meaning and significance of 'ordinary residence', see **6.4**.

out in such manner and take such form as the local authority consider appropriate'. Section 3 requires local authorities to allow disabled clients, or their representatives, to make representations as to their needs before an assessment is carried out. It also provides that authorities must give written statements of their decisions as to needs, with reasons, and must explain decisions not to provide services to meet identifiable needs. Such requirements manifestly constitute best practice, but s 3 has not so far been brought into force. Similarly, the Secretary of State has not taken the opportunity to issue directions. Therefore, assessment procedures are for each local authority to determine, subject, however, to policy and practice guidance[1] and also to the principles of natural justice.

5.4   WHAT IS 'NEED'?

The guidance defines 'need' as '. . . the shorthand for the requirements of individuals to enable them to achieve, maintain or restore an acceptable level of social independence or quality of life, as defined by the particular agency or authority. . .'.[2] It identifies five categories of need which should be explored on an assessment, viz:

(1)   personal/social care;
(2)   health care;
(3)   finance;
(4)   education, employment or leisure; and
(5)   transport/access.[3]

The Practitioners' Guide suggests that, in practice, most people who ask for, or are referred for assessment will fall into one of four categories:[4]

(1)   those for whom community living is no longer possible, or who are at risk (for example people with intensive personal care needs);
(2)   those reliant on others for survival, requiring help with, for example, feeding or toileting;
(3)   those reliant on others for support, requiring help with day-to-day household tasks, such as cleaning or shopping; and
(4)   those whose functioning or morale is impaired, for example as a consequence of a depressive illness.

---

1   *Community Care in the Next Decade and Beyond: Policy Guidance* (HMSO, 1989), *Care Management and Assessment: Practitioners' Guide* (HMSO, 1991).
2   *Care Management and Assessment*, Summary of Practice Guidance (HMSO, 1991), para 11.
3   Ibid.
4   Ibid, at para 2.22.

5.5 LEVELS OF ASSESSMENT

The Policy Guidance states that 'assessment arrangements should normally include an initial screening process to determine the appropriate form of assessment'.[1] Some people may need advice and assistance which do not call for a formal assessment; others may require only a limited or specialist assessment of specific needs; others may have urgent needs which require an immediate response. Procedures should be sufficiently comprehensive and flexible to cope with all levels and types of need presented.

Given the clear legal duty to carry out a s 47 assessment, it will be unlawful for a local authority to screen people out, without assessment, at a preliminary stage.[2] It is clear, therefore, that a simple assessment must be part of the initial screening process and may or may not lead on to a more comprehensive assessment.

The Practitioners' Guide emphasises that the assessment process should be as simple, speedy and informal as possible. It should be based on the minimum level of enquiry needed to give a clear picture of need and form a basis for a decision to invest public resources. The Guide describes six levels of assessment which an authority might use, ranging from simple tests of need for people requiring basic provision, through to comprehensive multi-agency assessments. The initial screening process should indicate the appropriate level of assessment.

The Guide is not prescriptive as regards this model and, in practice, it appears that most local authorities use three levels of assessment:

(1) 'simple': where people require basic provision, such as bus passes, which are available from a single agency in well-defined circumstances;
(2) 'specialist': where people need straightforward packages of homecare services, but various eligibility criteria will have to be taken into account; and
(3) 'comprehensive': where people have multiple needs and are at risk of harm if services are not provided. Such assessments are likely to involve several agencies, as will the ultimate provision of services under a care plan. They should be offered to individuals who, on preliminary screening, appear to be disabled.[3]

5.6 WAITING FOR AN ASSESSMENT

The legislation does not prescribe how quickly an assessment must be carried out. All the guidance emphasises that the greater the apparent need, the more

---

1 DoH Circular LAC (96) 7 at para 3.20.
2 *R v Bristol City Council ex parte Penfold* (1998) 1 CCL Rep 315. However, what will be an 'adequate' as opposed to a 'token' assessment is a moot point.
3 DoH Circular CI (92) 34; see **5.10**.

expeditious should be the assessment.[1] There is power under s 47(5) to provide services, as a matter of urgency, without a prior assessment of need.

There is a danger that non-priority cases remain at the bottom of the list. It seems that priority is given to assessments on hospital discharge and that assessments in the community may be subject to extreme delays, or may be carried out in emergencies only.

5.7 WRITTEN ASSESSMENTS

The current legislation does not expressly require that assessments should be recorded in writing, and simple decisions may sometimes be communicated orally. However, local authorities are generally expected to pass on to service users the full results of assessment, irrespective of whether the identified needs will in fact be met, and the Practitioners' Guide indicates that a copy of the assessment should be shared with service users, their representatives and those who have agreed to provide a service. It will normally be combined with a written care plan.[2]

Advisers should always seek to ensure that their clients are provided with full written records of all aspects of their assessments. These will be essential documents if clients subsequently wish to challenge assessments. In addition, all service users have a statutory right of access to their social services file and, consequently, to the assessments themselves.[3]

5.8 THE ASSESSMENT OF DISABLED PEOPLE

As stated above, a local authority must offer a comprehensive assessment to a person who appears to be 'disabled', irrespective of the scale of need that is actually presented. The reason for this is that s 4 of the DPSCRA 1986 requires an authority, on request by a disabled person, his or her carer or authorised representative, to decide whether his or her needs call for the provision of any services under the CSDPA 1970. To discharge this duty the local authority must carry out an assessment, and the duty to assess is, therefore, implicit. Section 47(2) of the NHSCCA 1990 extends the duty by removing the stipulation that it arises only on request.

---

1   See, for example, DoH Circular CI (92) 34.
2   See **5.16**.
3   The Data Protection Act 1998 has replaced the Data Protection Act 1984, the Access to Personal Files Act 1987 and the Access to Health Records Act 1990, with effect from 1 March 2000. It confers a right of access to personal information, whether stored electronically or manually, supported by enforcement provisions. The DoH has issued new guidance to social services departments on the Act and access to social services records (LASSL (99) 16 and LASSL (2000) 2). There are some exemptions from disclosure – for example, where it would cause serious harm to the physical or mental health of the applicant.

The Policy Guidance goes on to emphasise the fact that there are no hard and fast rules for defining disability. The statutory definition in s 29 of the NAA 1948 is very broad, and, therefore, the assessor will have to have a clear understanding of the local authority's interpretation of a 'disabled person' and ensure that staff implement the requirement for a comprehensive assessment consistently. As with 'need' itself, the framework for service operation is still organisationally defined.

5.9 THE ASSESSMENT OF CARERS

In the UK, there are more than 6 million informal carers, 75 per cent of whom look after older people. Most carers are spouses or adult children. The Policy Guidance on community care acknowledges the role of carers and the importance of partnership between carer, user and statutory authority:

> 'The assessment will need to take account of the support that is available from . . . carers. They should feel that the overall provision of care is a shared responsibility between them and the statutory authorities and that the relationship between them is one of mutual support. The preferences of carers should be taken into account and their willingness to continue caring should not be assumed'.[1]

However, the NHSCCA 1990 itself makes no direct reference to carers.[2] Section 47 requires social services authorities to assess only the needs of someone who may need community care services, and to determine provision in respect of the needs of that person alone. Carers have no entitlement to an assessment of their needs unless they themselves also require community care services. Section 8 of the DPSCRA 1986 goes a little further in requiring local authorities, when assessing the needs of a disabled person, to have regard to the ability of a carer to continue providing care on a regular basis. However, it creates no obligation to follow that up by providing services or support for the carer.

The CRSA 1995 was passed with all-party support after extensive lobbying on behalf of carers. Its advent was timely, given the evidence of increasingly early discharge from hospital of elderly people needing a high level of care.

Section 1 of the CRSA 1995 provides that, where a local authority is assessing (or reassessing) a person's needs under s 47 of the NHSCCA 1990, a carer[3] who is providing or intends to provide 'a substantial amount of care on a regular

---

1   DoH Circular LAC (96) 7 at para 3.2.8.
2   Paragraph 17 of the Policy Guidance (DoH Circular LAC (96) 7) states: 'carers may have community care needs in their own right by reason of their old age, physical or mental ill health, physical or learning disability. Where it appears to the local authority that a carer who is over the age of 18 may have need for community care services, then the local authority should carry out an assessment under s 47(1)(a) of the NHS and Community Care Act'.
3   The term 'carer' excludes someone who is employed to care, or who acts as a volunteer for a voluntary organisation; s 1(3).

basis' for that person may, at the same time, ask the local authority to assess his or her ability to provide and to continue to provide that care.[1] Having done so, the local authority must then take into account the result of that assessment in making its decision as to services. The CRSA 1995 does not require that the carer should actually be providing care at the time of the assessment, and the assessment should not assume willingness to go on providing care.

The CRSA 1995 creates a 'piggyback' right. A carer is entitled to a separate assessment only where the person cared for has had, or is having a s 47 assessment. Sometimes older clients who are comfortably off may not wish to be assessed by the local authority and will be content to rely on a caring relationship, supplemented perhaps by services which they purchase themselves. The perspective of the carer may be different and, therefore, conflicts of interest may arise.

There is likely to be some debate as to when care is 'substantial' and provided on a 'regular basis'. Entitlement to the invalid care allowance (the designated benefit for carers)[2] is based on caring 'regularly and substantially' for a disabled person, and this requirement is met by giving care for 35 hours per week or more. If, in any week, care falls below 35 hours, it is not regular and substantial, and benefit is not payable. The government has made it clear, however, that not all carers will be eligible for an assessment under the CRSA 1995, and that it is up to local authorities to determine the meaning of 'regular' and 'substantial'. Clearly, the test will be subjective; what is 'substantial' for a frail older person may not be so for a middle-aged person in excellent health.

Finally, it is clear that, while the CRSA 1995 creates a right to assessment, it gives carers, as carers, no separate entitlement to service provision. The local authority must determine only whether the assessed needs of the older person call for some provision. There may be some implication that any services provided by the local authority for the older person will reflect the carer's ability to cope, as well as the older person's needs, but the Act provides no real clues as to what 'carers' services' might include.

Possible examples of services which may meet the needs of an older person and, at the same time, assist carers to go on providing care include:

- provision of day centres (NAA 1948, s 29);
- night-sitter services (NHSA 1977, Sch 8);
- home help and laundry facilities (NHSA 1977, s 21 and Sch 8);
- recreational facilities (HSPHA 1968, s 45); and
- above all, respite care (NAA 1948, s 21).[3]

---

1   The guidance on the CRSA 1995 emphasises that local and health authorities will need to ensure that hospital discharge procedures take account of its provisions, and that carers are involved as soon as planning for discharge starts, DoH Circular LAC (96) 7, para 16. (This is s 7 guidance); see **3.5**.

2   SSCBA 1992, s 70; ICA Regulations 1970, reg 4.

3   This was acknowledged in the Parliamentary debates on the CRS Bill. See **5.9.1**.

Nevertheless, the question remains: what will be the position, when, for example, a carer wants/needs a day centre placement for an elderly relative when the latter prefers to remain at home? Such tensions are, or course, an inescapable part of the caring process, but the CRSA 1995 offers no obvious resolution.

The legal position will change once the Carers and Disabled Children Act 2000 comes into force. This gives local authorities powers to provide services directly to carers who, in turn, will be entitled to a freestanding assessment of their needs.[1]

5.9.1 Respite care

The service most likely to enhance a carer's ability to continue caring may be respite care. Local authorities may arrange such care under s 21 of the NAA 1948, but the NHS guidance on meeting continuing health care needs[2] also lays down criteria for respite care funded by the NHS, which is said to be an integral part of NHS provision for elderly and incapacitated people. There are strong arguments in favour of targeting resources towards respite care in order to postpone or avert the need for full-time residential care, and the Department of Health has now allocated additional resources to local authorities for the period 1999 to 2002 to develop short-term breaks and other services for carers.

Although the CRSA 1995 impliedly designates respite care as a service for carers, rather than for people in need of care, provision at present is based not on the caring role, but on assessment of the person in need of care and, hopefully, of the carer. If the service user does not need respite care, but the carer does, the local authority has to resolve that conflict. This point was raised in the parliamentary debates on the CRSA 1995:

> 'Although the elderly person did not mention respite care, the carer is crying out for it, and among the services that we will provide, albeit to the cared-for person, respite care will be there regularly.'[3]

A High Court ruling on respite care demonstrates that a carer is entitled to seek a review of service provision based on the assessed needs of someone else. Dyson J upheld a carer's application to review the local authority's decision to alter a long-standing respite care arrangement on the basis of a new assessment of the service user's needs.[4] The decision was quashed because the local authority had failed, in breach of the guidance, to ascertain the carer's wishes and preferences in relation to respite care.

---

1   See **5.14**.
2   DoH Circular HSG (95) 8; see **2.4.3**.
3   *Hansard* C, vol 258, col 432 and vol 564, col 630.
4   *R v North Yorkshire County Council ex parte Hargreaves* (1997) 1 CCL Rep 104.

5.10   REVIEWING ASSESSMENTS

The emphatic drafting of s 47(1)(a) of the NHSCCA 1990 appears to impose a
continuing duty on local authorities to review their assessments from time to
time and to reconsider initial assessments which are adverse to the user.
Undoubtedly, an individual may ask the local authority to review his or her
assessment, but, additionally, Circular CI (92) 34 states:

> 'The clear plans of all users should be subject to regular review. For frail people in
> the community, frequent reviews and adjustments of their care plans are likely to
> be needed. Before any changes in services are made for existing users, they should
> be reassessed' (para 31).

This last point is underlined by the decision in *R v Gloucestershire County Council
ex parte Mahfood and Barry*,[1] discussed at **5.15**, where the Divisional Court ruled
that a reassessment of a service user's needs is a prerequisite before any decision
to alter or reduce services is taken.

In addition, the unimplemented s 3 of the DPSCRA 1986 creates a right to
have an assessment reviewed where a user is unhappy about its outcome. The
Policy Guidance states:

> 'Decisions on service provision should be reached in discussion with users and
> carers and every effort should be made to ensure that the result is acceptable to
> them. A formal judicial appeal procedure would be foreign to such arrangements
> and it would not be appropriate to introduce one' (para 3.54).

Accordingly, the first step towards a review, based not on change of
circumstances but on dissatisfaction with the original assessment, will be to
invoke the local authority's complaints procedure.

5.11   THE DUTY TO MAKE A DECISION AS TO SERVICES

Once the assessment of need has been carried out, s 47(1)(b) of the NHSCCA
1990 comes into play. It states that:

> 'having regard to the results of that assessment, the local authority shall then decide
> whether the user's needs call for the provision by them of any such [community
> care] services'.

Therefore, the local authority must make a decision about service provision and
must also communicate this, with reasons, to the user. However, it has a clear
discretion to determine the scope of the provision that it will make and, in some
cases, may determine that there will be no provision. Section 47(1)(b) does no
more than emphasise that the creation of a qualified right to assessment has not
altered the fact that the community care legislation creates, for the most part,
powers and general responsibilities rather than specific duties which are owed

---

1   (1997) 1 CCL Rep 7, QBD.

to individuals. The local authority must now, as in the past, exercise its judgment in the light of the assessment, rationally, consistently and fairly, and, in most circumstances, by reference to available resources.[1]

Section 47(3) of the NHSCCA 1990 requires a local authority to take account of the likelihood of any provision being made by the health authority[2] or local housing authority when making its own decision as to services. Although there are important overlaps in responsibility for care services between health and social services authorities, s 47(3) explicitly allocates the lead role to social services, giving health authorities an option to pursue other priorities, as described in Chapter 2.

5.12 SERVICE PROVISION FOR DISABLED PEOPLE

Section 47(2) of the NHSCCA 1990 runs as follows:

'(2) If at any time during the assessment of the needs of any person under sub-section (1) it appears to a local authority that he is a *disabled person*, the authority –

(a) shall proceed to make such a decision as to the services he requires as is mentioned in s 4 of the Disabled Persons (Services Consultation and Representation) Act 1986 without his requesting them to do so under that section;

(b) shall inform him that they will be doing so and of his rights under that Act.'

Section 4 of the DPSCRA 1986 referred to in para (a) above, states that a local authority must decide whether the needs of a disabled person call for the provision of services under s 2 of the CSDPA 1970. This duty arises on request by a disabled person, or by his or her carer or authorised representative and, in order to discharge it, the local authority must first carry out an assessment of need. Subsections 47(1) and (2) of the NHSCCA 1990 go further in making unconditional both the duty to assess and the duty to take decisions about service provision.

As regards any 'rights' to services, s 2 of the CSDPA 1970 requires a local authority to make arrangements to provide specified services where it is satisfied both as to the needs for such services and as to the necessity for making arrangements to meet those needs. It is clear, therefore, that s 47(2), like s 47(1), requires a local authority only to make a *decision* as to what, if any, services it should provide and that individuals whose needs have previously been assessed cannot expect provision unless it is *necessary* to meet those needs.

Prior to 1995, however, there was a view that s 2 of the CSDPA had created a duty which is owed to individual disabled people rather than to the community

---

1   See **5.15**.

2   The responsibility of the NHS for funding long-term care is considered in Chapter 2.

at large, and which may be directly enforceable. This view was largely derived from the parliamentary debates at the time the legislation was passed. It was also considered that the s 2 duty could not be qualified by the application of eligibility criteria or, in particular, by the argument that available resources are inadequate to meet all assessed needs.

Two decisions of the High Court on judicial review lent credence to this assumption.[1] In fact, neither ruling directly addressed the question of whether lack of resources will afford a defence to a local authority which is challenged after failing to provide services following an assessment of need. In *R v Gloucestershire County Council ex parte Barry*, however, the House of Lords confronted this and related issues. Its decision is of fundamental importance for local authorities, and is reviewed in some detail at **5.15**.

5.13 DETERMINING SERVICE PROVISION

The Policy Guidance indicates (at para 3.24) that, as community care policies aim to preserve or restore normal living as far as possible, the following order of preference is implicit in determining service provision:

(1) support for the user in his or her own home, including day and domiciliary care, respite care, the provision of disability equipment and adaptations to accommodation as necessary;

(2) a move to more suitable accommodation which might be sheltered or very sheltered housing, together with the provision of social services support;

(3) a move to another private household, to live with relatives or friends, or as part of an adult fostering scheme;

(4) residential care;

(5) nursing home care; and

(6) long-stay care in hospital.

It is accepted that care packages will include health provision, both primary and specialist, and housing provision as well as social services provision. The prioritisation manifestly relies on the availability of NHS resources for long-term care, but guidance on continuing health care[2] has confirmed the contraction of NHS services in this area whilst purporting to clarify the responsibilities that the NHS will accept.

The Policy Guidance emphasises that the aim must always be to devise a cost-effective package of services to meet the users' care needs. However, local authorities also have a responsibility to act within the resources available, which 'will sometimes involve difficult decisions where it will be necessary to strike a balance between meeting the needs identified within available resources and

---

1   *R v Ealing Borough Council ex parte Leaman* (1984) *The Times*, 10 February. *R v Hereford and Worcester County Council ex parte Chandler* (CO/1759/91).

2   DoH Circular HSG (95) 8; LAC (95) 5; see Chapter 2. New guidance is awaited.

meeting the care preferences of the individual'.[1] Given recent case-law, this statement, and indeed much of the Policy Guidance, appear disingenuous. The real issue for local authorities is the allocation of priority between identified needs, and the 'rationing' of their resources.

5.14 SERVICES FOR CARERS

The CDCA 2000 is intended to enable local authorities to offer direct support to carers, and forms part of the present Government's National Strategy for Carers.[2] It addresses the obvious weakness of the CRSA 1995 in creating only a 'piggyback' right for carers,[3] by requiring local authorities to carry out carers' assessments even where those cared for have refused to be assessed for, or to receive, community care services. Local authorities will also have power to provide services (unspecified) which will help carers to provide care, and which may take the form of physical help.[4]

The CDCA 2000 does not repeal the CRSA 1995, and contains complex provisons which obviously envisage that assessments may be carried out either under the CRSA 1995 or under the CDCA 2000.[5] In addition, there is provision for services which could fall within the definition of 'community care services' to be delivered either to the carer, or to the person cared for subject, in some cases, to agreement by both people concerned and, in other cases, to a decision by the local authority.[6] It is difficult to predict how far this tortuous piece of legislation will bring about any significant, practical change in the position of carers. Some services, such as respite care, simply cannot be delivered if the cared for person does not agree, irrespective of who is supposed to be the recipient.

The Act is expected to come into effect in April 2001.

5.15 ELIGIBILITY CRITERIA AND THE GLOUCESTERSHIRE RULING

In *R v Gloucestershire County Council ex parte Mahfood and Barry*,[7] five elderly and disabled people sought judicial review of the local authority's decision to withdraw services which it had previously provided under s 2 of the CSDPA 1970. The county council argued that, because of cuts in central government provision for community care, it no longer had the resources to meet the needs

1   DoH Circular LAC (96) 7, para 3.25.
2   DoH Circular LASSL (99) 2 *Caring About Carers: A National Strategy for Carers.*
3   See **4.1**, and CDCA 2000, s 1.
4   CDCA 2000, s 2.
5   Ibid, ss 1(1) and 4(1).
6   Ibid, ss 2 and 4.
7   (1997) 1 CCL Rep 7 at 19 and 40.

of the five applicants or, indeed, of perhaps 1,500 other people in a similar position. The applicants maintained, however, that individual need is the only criterion for service provision under s 2 of the CSDPA 1970, and that the duty to meet need is absolute and specific, and is not tempered by shortage of resources or the competing needs of others.

In the Divisional Court, McCowan LJ expressed some sympathy for the applicants' contention, but concluded that their interpretation of s 2 would be 'impractical and unrealistic', given that any local authority faces an impossible task unless it can have regard to the size of its financial cake in order to determine how fairest and best to cut it. Nevertheless, the court granted declaratory relief to the applicants because the county council had acted unlawfully in cutting services without reassessing their needs.

On appeal, the Court of Appeal, by a majority of two to one, determined that, in considering whether, under s 2 of the CSDPA 1970, it is necessary to make arrangements for meeting assessed needs, a local authority is not entitled to take account of the resources available to it. On a further appeal, the House of Lords, by a majority of three to two, held that 'needs' and 'necessity' are relative concepts, and that local authorities are entitled to take their resources into account when determining what provision is necessary in order to meet assessed needs.[1]

Gloucestershire is seen as a landmark decision which carries profound implications for all areas of social welfare provision. There is still an ongoing debate as to whether a local authority can be regarded as having 'pure' duties to which resources 'must' be directed, and increasingly too, the scope of NHS responsibilities is being tested.[2] Most noteworthy is the sheer volume of case-law since 1993 when, as has been noted elsewhere, the main changes were financial and cultural rather than legal. The reasons for this increased use of the legal process lie beyond the scope of this book, but it is clear that, as a result, the boundaries of our Welfare State are being redefined in a way which is unprecedented and which raises some very important political questions.

In practical terms, the most important immediate outcome of the *Gloucestershire* decision has been its endorsement of the use of eligibility criteria in relation to all community care services. Guidance written before 1993 explained how policy statements or eligibility criteria were to be used to bridge the gap between assessed needs and what the local authority could be expected to provide,[3] but prior to the *Gloucestershire* case the courts had done little to explore the principles of distributive justice, which the clash between spending cuts and consumer demands has placed before them many times since 1993.

---

1   See also *Taking Care* Audit Commission, 1993.
2   *R v North and East Devon Health Authority ex parte Coughlan*; see **2.4.5**.
3   See CI (92) 34, the so-called 'Laming Letter'. It was cancelled in 1994, but its content remains relevant.

In the House of Lords, Lord Clyde stated:

> '... in deciding whether there is a necessity to meet the needs of the individual some criteria have to be provided. Such criteria are required both to determine whether there is a necessity at all or only, for example, a desirability, and also to assess the degree of necessity ... it is possible to draw up categories of disabilities, reflecting the variations in the gravity of such disabilities which could be experienced ... but in determining the question whether in a given case the making of particular arrangements is necessary in order to meet the needs of a given individual it seems to me that a mere list of disabling conditions graded in order of severity will still leave unanswered the question at what level of disability is the stage of necessity reached. The determination of eligibility for the purposes of the statutory provision requires guidance not only on the assessment of the severity of the condition or the seriousness of the needs but also on the level at which there is to be satisfaction of the necessity to make arrangements. In the framing of the criteria to be applied it seems to me that the severity of a condition may have to be matched against the availability of resources ... once it is recognised that criteria have to be devised ... in one sense there will be an unmet need. But such an unmet need will be lawfully within what is contemplated by the statute.'

The implications of the *Gloucestershire* ruling are as follows.

(a) Local authorities may be expected to use a system of banding,[1] expressing the level of priority attached to different groups of people, and probably the level of service/hours of provision to be made available. Possible bands might be:

   - levels of risk, for example abuse or lack of support;
   - tasks of self-care, for example feeding and toiletting;
   - needs of carers, for example respite care; or
   - other 'quality of life' elements, such as social contact.

(b) Eligibility criteria will be based on risk assessment. If the risk of not providing services for certain groups, or in certain situations, is unacceptably high those services will be given highest priority. It is already clear that a major consequence of such an approach has been to concentrate resources on high-dependency service users, (the first category above). In many areas, a whole range of basic services, for low-risk needs, but which enable older people to remain at home and retain their independence, have been cut in favour of high-intensity provision.[2] Such developments do, of course, run counter to the philosophy expressed in the White Paper on Community Care.

---

1   In relation to special educational needs, local education authorities commonly band children in terms of levels of learning difficulties/sums of money to be made available for provision. The direct payments scheme offers a similar option.

2   See, for example, Watson, L *High hopes: Making Housing and Community Care Work* (Joseph Rowntree Foundation, 1997).

(c) Lack of resources alone cannot justify a withdrawal or reduction of
     services, and reassessment of a service user's needs will be a prerequisite
     before any decision to reduce services is taken. It is lawful to carry out any
     reassessment in the light of revised eligibility criteria, which take into
     account new resource constraints, but the local authority would also have
     to be satisfied that a reduction in services would not leave the user at severe
     risk.
(d) Having carried out an assessment of need and applied the eligibility criteria,
     a local authority *must* make a decision under s 47(1)(b) of the NHSCCA
     1990, and, if the criteria are met, the service must be provided.[1]
(e) The Policy Guidance emphasises that the provision of services, whether or
     not the local authority is under a duty to provide them, should not be
     related to users' ability to pay for them. 'The assessment of financial means,
     should, therefore, follow the assessment of need and decisions about
     service provision.'[2] In the residential care sector, however, this guidance
     no longer holds good and the present legal position is that eligibility
     criteria, which would exclude service users with capital in excess of
     £16,000, are lawful.[3]

As explained above, the *Gloucestershire* decision endorsed what amounts to the
explicit 'rationing' of many public services. It has been followed in respect of
residential care services.[4] However, other decisions since 1997 have taken a
different line. In *Re T*,[5] the House of Lords distinguished *Gloucestershire* in an
appeal concerning the duty of a local education authority to make provision of
'suitable' education for children unable to attend school because of illness.[6] By
any standards, this is one of the lesser duties imposed on a local education
authority, but the House of Lords came to the conclusion that s 19 of the
Education Act 1996 creates an immediate obligation to provide suitable
education which cannot be qualified by a lack of resources. In many respects,
this decision is deeply unconvincing, but in *R v Birmingham County Council ex
parte Taj Mohammed*,[7] Dyson J took a similar position in respect of a disabled
facilities grant. At present, it appears that the *Gloucestershire* approach is to some
degree in conflict with the willingness on the part of certain judges to interpret
statutory language as creating absolute duties without reference to the
underlying policy of the legislation, or to the relative importance of the
provision under discussion. This division of opinion reflects a fundamental
shortcoming of the English common law system, in failing to develop an
adequate response to the rationing of most social welfare provision, which is

---

1   *R v Sutton London Borough Council ex parte Tucker* (1998) 1 CCL Rep 251.
2   DoH Circular LAC (96) 7, para 3.31.
3   See **6.9**. The capital threshold increases to £18,500 from 9 April 2001.
4   *R v Sefton Metropolitan Borough Council ex parte Help the Aged* [1997] 4 All ER 532; *R v
     Wigan Metropolitan Borough Council ex parte Tammadge* (1998) 1 CCL Rep 581.
5   (1998) 1 CCL Rep 352.
6   Education Act 1996, s 19.
7   (1998) 1 CCL Rep 441.

now taken for granted by politicians and policy makers. Our public law is focused on judicial review, which purports to promote due process in decision-making, but in fact addresses individual grievances, and does not allow relative claims on cash limited resources to be determined judicially.

5.16 THE CARE PLAN

Following the decision as to services, the guidance envisages that the local authority will set up, fund and monitor a care plan,[1] a copy of which will be provided for the service user. Where individual needs are complex, a care manager, usually based in the social services department, will be responsible for devising a package of services. Budgets are normally devolved to care managers and will be used to commission services, both internal and external to the local authority. The ongoing responsibility of the care manager will be to harmonise interagency inputs and monitor the quality of service. Managing commissioning budgets requires the development of new skills, including cash-flow management, and it is not intended, therefore, that care managers should be directly involved in service delivery. Consequently, many social services departments have now effected an internal split between purchaser and provider functions.

The guidance observes:

> 'The care plan does not have a legal standing as a contract but, to reinforce the sense of commitment, contributors (including the user) may be asked to signify their agreement by signing. With or without signatures, the expectation is that contributors will honour their commitments and the care plan will be the means of holding them to account. As such, a care plan may be used as evidence in the consideration of a complaint.'[2]

5.17 CHOICE OF SERVICES

Choice was a selling point of the community care reforms. Community care plans should identify how they intend to increase consumer choice; assessments should 'enable users and carers to exercise genuine choice'; care management systems should seek to promote 'individual choice and self-determination'. The supermarket analogy is defective, however, for where the fulfilment of an individual's choice is dependent on the allocation of limited resources by a publicly accountable body and on the outputs of commissioning arrangements between that body and third party providers, the meaning of the term is fundamentally altered. As a result, the early research now shows some disillusionment with the actual outcomes.

---

1   *Care Management and Assessment*, Practitioners' Guide (HMSO, 1991), p 61.
2   Ibid, p 68.

For instance, the 'choices' of users and carers may be in conflict. Whose choice takes priority where maintaining the user's independence restricts the carer's capacity to choose?[1] Again, in some areas, local authorities' charging policies for home-based services are having the effect that the only real choice may be not to have expensive services. Research by Age Concern refers to 'pressure which new charging policies, cuts in local services and targeting of services bring in placing the costs of care squarely on the shoulders of many who can least afford to pay'.[2]

The Secretary of State has not issued directions or specific guidance on choice in respect of domiciliary services. There are, however, two directions on choice of residential accommodation[3] which are considered in detail in Chapter 6. They cover the choices available once a local authority has agreed, after assessment, to arrange a residential placement. However, the imposition of financial ceilings within eligibility criteria is not unusual. Some local authorities operate 'normal limits' policies, which set a ceiling on the cost of domiciliary packages, equivalent to the gross cost of arranging suitable residential placements. The Divisional Court has held that where a frail elderly person 'needs' 24-hour care, a local authority is entitled to offer only a residential placement rather than a domiciliary package where that would be a more efficient use of its resources.[4] It is not difficult to identify, in such criteria, a new 'perverse' incentive towards residential care. More generally, where it is possible to meet assessed needs in different ways it will be lawful for a local authority to use the more cost-effective provision. Again, individual choice may be a marginal consideration.

In theory, no one can be forced to accept a community care service that he or she does not want. In practice, budgetary issues may pre-empt choice. Furthermore, it appears that some older people assessed as needing residential care are seeking to remain at home because, under the statutory means test, which is confined to residential placements, the value of their homes will be taken into account. In response to this, some local authorities now impose legal charges on property in order to recover the full economic costs of home-care services.[5] If choice exists at all, the key to it must be information about available services, available resources and priorities, plus the ability to exert some influence on the assessment process. Many older people may need to call upon a 'more powerful voice' to help in this, and as noted already, there is an important role for the adviser.

---

1   See **5.9**.
2   Age Concern *Mapping the Change: No Time to Lose* (1993), p 16.
3   DoH Circulars LAC (92) 27 and LAC (93) 18.
4   *R v Lancashire County Council ex parte Ingham* (1995) unreported.
5   See Chapter 8.

Chapter 6

RESIDENTIAL CARE SERVICES

'The old institutions or workhouses are to go altogether. In their place will be attractive hostels or hotels, each accommodating 25 to 30 old people, who will live there as guests not inmates. Each guest will pay for his accommodation – those with private income out of that, those without private income out of the payments they get from the National Assistance Board – and nobody need know whether they have private means or not. Thus, the stigma of "relief" – very real too, and acutely felt by many old people – will vanish at last'.[1]

6.1 INTRODUCTION

There are about half a million care places in residential and nursing homes in the UK. More than 70 per cent of all residents are female and over the age of 74; about half are over 85.[2] An estimated 75 per cent of residents have some level of dementia. In 1999, 53 per cent of residents in independent sector homes were financially supported by local authorities.

Privately run homes accommodate more than half of all those currently in residential care. Local authorities' own provision was reduced by nearly 50 per cent between 1988 and 1998. Most providers are independent small businesses, each running just one or two homes. The larger operators, such as the British United Provident Association (BUPA), are focused on the nursing-home and dual-registered home sectors. The average number of places provided has continued to rise in both nursing and residential homes, although that average is significantly lower in the residential sector than in the nursing sector. Very small homes (with fewer than four residents) tend to specialise in residential care for younger, physically disabled individuals and those with multiple disabilities, rather than older people.

There is a trend towards larger homes. In the nursing-home market the average size has increased by more than one-third in 10 years. In 1996, on average, nursing homes provided 37 places, dual-registered homes 45 places, and residential homes 19 places, although new nursing homes set up by major providers now average nearer 65 places. Commentators suggest that, from a profit point of view, the optimum size for a nursing home, based on a staff-to-resident ratio, is 50–60 beds.

The average fees charged by both nursing and residential homes have followed a path intermediate between average costs and changes in support limits. Recently, average fees have increased by less than the average earnings index, the retail price index or the weighted average income-support uprating. For the

---

1   Garland, R 'End of the Poor Laws' (1948) *Social Welfare*, vol 11, no 2 at p 36.
2   *Older People as Consumers in Care Homes* (Office of Fair Trading, 1998).

year 1999/2000 fees increased by less than 3 per cent, which is way below cost increases resulting from inflation, the national minimum wage and the Working Time Directive. Beyond that, there is evidence of a decline in admissions to care homes, brought about mainly by the tight eligibility criteria set by local authorities.[1] There is now perceived to be a real risk of widespread home closures which, in years to come, will mean that there will be a shortage of supply. Given the age and dependency profile of the residential care population such a change in circumstances is likely to have serious consequences. This chapter will explore local authority responsibilities for providing or arranging residential care services.

For many older people, the change in the organisation and delivery of residential care services has been the most important outcome of the implementation of Part III of the NHSCCA 1990, notwithstanding that the thrust of the legislation was towards keeping people out of residential accommodation wherever possible. The post-1993 financial regime remains a source of confusion and, therefore, anxiety for older people and their advisers. Thus, it will be helpful to explain the 1993 transition, before moving on to consider the present legal position in some detail.

6.2   THE SITUATION BEFORE APRIL 1993

6.2.1   Part III accommodation

Since the 1940s, local authorities have had a duty to provide residential accommodation for the elderly and infirm and others needing care. Section 1 of the NAA 1948 provides:

> 'the existing poor law shall cease to have effect, and shall be replaced by the provisions of . . . Part III of this Act as to accommodation and other services to be provided by local authorities . . .'

The responsibility for providing a safety net for the most vulnerable members of society was, therefore, a natural successor to the previous parish responsibilities under the Poor Law 1832. It devolved to social services departments of local authorities under s 195 of the Local Government Act 1972. Before responsibility for homelessness passed to housing departments in the 1970s, s 21 also covered provision for homeless people.[2] Under s 24, the whole range of the local authority's responsibilities was owed to people ordinarily resident in its area, although it nevertheless had a residual power to provide for those with no settled residence, and others in urgent need of residential accommodation.

---

1   Approximately 760 homes closed in 1999, and there was a drop in new registrations from 280 in 1998 to 185 in 1999; Laing & Buisson *Care of Elderly People Market Survey*, 2000.

2   Section 21(1)(b) gave power to provide temporary accommodation for people 'in urgent need thereof'.

Authorities could discharge their s 21 duty by providing accommodation in their own, managed, premises;[1] through arrangements made with another local authority; or by 'sponsoring' beds in the voluntary or private sectors. The extent to which the latter powers were used varied considerably between local authority areas, and was influenced by political factors. Inner London boroughs, and many metropolitan authorities regarded it as important to maintain a substantial stock of Part III homes. Other authorities were always prepared to sponsor beds and avoid the costs of running their own accommodation. By the 1970s, some authorities were transferring their Part III accommodation to the independent sector in order to release resources for other purposes. The Local Government Act 1988 allowed authorities to provide financial assistance to transferees in connection with the disposal of residential establishments.

Section 22 of the NAA 1948 required local authorities to fix a standard rate of charge for Part III residents, whether they were providing directly for them, or sponsoring them.[2] A means test was prescribed, latterly based on Sch 3 to the Supplementary Benefits Act 1976. A minimum charge was payable, and residents could claim social security benefits (national assistance, then supplementary benefit, and, since 1988, income support) if their resources were insufficient to meet it.

6.2.2   Schedule 8 to the NHSA 1977

This part of the NHSA 1977, originally enacted in 1946, described certain functions that were exercisable under s 21 of the Act by social services departments. They included making arrangements for the care of persons suffering from illness, for prevention of illness and for after-care. Departments were expected to arrange various services and, in particular, to provide and maintain residential accommodation. 'Illness' here included mental disorders within the meaning of the mental health legislation, latterly the MHA 1983. The Sch 8 powers overlapped with the duty laid on the Secretary of State for Health under s 3 of the NHSA 1977 to make provision for nursing care and after-care.

6.2.3   The independent sector

Comment has already been made in Chapters 1 and 2 on the demographic and economic factors which combined to produce a 500 per cent increase in private residential provision made by voluntary or commercial organisations between 1983 and 1993. Before implementation of Part III of the NHSCCA 1990 on 1 April 1993, the independent providers relied on the following two main client groups.

---

1   NAA 1948, s 21(4).
2   NAA 1948, s 26(1).

(1) People taking up beds 'sponsored' by local authorities under s 26 of the NAA 1948. The willingness of local authorities to use this option had some influence on the extent and range of independent provision.

(2) People entering residential establishments by a direct route, making individual arrangements with providers. Some would fund their own placements from beginning to end, so that the arrangements would always be 'private'. Others, initially or at a later stage, would need financial help to maintain placements, and could claim income-related benefits from central government through the Benefits Agency and the DSS. The ready availability of such funding was, of course, a considerable incentive to the growth of the independent sector. Even after benefit was claimed, however, accommodation arrangements were still made directly between resident and provider, without the involvement of the local authority, and state funding was conditional on financial need, rather than the need for residential care.

6.2.4   Residential care homes and nursing homes

The complex history and development of the NHS alongside social services provision meant, for many years, that residential establishments provided places for those needing either 'social care' or 'nursing care', but without funding necessarily following the event. For example, the NHS did not consistently fund nursing home placements, notwithstanding its statutory responsibilities to provide nursing care, and local authorities made arrangements for care in nursing homes under Sch 8 to the NHSA 1977. Meanwhile, individuals made their own arrangements, at their own expense, for both personal and nursing care, and the market responded to their needs. The DSS funded placements in either sector. Until the 1970s, the health service and social services were both run locally, which meant that a seamless web of service provision could more easily be maintained. After that, the complexity of funding arrangements, plus political and economic pressures, meant that older people facing important decisions about future care found it very difficult to understand how the system worked.

The legal distinction between residential care homes and nursing homes has been made only in legislation which purports to lay down quality standards for all residential care provided by the independent sector. The NAA 1948 originally contained requirements for the registration, conduct and inspection of residential care homes, and the Nursing Homes Registration Act 1927 did the same for nursing homes – long before the NHS was set up. The legislation has been updated over the years, and the two strands are now consolidated in the Registered Homes Act 1984 (RHA 1984).[1]

---

1   For a full discussion of quality standards and the inspection process, see Ridout, P
     Registered Homes (Jordans, 1997).

However, the RHA 1984, with its emphasis on basic physical standards, rather than 'quality of life' issues, has been left behind by a service culture which insists on dignity, respect and 'empowerment' of service users. The Care Standards Act 2000 (CSA 2000), which will come into force in 2002, will overhaul the care system, replacing the RHA 1984 with new registration standards, and a new framework for inspection. A National Care Standards Commission will be established as the registration body for England, and will also be responsible for disseminating best practice and enforcing minimum national standards which will be set by the Government.

Local authority care homes, domiciliary services and primary care services will be regulated for the first time.[1]

6.3 POST-1993: LOCAL AUTHORITY RESPONSIBILITIES

On 1 April 1993, Part III of the NAA 1948 was substantially amended by Part III of the NHSCCA 1990, and the power contained in Sch 8 to the NHSA 1977 to make residential arrangements in respect of illness and for after-care was removed. As has been seen, the policy behind the legislative changes was to encourage local authorities to act as facilitators and purchasers of services rather than providers. The new funding arrangements provided such 'encouragement'.

The purchasing power now extends to:

– residential care homes;
– nursing homes and mental nursing homes; and
– homes that have a dual purpose.

The duty in s 21 of the NAA 1948 to 'make arrangements' as the Secretary of State directs, remains. However, the description of the client group is amended to: 'persons who by reason of age, illness, disability or other circumstances are in need of care and attention which is not otherwise available to them'.[2] The explicit inclusion of 'illness' rather than 'infirmity' in this description is the key to local authorities' new responsibilities for arranging nursing home care. Section 21(4), which provides for local authorities to exercise their functions by making residential care arrangements in their own premises, survives intact.

The Department of Health originally took the view that authorities must continue to make some direct provision for residential care in order to maintain a full range of choice for users.[3] However, in *R v Wandsworth London Borough*

---

1   Standards relating to minimum room sizes in residential care homes and nursing homes have already been announced.
2   Section 21(1).
3   DoH Circular LAC (91) 12.

Council ex parte Beckwith[1] a resident challenged Wandsworth Council's decision to close and sell off all its own Part III accommodation and rely solely on purchasing arrangements with the independent sector. The House of Lords ruled that the Council was entitled to discharge its statutory duty by means of such arrangements, and was not required to maintain accommodation under its own management.

Inevitably, therefore, the focus of attention for most local authorities is the *purchasing* or *commissioning* of residential services, under s 26 of the NAA 1948, which has been considerably amended and which imposes conditions on the exercise of the purchasing power.

6.4   ORDINARY RESIDENCE

As has already been observed, the NAA 1948 gave local authorities powers and duties to provide residential accommodation (and certain other welfare services) for people 'ordinarily resident' in their areas.[2]

The concept of 'residence' has been used since the days of the Poor Law 1832 as a connecting factor linking individuals with jurisdictions under which they may claim to have substantive rights or at least locus standi. 'Ordinary' residence, 'normal' residence and 'habitual' residence are all familiar terms, and there has been an active but inconclusive debate as to whether there is a significant difference in meaning between them.[3]

It is accepted that the decision by the House of Lords in *R v Barnet London Borough Council ex parte Shah*[4] lays down the correct approach to disputes under Part III of the NAA 1948, namely that 'ordinarily resident' refers to 'a man's abode in a particular place or country, which he has adopted voluntarily and for settled purposes as part of the regular order of his life for the time being, whether of long or short duration'.[5] Guidance issued in 1993[6] confirms that ordinary residence is a question of fact and that intention plus length and continuity of residence will have to be taken into account. Of paramount importance is the question of 'how long' it takes to become ordinarily resident in a new area. Some authorities refer to an 'appreciable' period, but the application of such a test in different contexts has produced periods ranging from 1 month to 6 months.

---

1   [1996] 1 All ER 129, HL.
2   NAA 1948, ss 21 and 29.
3   See *Ordinary Residence and Community Care: An Overview* (1999) 2 CCL Rep 100, which explores these issues and the problems in defining 'ordinary residence' in some detail.
4   [1983] 2 AC 309. In fact the issue in that case was the sphere of responsibility of a local education authority.
5   *Per* Lord Scarman.
6   DoH Circular LAC (93) 7: *Ordinary Residence*.

Disputes between local authorities as to where individuals are ordinarily resident are not infrequent, because provision for long-term care is so expensive. Section 32(3) of the NAA 1948 provides that such disputes must be referred to the Secretary of State, rather than to the courts, which means that there is an absence of authority, and some uncertainty as to the legal position. The present rules, guidance and grey areas may be summarised as follows.

(i) Where older people purchase their own residential care, they will be considered to be ordinarily resident in the local authority area where the home is situated. Consequently, if their chosen home is outside the area where they have previously lived, they will acquire a connection with a new local authority. This may be significant if, over time, their private resources are exhausted and they need to seek local authority financial support, because budgets and quality of service vary from area to area.

(ii) Where an older person is assessed by his or her local authority as needing residential care, and chooses to go into a home in another local authority area, that choice must, in principle, be respected.[1] Section 24(5) of the NAA 1948 states that where a person is provided with residential accommodation he or she *shall* be deemed to be ordinarily resident in the area in which he or she was ordinarily resident before the accommodation was provided. Consequently, the placing authority will retain responsibility for that person, and *shall* notify the receiving authority.[2] There should be clear agreements about all financial aspects of the care to be provided before the placement is made.[3]

(iii) Where an older person moves into a new area, and subsequently requires residential care, the receiving local authority must undertake an assessment of need, irrespective of ordinary residence. The decision about service provision will, however, depend initially on ordinary residence, determination of which may then trigger a dispute between the local authorities, either of which might be required to subsidise residential care. This is not a recipe for a peaceful transition into a residential home. Where the older person lacks mental capacity, the situation becomes even more difficult. The courts have held that young people with severe learning disabilities will be ordinarily resident with their parents because, like children, they are unable to exercise an independent choice.[4] As regards older people, it may be argued in some cases that they are ordinarily resident where family members live, but there seems to be no clear authority on this point.

---

1   For further discussion, see **6.6**.
2   DoH Circular LAC (93) 7, paras 7 and 8.
3   It is not unheard of for one local authority to provide advice and assistance which results in an older person moving to another area and *subsequently* seeking residential accommodation. This means that the receiving local authority may have responsibility.
4   *R v Kent County Council ex parte S* [2000] 1 FLR 155.

(iv) Section 24(6) states that a patient in a NHS hospital will be deemed to be ordinarily resident in the area in which he was 'ordinarily' resident before admission to hospital. However, the responsibility of a health authority for a patient is determined by 'usual' residence.[1] Where there is no 'usual' address, the patient will generally be treated as usually resident in the area where he or she is found to be in need of treatment. That area may not necessarily be the patient's 'ordinary' residence. DoH Circular LAC (93) 7 states that in 'the majority of cases the area of ordinary residence for social services care and the area where a person needing health care is usually resident will be the same'. Nevertheless there is room for dispute where patients are being discharged from hospital into residential care. When a patient is placed in a residential care home or nursing home away from his or her 'usual' residence, the health authority in which the home is situated becomes responsible for providing appropriate health services.

(v) Section 24(3) permits local authorities to provide accommodation for people with no settled residence where they are in 'urgent need'. Where an individual is not considered to be ordinarily resident in a particular area, the receiving authority may act under s 24(3) where resources permit.[2]

6.5 THE EXTENT OF A LOCAL AUTHORITY'S ENHANCED POWERS

(i) A local authority may not make arrangements for an individual in any establishment providing nursing care without the consent of the health authority. The Residential Accommodation (Determination of District Health Authority) Regulations 1992[3] identify the 'relevant' health authority in each case. In an emergency, the local authority may place a person in a temporary nursing home placement without reference to the health authority, but the necessary consent must be sought as soon as possible after that.[4]

(ii) As a general rule, arrangements may only be made with homes which are registered under Parts I or II of the RHA 1984, or are specifically exempt from registration. Since April 1993, registration has been extended to 'small homes', which provide residential accommodation with board and personal care for fewer than four persons (relatives excepted).[5] In addition,

---

1   DoH Circular LAC (93) 7, para 18. National Health Service Functions (Directions to Authorities and Administration Arrangements) Regulations 1991, SI 1991/554.
2   See, for example, *R v Westminster City Council ex parte M* (1997) 1 CCL Rep 85, and other recent judicial review decisions exploring the scope of the s 24(3) responsibility in respect of asylum seekers.
3   SI 1992/3182.
4   NAA 1948, s 26(1B), (1C) and (1D).
5   Registered Homes (Amendment) Act 1991, amending RHA 1984, s 1.

authorities are expressly prohibited from making arrangements with providers who have been convicted of any offences created by the RHA 1984, or by regulations made under it.[1] The range of such offences is broad; not all reflect directly on the 'fitness' of the providers to have care of elderly people.[2]

Restricting local authority purchasing power to registered establishments was new; the NAA 1948 originally permitted residential accommodation arrangements to be made without such restriction. The effect was to render ultra vires placements made in establishments such as Abbeyfield homes, which do not provide 'board or personal care' within the definition in s 1 of the RHA 1984 and so do not fall within the scope of the registration system. As such establishments are regarded as exemplifying best practice in community care, a small amendment was made to the drafting of the new s 26(1A) of the NAA 1948 by the Community Care (Residential Accommodation) Act 1992. This makes clear that the requirement to deal with registered premises applies only where the local authority is specifically making arrangements for 'board and personal care'. Arrangements may, therefore, be made without statutory restriction in establishments where a more independent regime is adopted, but, of course, they will be subject to the local authority's own service specifications.

(iii) Residential care homes must be inspected by the local authority's inspection unit. This is a new requirement, and goes beyond the inspection requirements laid down in the RHA 1984. As noted earlier, from 2002, the National Care Standards Commission will replace all existing local authority and health authority inspection units, and will regulate and inspect services across the whole area of social care, including the non-residential sector.[3]

(iv) Local authorities are also prevented from arranging accommodation under s 21 or s 26 of the NAA 1948 for any person who was ordinarily resident in relevant premises before 1 April 1993. 'Relevant premises' are residential care homes or nursing homes registered under the RHA 1984, or those exempt from registration, or 'such other premises' as are prescribed by regulations.[4] The regulations referred to are the Residential Accommodation (Relevant Premises, Ordinary Residence and Exemptions) Regulations 1993.

---

1   NAA 1948, s 26(1E).
2   See, for example, RHA 1984, s 5(3), which permits conditions regarding numbers, age or sex of residents to be attached to a registration certificate. Breach of such conditions may lead to deregistration.
3   CSA 2000. The National Care Standards Commission is one outcome of the work done by the Royal Commission on Long-term Care.
4   NAA 1948, s 26A. The CSA 2000 creates the generic term 'care home' which will apply to all residential homes from April 2002.

Most people covered by this exclusion have 'preserved rights' to income support, and so can claim income support to meet all, or most of the costs of a residential placement. Nevertheless, advisers are increasingly coming across situations where local authorities' lack of vires prevents them from intervening in support of very elderly, very vulnerable people.[1]

6.6   INDIVIDUAL CHOICE OF HOME

Assessments will specify whether residential care home or nursing home accommodation is required and whether an individual needs a place in a specialist unit, offering care to, for example, elderly people with dementia. The local authority will be expected to provide a range of options within this specification. Most authorities publish lists of providers which they are prepared to recommend to users. In some instances, complaints have been made against local authorities on the basis that the choice offered is too narrow. If homes do not fulfil the criteria in ss 26 and 26(A) of the NAA 1948, they cannot be offered to users, but local authorities themselves may also create ineligibility by adopting overly stringent specifications for their providers. Either way, choice will be restricted.

An underlying factor is cost. As a result of pressures on their budgets, local authorities will expect prices to be keen, and many simply ignore providers who cannot compete on price. One danger here is that large public limited company providers can offer residential accommodation at a lower unit cost than smaller more 'homelike' establishments, and already the growth of large residential units is being noted. Such a development clearly does not equate with community care policies and is driven wholly by market forces. Local authority lists will be similarly price-driven.

Early research on the effects of the community care changes indicated that prices throughout the residential sector, but for nursing home care in particular, were being held down to former DSS rates.[2] Bearing in mind that such rates did not usually match full bed fees, it is clear that prices have fallen, relatively speaking, since before April 1993. There is further evidence that some local authorities are placing in residential care homes people who would have had nursing home care before April 1993.

The Secretary of State has issued directions which are intended to ensure that people entering residential care homes or nursing homes have a genuine choice as to where they should live. The National Assistance Act (Choice of Accommodation) Directions 1992[3] provide that a local authority, having determined that it will make residential accommodation arrangements, must give effect to an expressed choice of placement provided that:

---

1   For further discussion, see Chapter 15.
2   Audit Commission, *Taking Care* (1993).
3   DoH Circular LAC (92) 27.

- the accommodation chosen is suitable in relation to the individual's assessed needs;
- to do so would not cost the authority more than it would usually expect to pay for accommodation for someone with the individual's assessed needs;
- the accommodation is available; and
- the person in charge of the accommodation is prepared to accept the placement subject to the local authority's usual terms and conditions.[1]

Cost factors underlie two of these four provisos. In particular, the local authority may argue against a preferred placement because it is too expensive by reference to other possible placements. The emphasis in the directions is, however, on provision for equivalent needs, not cheaper and less appropriate provision. The local authority may not put a ceiling on what it is prepared to pay for residential placements, and must be prepared to meet appropriate fees of establishments which provide for certain types of need and deliver a service which is not available elsewhere. In *R v Avon County Council ex parte M*,[2] it was held that the local authority was obliged to provide residential accommodation which was appropriate to the assessed needs of a man with learning disabilities. He required a placement outside the county which would cost £3,000 per year more then the local placement proposed by the authority.

The guidance in DoH Circular LAC (92) 27 envisages 'circumstances where an authority might judge the need to move to another part of the country (where cost might be higher) to be an integral part of an individual's assessed needs (for example to be near a relative) and therefore one of the factors to be considered in determining what the authority would usually expect to pay'. Local authorities should not restrict choice to their approved lists of providers; suitability cannot reasonably be related to inclusion in a list, which is simply a convenient tool for allocating placements when no preference is expressed.

The presumption of choice extends everywhere in England and Wales. Neither s 26 of the NAA 1948 nor the RHA 1984 applies in Scotland, so English authorities may make arrangements only with residential or nursing care providers in England or Wales. However, DoH Circular LAC (93) 18 clarifies circumstances in which English, Welsh or Scottish authorities may lawfully combine forces, under their separate legislative powers, to achieve cross-border placements.[3]

---

1   See also DoH Circulars LAC (92) 27 and LAC (93) 18.
2   [1994] 2 FLR 1006.
3   Clause 55 of the Health and Social Care Bill, published in December 2000, authorises regulations specifying the conditions in which cross-border placements may be made. They will apply to s 21 arrangements made in Scotland, Northern Ireland, the Channel Islands or the Isle of Man.

6.7   TOP-UPS

Where a local authority considers that the prospective resident's preferred home is too expensive, but a third party is able and willing to make a sufficient contribution towards the cost of the placement, the preference must, in principle, be respected.[1] The amount of the third-party contribution will be the difference between the actual fee for the accommodation chosen and the amount that the local authority would usually expect to pay for someone with the individual's assessed needs. Bearing in mind that the contractual obligations to the provider will rest on the local authority, it will be entitled to satisfy itself that the offer of financial help is a serious one, and that there are resources to back it.

Third parties are likely, therefore, to be subjected to financial checks and may be asked to enter into a top-up contract with the local authority. They will be told that they must cover fee increases, which will not necessarily be apportioned equally between themselves and the local authority. In addition, they will be advised that, if fees are not met in the future, the local authority will normally move the resident to cheaper accommodation.[2]

The direction on topping-up arrangements does not apply to 'liable relatives' (spouses) who have a duty to contribute to the cost of accommodation under s 42 of the NAA 1948. The guidance states that:

> '. . . such people cannot act as third parties for the care of the relative to whose care they are already obliged to contribute.[3] However, local authorities are not precluded from entering into "similar" arrangements with liable relatives who have the resources to both meet their s 42 liability and make an additional third party payment. Elderly spouses should always be advised that, if the local authority accepts their offer to top-up the fees of a spouse in residential accommodation, it will nevertheless retain the option of enforcing the liable relatives' obligation.'[4]

DoH Circular LAC (92) 27 states that there is no reason why local authorities should not 'at the request of the resident, arrange more expensive accommodation for someone who can, from their own resources, afford to pay the original cost'. This implies that residents may make their 'own top-ups' out of residual capital. Given, however, that such 'payments' will only be in issue where a local authority has undertaken to provide financial assistance to the resident, there must be some incongruity in a situation where public funds are supporting an arrangement which the authority considers more expensive than is legally necessary and which depends on the resident using up disregarded capital below the £16,000 threshold as though it were income. If that capital were exhausted, the local authority would be forced either to allocate additional

---

1   DoH Circular LAC (92) 27, para 4.
2   Ibid, para 11.9.
3   Ibid, para 11.13.
4   See **9.6.4**.

funds to support the placement, which would be unfair to other older people needing services, or to take the risk (with attendant criticism or blame) of moving the resident to a cheaper home.

In 1998, the Department of Health issued fresh guidance,[1] stipulating that residents cannot 'act as their own third party'. Arrangements made prior to the new guidance will be at the discretion of local authorities, but, given that residents' needs may, over time, incorporate the need to remain settled and secure, upheavals will be unlikely, although any shortfalls in fees will have to be met from the public purse.

The legal position remains interesting. Own top-ups are now considered to be unlawful, but the original Directions on Choice, which both the 1992 and the 1998 guidance seek to amplify, are altogether silent on the matter – neither authorising nor prohibiting such arrangements. The primary legislation is also silent. In order to square the circle, it has to be argued, rather unsatisfactorily, that what is not expressly permitted is unlawful.

When the new Health and Social Care Bill is implemented,[2] the gap in the law will be filled. Clause 53 authorises 'additional payments' (top-ups) by residents themselves or by 'other persons', including liable relatives. It appears that residents' own top-ups will have to be made only out of specified resources, perhaps leaving some residual capital intact.

6.8 RESOURCES AND THE DUTY TO PROVIDE RESIDENTIAL ACCOMMODATION

As explained at **6.3**, above, s 21 of the NAA 1948 states that it shall be the 'duty' of every local authority to 'provide residential accommodation for persons ... who are in need of care and attention which is not otherwise available to them'.

Before 1993, the nature and scope of this core local authority responsibility had not been considered by the courts. However, two recent decisions by the Court of Appeal have now examined s 21 of the NAA 1948 in some detail.

6.8.1 *R v Sefton Metropolitan Borough Council ex parte Help the Aged*[3]

This judicial review was brought against Sefton Metropolitan Borough Council on behalf of Mrs Charlotte Blanchard, a lady in her 80s, who had been assessed as needing care in a nursing home. When admitted to the home, she had capital of approximately £17,500. Three months later, she sought financial support from the local authority.

---

1   DoH Circular LAC (98) 8.
2   The Bill was published in December 2000. The Government intends that it will be brought into effect in stages from April 2001.
3   (1997) 1 CCL Rep 57, CA.

Sefton Metropolitan Borough Council has a large population of elderly people, and in the early 1990s there was a substantial deficit on the social services' budget. The social services department implemented a new policy of not providing or arranging residential accommodation for anyone, irrespective of need, who had capital resources in excess of £1,500. The policy purported to ignore the capital threshold of £16,000 set in the National Assistance (Assessment of Resources) Regulations 1992 (NA(AR) Regs 1992).[1] Therefore, although Mrs Blanchard's needs were acknowledged, her application for local authority support was deferred for one year, until her capital fell below £1,500.

The Court of Appeal ruled that Sefton Metropolitan Borough Council was entitled to have some regard to its limited financial resources in deciding whether applicants for residential accommodation were in need of care and attention, but that where an individual's need was manifest there was a duty to make provision, irrespective of resources.

This ruling followed shortly after the decision by the House of Lords in the *Gloucestershire* case.[2] The decision in that case was that a local authority may take its resources into account when determining the level of services to be provided under s 2 of the CSDPA 1970. In *Sefton*, however, although Lord Woolf MR expressly followed the House of Lords in concluding that a local authority may legitimately take resources into account when making its decision as to an individual's need for care and attention, he expressly restricted the scope of financial considerations to a 'limited subjective element'. In any event, it was not disputed that Mrs Blanchard had been assessed by Sefton Metropolitan Borough Council as qualifying for assistance under s 21 of the NAA 1948, and that the real issue was the deferment of such assistance pursuant to Sefton's policy.

6.8.2   *R v Kensington and Chelsea Royal London Borough Council ex parte Kujtim*[3]

This application was brought by a Kosovan refugee who had been assessed by Kensington and Chelsea Royal London Borough Council as needing residential accommodation under s 21 of the NAA 1948, and placed in bed and breakfast accommodation, from which he was subsequently twice evicted for allegedly violent and disruptive behaviour.

The Court of Appeal held that if, following assessment of need under s 47 of the NHSCCA 1990, an individual is accepted as being 'in need of care and attention' within s 21(1)(a) of the NAA 1948, there is then a duty to provide residential accommodation, which continues for as long as the assessed needs

---

1   Referred to throughout this book as 'the charging regulations'.
2   See **5.14**.
3   (1999) 2 CCL Rep 340, CA, followed in *Batantu v Islington LBC* (2000) LTL, 8 November.

remain unchanged. If, however, a service user unreasonably refuses to accept the accommodation provided, or fails to observe reasonable requirements in relation to its occupation, the local authority is then entitled to treat its duty as discharged.

Here, the Court of Appeal followed and extended *Sefton*, in holding that where an assessment reveals a need for care and attention, the local authority's duty to provide residential accommodation is directly enforceable by judicial review. No comment was made, however, regarding Lord Woolf's other conclusion that a local authority's resources (or lack of them) must provide part of the context in which the decision as to whether there is a need for care and attention is actually made. Perhaps decisions about residential care should not be treated in the same way as decisions about non-residential services. Given the present community care policies, residential care is the option of last resort, and it must either be provided 'in full' or not at all. It is also likely to be a less expensive option than provision of an appropriate level of service within the community.

6.9 'NOT OTHERWISE AVAILABLE'

In *Sefton*, the Court of Appeal considered the meaning of a further phrase in s 21(1)(a) of the NAA 1948. Can it be said that residential accommodation is '*otherwise available*' to a would-be resident who has resources with which he or she could purchase care independently of the local authority? In other words, is the local authority's duty to provide a service to meet assessed needs affected by the prospective resident's financial situation, even where that service must ultimately be charged for?

On this point, the court ruled that care and attention cannot be said to be 'otherwise available' to people who are financially eligible for support under the charging regulations.[1] Therefore, Sefton Metropolitan Borough Council's policy was unlawful, and Mrs Blanchard, with resources of well below £16,000, was entitled to financial support in respect of her residential care.

However, the judges did not explore the position where an individual seeking local authority support in fact has resources in excess of £16,000, although in practice this is an issue which affects a great many older people. It may be argued that, in 1948, '*not otherwise available*' was referring to other physical accommo-dation which would meet the needs occasioned by old age or infirmity. At that time, the independent sector hardly existed. This is supported by the fact that s 22 of the NAA 1948 quite clearly envisages circumstances where a local authority may make residential care arrangements for an individual who needs care and attention in the full expectation that he or she will be in a position, at least for the time being, to reimburse the care fees in full. As explained elsewhere in this chapter, there are advantages, particularly for older people who lack mental capacity, in accessing local authority support in respect of

---

1   NA(AR) Regs 1992, SI 1992/2977.

residential care.[1] However, a short piece of legislation which came on to the statute book after *Sefton*, via the Private Members' Bill procedure has unfortunately made it more difficult for people, even with very modest capital, to be able to gain the benefit of the relative security offered by a local authority placement at a time when economic forces are beginning to pose a real threat to the stability of the residential sector.

6.9.1   The Community Care (Residential Accommodation) Act 1998

This short Act amends s 21 of the NAA 1948 by adding the provision that, in determining whether care and attention are *otherwise available* to a person, a local authority shall disregard so much of the person's capital as does not exceed the capital limit prescribed in the NA(AR) Regs 1992.

Guidance was issued to accompany this amendment.[2] In addition, the charging regulations themselves were amended so that the definition of 'resident', which is used throughout, is now to include a person for whom it is 'proposed to' provide accommodation under Part III of the NAA 1948, as well as a person for whom accommodation is provided. This means that local authorities may now carry out financial assessments *before* determining whether care and attention are 'otherwise available' to an individual.[3]

The changes to the regulations make it clear that the importance of the amendment to s 21 of the NAA 1948 lies not in what is stated, but in what is not stated. There now appears to be a statutory implication that care and attention are to be regarded as *'otherwise available'* to a person whose capital exceeds £16,000,[4] and the interface between ss 21 and 22 of the NAA 1948 has become an awkward one, which is smoothed over to some extent, by the new guidance. The latter is of considerable importance, and practitioners will need to be familiar with the detail. It states, in particular, that where a resident's assessed capital is above £16,000, he or she will have to pay the full charge, and 'may be in a position to make their own arrangements'. However:

> '... that does not exempt a Social Services Department from its duty to make arrangements for those people who are themselves unable to make care arrangements and have no one to make arrangements for them ... it is the Department's view that having capital in excess of the upper limit of £16,000 does

---

1   See **6.11**.

2   DoH Circular LAC (98) 19: Community Care (Residential Accommodation) Act 1998.

3   In *Robertson v Fife Council* (Scottish Court of Session, December 1999) the local authority declined to make nursing home arrangements for an elderly lady who had transferred her flat to her children some two and a half years previously. The value of the house was assessed as notional capital, with the result that her total assets exceeded £16,000. The Social Work (Scotland) Act 1968 does not include the phrase 'not otherwise available' which would perhaps prevent a similar decision in England. See Chapters 11–13 for a discussion of the notional capital rule.

4   The capital threshold will increase to £18,500 from April 2001.

not in itself constitute adequate access to alternative care and attention. Local authorities will wish to consider the position of those who have capital in excess of the upper limit of £16,000 and must satisfy themselves that the individual is able to make their own arrangements, or has others who are willing and able to make arrangements for them, for appropriate care. Where there is a suitable advocate or representative (in most cases a close relative) it is the Department's view that local authorities should provide guidance and advice on the availability and appropriate level of services to meet the individual's needs. Where there is no identifiable advocate or representative to act on the individual's behalf it must be the responsibility of the local authority to make the arrangements and to contract for the person's care.'[1]

The guidance goes on to say that, having determined that they will make arrangements for residential accommodation, local authorities should do so without undue delay. This applies particularly where the assets of a resident who has previously been self funding have been reduced to the £16,000 threshold.[2] Where residents who have been placed by local authorities subsequently become 'self funding' following the sale of their former home, the guidance envisages that local authorities will terminate their contractual arrangements with providers, leaving residents to fend for themselves, if they are satisfied 'that the person is able to manage their own affairs or has someone who can take over the arrangements on their behalf'.[3]

It is clear throughout DoH Circular LAC (98) 19 that '*otherwise available*' is now defined, almost exclusively, in financial terms.[4] The exception for residents who lack mental capacity and have no attorney, receiver or advocate is a narrow one, although it can at least be said to fall within the spirit of the NAA 1948. The implications for older people with modest resources are considerable and their advisers will need to bear the following points in mind.

– It is essential to monitor the diminution of resources of an older person who has been self-funding. There is no guarantee that a local authority will respond instantly when asked to carry out an assessment, and it is probably negligent for a legal adviser to permit his or her resources to fall below the capital threshold without making appropriate efforts to access public funding.

– In many cases, residents will be entitled to income support as well as local authority funding once their capital falls to £16,000 (£18,500 from April 2001), and the claiming process should be straightforward. Regulation 13 of the Social Security (Claims and Payments) Regulations 1987 permits the claim to be made up to 3 months before a resident will qualify for benefit.

---

1   DoH Circular LAC (98) 19, para 10.
2   Ibid, para 11.
3   Ibid, para 12.
4   The Health and Social Care Bill 2000 adopts the same approach. Clause 57 further amends NAA 1948, s 21 to specify that, in determining whether care and attention are *otherwise available* to a person, certain resources are to be disregarded. See **10.1**.

– A decision by a local authority to 'privatise' care arrangements once the resident's property has been sold should always be resisted unless the proceeds of sale are very substantial. Vulnerable clients must be protected against any disruption of a settled placement and, at the very least, advisers should seek local authority agreement to maintain the same placement, on the same terms, should the capital released fall below the prescribed threshold during the resident's lifetime.

– In some cases where there is a property to sell the resident may opt for 'loophole' funding under a private care arrangement.[1] This course of action is likely to suit the local authority, but, again, it is imperative to seek to negotiate a fall-back position should the property prove difficult to sell, should the proceeds of sale be depleted to £16,000 (£18,500), or should home fees substantially exceed benefit rates.

6.10 LOCAL AUTHORITY CONTRACTS FOR RESIDENTIAL CARE

The contractual role of the local authority, as commissioner of services, has already been referred to in Chapter 1. Residential accommodation arrangements under s 26 of the NAA 1948 will be made between the local authority and the care provider on behalf of a third party, the resident, whose identity may or may not be known, depending on whether the local authority has negotiated block contracts, or whether it is spot purchasing. Where, however, the local authority is arranging care in its own Part III accommodation under s 21 of the NAA 1948, there will be a direct relationship between the local authority and the resident, which lies in statute rather than contract.

6.10.1 Standard terms and conditions

Local authority contracts for residential care services will contain:

– basic contractual conditions, such as would be found in any commercial contract; and
– detailed service specifications, which should cover all aspects of the service being contracted for and should include quality standards and provision for monitoring.

As a result, contracts tend to be very long, very legalistic and not very user-friendly. The practice guidance states that it is essential for a local authority to seek legal advice on a proposed contract at the outset of the negotiations. Providers will be well advised to take the same course of action, especially since local authorities will have a dominant bargaining position.

---

1   See **14.4.6**.

Authorities are expected to involve service users, carers and other bodies in determining the service specifications.[1]

Standard conditions should cover:

- duration of the contract (fixed or renewable);
- purchasing arrangements;
- variation procedures;
- procedures for resolving disputes;
- default arrangements;
- insurance;
- authorised officers;
- details of any sub-contracting;
- complaints procedures for users or carers;
- review procedure (for both specifications and conditions).

Section 26(1E) of the NAA 1948 requires that residential care arrangements be terminated forthwith if the proprietor of the home is convicted of any offence under the RHA 1984.

6.10.2 Fees

The local authority will always contract to pay the accommodation fees to the care provider and will then expect to recoup contributions from residents. The statutory duty to charge residents for their accommodation is laid down by s 22 of the NAA 1948 which also authorises means testing. The duty to impose and recover charges is, legally, quite independent of the s 21 duty and this important point is reinforced by the contractual structure which makes the local authority liable to pay providers the contracted price for beds, whether or not contributions are recovered from individual residents.[2] Therefore, providers have a degree of financial security, even if the contracted fees may not be the best obtainable in the open market place.

Section 26(3A) of the NAA 1948 creates a different payment option. The local authority may agree with providers and with residents that contributions by the latter will be paid direct to the providers and not collected by the local authority. The advantage of such an arrangement (illustrated in Figure 2, below) is that it gives residents status *vis-à-vis* providers rather than leaving them as the objects of contractual arrangements made between third parties. Different types of arrangements are permitted by s 26(3A) of the NAA 1948, but the net effect is to involve residents directly as 'part-purchasers' of their own care services, which fits in with the user-led approach to long-term care emphasised in the White Paper on Community Care. Legally, a resident will become 'liable' to pay his or her assessed contribution direct to the provider. The local authority will, in turn, make net payments to the provider. If a resident fails to

1   Policy Guidance (DoH Circular LAC (96) 7), para 4.20.
2   NAA 1948, s 26(2).

meet payments, however, the local authority's obligation to the provider to cover the full cost of the placement is revived, and the *local authority* (not the provider) is empowered to take steps to enforce the contributions. When this model is used, there may be a single contract between local authority, provider and resident, or two linked contracts between local authority/provider and provider/resident.

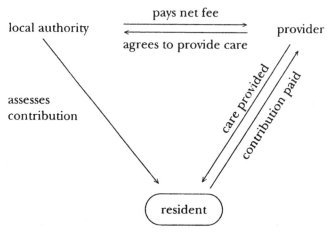

Figure 1. Contractual arrangements between local authorities, residential care providers and residents made under s 26(3A) of the NAA 1948.

Many local authorities favour the arrangement described above, largely because it relieves them of an administrative burden. However, advisers are reminded that the legislation does not permit local authorities to override the wishes of residents in this respect. Should problems ever arise regarding payment of a resident's contribution (for instance because an income support claim is delayed or changed) it is better for the local authority to take the burden, rather than for the resident to have to face correspondence, (sometimes hostile), or even the threat of proceedings, from the care provider.[1]

6.10.3   Quality assurance

Since April 1993, social services authorities have sought to use their purchasing power to promote higher standards of care, especially in the residential sector, where most of the contractual activity is concentrated. Stringent service specifications have put providers under pressure, and there have been applications for judicial review, whereby providers have sought to challenge local authority contracts on grounds of unreasonableness. The underlying question is: are contracts for care simple commercial contracts, and so subject to

---

1   Such proceedings would in fact be wrongly directed, as the local authority always carries the residual responsibility to pay the agreed fee; however, providers often misunderstand the legal position.

individual bargaining power and pure market forces? Or is there a public interest factor which requires the local authority to restrain its superior bargaining power and make only 'reasonable' demands on its contracting partners? The present judicial view is that local authority contracts with providers of residential care are subject to general contractual principles and that remedies lie in private law only. The concept of 'public law contract', which is familiar to some European legal systems, is not recognised in English law.[1]

It is clear, however, that the economic power of local authorities in relation to residential care contracts, in particular, does raise some very difficult questions. There is, on the one hand, powerful research evidence to confirm the widely held view that privately funded residents usually pay more than state funded residents for the same level of service. This is a direct outcome of the purchasing power of local authorities.[2]

On the other hand, it is also becoming clear that constant downward pressure on prices exerted by local authorities is forcing providers of residential care out of business, and concerns are being expressed as to the adequacy of residential provision in years to come if this trend continues. At present there are conflicting views as to the application of competition law to local authorities, but now that the Competition Act 1998 is in place, this issue is likely to be raised before the courts in the near future.

6.11   PRIVATE RESIDENTIAL CARE CONTRACTS

It is popularly assumed that local authority arranged care is inherently inferior to private arrangements. For the reasons given above, that is a myth. On the whole, the residential care providers with which local authorities have purchasing arrangements also offer their services to private purchasers. The care is the same. Local authority managed accommodation[3] does labour under a particularly negative reputation, but again there is no evidential basis for this.[4]

There may be a number of advantages in seeking to access local authority arranged care. As explained above there is usually a clear financial advantage to

---

1   See, for example, *R v Newcastle-Upon-Tyne CC ex parte Dickson* [1994] COD 217: *R v Coventry City Council ex parte Coventry Heads of Independent Care Establishments (CHOICE)* (1998) 1 CCL Rep 379.

2   Laing, W *A Fair Price for Care* (Joseph Rowntree Foundation, 1998). This paper is based on the results obtained from Laing and Buisson's CRASSCH survey carried out in 1997/98, and two further specific pieces of research.

3   Older people cannot purchase their own care in local authority owned or local authority managed accommodation. The local authority is the provider of the service, on the basis of need.

4   The Audit Commission has suggested that 'good' homes do not have significantly higher overall costs than homes which provide a lower quality of service, and that it is important for all purchasers of care to get a better understanding of quality. See Audit Commission *The Coming of Age* (1997), paras 125–129.

be gained from arrangements under the NAA 1948. In addition, the fact that attendance allowance is available where the claimant is in residential care arranged under s 26 of the NAA 1948, but reimburses the local authority in full, adds to the financial benefit.[1]

There may also be advantages in having the protection of a local authority contract, which will almost certainly specify quality assurance standards which are substantially in excess of registration requirements.[2] It may be difficult to secure equivalent standards in a privately negotiated arrangement, and individual purchasers may, therefore, miss out on a layer of contractual protection. Legal advisers must, of course, strive to offset this inherent disadvantage (see **6.10.5**).

If a home has to be closed down, for breach of registration standards, a local authority must take responsibility for all residents who are displaced. However, it is possible that 'troublesome' residents may have less security as private purchasers than under a local authority arrangement and, of course, failure to pay fees (following default by an attorney, for instance) may lead to eviction for a private purchaser. Where arrangements are made under the NAA 1948, on the other hand, default in payment of a contribution, or even the full fee, must always be compensated for by the local authority.[3]

6.11.1   Terms of the contract

The relationship between a private purchaser and a provider of residential care services rests entirely on contract. There is no legal requirement for a written contract, but it is of the utmost importance for vulnerable, older clients that arrangements for accommodation and care at the end of their lives should not rely on inference. Most written contracts that are offered to prospective residents are brief and cover basic issues, without specifying service levels or quality standards.

It is suggested that the following minimum conditions should be stipulated as a matter of best practice and, if absent, should be fought for.

(i) Services to be provided
The contract should define the service to the extent that it will be clear exactly what is included in the agreed fee, and whether the service has been fully delivered. Local authority contracts will always specify the service package, and private purchasers are entitled to expect the same treatment.

---

1   DoH Circular LAC (98) 19, discussed at **6.9.1**, indicates that there will be some
    circumstances where elderly people, who have capital assets in excess of £16,000, but
    whose income is modest, may be eligible for local authority arrangements. On the
    attendance allowance point, see **14.4.7**.

2   The courts have endorsed this practice: see *R v Coventry City Council ex parte CHOICE*
    (1998) 1 CCL Rep 379, QBD.

3   NAA 1948, s 26(2). See *Chief Adjudication Officer v Quinn & Gibbon* [1996] 4 All ER 72;
    and *Steane v Chief Adjudication Officer* [1996] 4 All ER 83.

(ii) Fees

The contract should specify the global fees, and how they are to be paid. It should state whether payment is to be made in advance or in arrears. The cost of any extra services, which are not included in the basic fee (for example hairdressing, chiropody, and incontinence services) should be specified.

(iii) Fee increases

The contract should state how fee increases are to be negotiated, and what notice has to be given before increases are implemented.

(iv) Security of tenure

Providers generally subscribe to the view that residents' occupation must be non-exclusive if care is to be managed effectively, and that security of tenure in the accepted sense is inappropriate. However, the Housing Corporation has made a public commitment to tenancies, rather than mere licences, for residential accommodation as well as for sheltered housing, and general concerns to empower and promote independence for service users lead in the same direction. Some contracts and management styles may eventually prompt challenges under the Human Rights Act 1998.

6.11.2   Absence from the home

Contracts should make clear the extent of the continuing obligation to pay fees where, for example, a resident is admitted to hospital. It may be appropriate for fees to be reduced after several weeks' absence, since the home owner's costs will be reduced. Where fees continue to be paid, the resident's room should not be used – for example, for respite care.

6.11.3   Termination

Contracts typically entitle home owners to a termination where fees are in arrears; where the resident's behaviour is disruptive and affects the well-being of other residents; and where the home is no longer able to provide the care which the resident needs. Residents themselves should be able to terminate arrangements if they are dissatisfied with the service provided, or if they wish to move elsewhere.

6.11.4   Death of the resident

The death of a resident creates a sudden void for the home owner, and loss of income. Most standard contracts provide that fees should remain payable for a period after the death to enable the home owner to fill the vacancy. Obviously it is in the interests of the resident and his or her family that the contract terminates immediately. This is an area where a reasonable balance has to be struck and where advisers should foresee the need to negotiate.

Contracts may be expected to specify that fees remain payable at least until all the resident's personal possessions have been removed. This is not unreasonable, and those acting in the administration of the estate should be aware of the need to collect personal items at the earliest opportunity.

6.11.5   Personal matters

Best practice requires that homes accommodate residents' lifestyle choices as far as possible, but specific needs and requirements should always be raised at the contract stage. Some clients will be smokers; others will wish to live in a smoke-free environment. Whether or not a home permits residents to keep small pets is often a very important issue for older people. Despite the evidence that the companionship of animals adds to general well-being, some homes still ban them or heavily restrict the type of pet that may be kept.

6.11.6   Gifts

Elderly residents often become very attached to their care staff, and may wish to make gifts or bequests to them. Obviously there is scope for financial abuse in this situation, and the code of practice for staff in any well-run home should address this. This issue is not perhaps for the care contract, but clients should always be advised about the need to take independent advice before making gifts or testamentary dispositions. The contract should, however, make it clear that additional payments/tips will not be solicited and should not be given.

6.11.7   Disputes

The contract should provide for some form of alternative dispute resolution in order to avoid the need to go to court should a dispute arise. All homes should have an internal complaints procedure which, it is hoped, will allow most difficulties to be resolved. Regulation 17 of the Residential Care Home Regulations 1984 requires homes to make available to residents and their relatives the address and telephone number of the registration authority, so that complaints which are not satisfied internally can be referred on.

6.12   HEALTH CARE SERVICES FOR RESIDENTS

Older people living in residential care homes and nursing homes will rely on NHS provision for most of their medical or health care needs, just as if they were still in their own homes. The guidance issued to local authorities emphasises that contracts for independent sector residential care should not include provision of any service which it is the responsibility of the NHS to provide.[1]

The health authority in whose area the elderly person is usually resident must purchase appropriate community health services. In this context, basic NHS

---

1   DoH Circular LAC (92) 24, *Local Authority Contracts for Residential and Nursing Home Care after April 1993.*

provision includes GP visits, district nursing services, physiotherapy, speech therapy and possibly incontinence services and aids. The guidance states that services should be provided on the same basis as to people in their own homes. There is some recent evidence that people in residential care in fact receive a better service.

The distinction between community health services[1] and personal care provided in residential care homes seems to be reasonably clear. For nursing home residents, however, the relationship between community health provision and the basic care available in homes is more complex. However, as regards nursing homes, which are supposed to deliver 'nursing care', the position is less clear. The guidance states that local authority packages purchased under s 26 of the NAA 1948 must include provision of all 'general nursing services', but that health authorities/GPs will be responsible for purchasing, 'within the resources available', specific physiotherapy, chiropody and speech and language therapy services, plus 'specialist' nursing advice, for example incontinence advice or stoma care. Quite apart from the fact that it may be difficult to distinguish between general or specialist nursing advice, the guidance also seems to indicate that health authorities have some discretion over what services they will purchase. Elderly people who purchase their own residential or nursing care should be advised to make enquiries as to the community health provision they can expect.

6.12.1 Incontinence services

Incontinence services which are not provided by the NHS can be a substantial addition to weekly home fees. Older people in residential care homes may find that incontinence supplies are charged for as 'extras'. This should always be questioned, as health authorities must publish criteria which should be even-handed between residents and users who live in their own homes. As far as nursing home residents are concerned, HSG (95) 8 states that incontinence supplies should be included in the basic fee, and so should be paid for by whichever agency, or individual, is responsible for fees.

6.12.2 The *Coughlan* decision

Chapter 2 contains an extended discussion of the interface between 'health' and 'social' care, and of the implications of the Court of Appeal's decision in *R v North and East Devon Health Authority ex parte Coughlan*. It will be seen that *Coughlan* does not altogether resolve the question *when*:

(a) it is appropriate for a patient's basic nursing care to be provided by social services under the NAA 1948 (and charged for), leaving the NHS to fund any specialist overlay; or *when*

(b) a patient's needs are such that the NHS must arrange, and fund, the whole package.

---

1   See **2.3**.

The introduction of a new provision for nursing care delivered by registered nurses in nursing homes to be funded by the NHS will make this interface more complex.[1]

---

1   Health and Social Care Bill 2000, clause 48.

Chapter 7

PUBLIC FUNDING FOR LONG-TERM CARE

'Simply describing the current system vividly demonstrates a number of complexities and confusion.'[1]

7.1 INTRODUCTION

As previously explained in Chapter 1, the hidden agenda for the new arrangements for community care was the capping of social security spending on residential care. Under the NHSCCA 1990, local authority social services departments became the lead agencies for arranging social care, and additional funds were transferred to local authorities through the STG. It was intended that local authorities should not, in future, be able to shift the costs of long-term care back to central government via the benefits system. As will be explained, this intended outcome has not been achieved.

From the perspective of older people needing, or receiving, long-term care, there have been three main consequences of the legislative and policy changes which took place in April 1993.

(1) Local authorities, through the assessment process[2] have become 'gatekeepers' of public funds. People who feel that they need services at home, or who wish to enter residential care homes or nursing homes, and who are not in a position to purchase their requirements in the open market, must 'pass' the needs test in order to qualify for local authority commissioned services, which now include all residential care arrangements. Services are supposed to be needs-led, but, as explained in Chapter 5, this does not necessarily mean that people get what they want. Even if needs/wants are met, or partly met, users must expect to pay for their services, to the extent that their circumstances allow.

(2) Most local authority charges are now means tested. People going into residential care by arrangement with the local authority will always be subject to a statutory means test. Where non-residential services are being provided, local authorities will normally charge users, as they have the power to do, and may either operate a means test or use some other charging device. Health care services, whether delivered in hospital or via community health providers, are still free of charge to users. It is apparent, however, that the demarcation line between the different community services is shifting. Services previously labelled 'health' and so free of

---

1   The Royal Commission Report on Long Term Care *With Respect to Old Age*, Cm 4192–I (Stationery Office, 1999), para 4.32.
2   See Chapter 5.

charge are being re-labelled 'social care' and are having to be paid for by users. There is more extensive discussion of this issue in Chapter 2.

(3) Income support rules have changed. Older people who have very low incomes, or who are without resources at all, can still claim means-tested benefits to raise their resources to a basic subsistence level, but the enhanced payments of income support which used to be available for residential care have stopped. Claimants living in their own homes used to receive less than half the amount of income support which was available to claimants in residential homes or nursing homes. This benefits incentive towards residential care has now largely disappeared.[1]

7.2   PAYING FOR RESIDENTIAL CARE BEFORE 1 APRIL 1993

As explained in Chapter 1, residential care arrangements before April 1993 were made either by local authorities, in pursuit of their responsibility under Part III of the NAA 1948, or by individuals purchasing on their own behalf. Local authorities owned and managed their own Part III accommodation and, in addition, there was a flourishing independent sector in which authorities were permitted to sponsor beds as an alternative means of discharging their statutory responsibility. They had no explicit duty to make arrangements for nursing home care. Individuals could, of course, enter nursing homes by their own arrangement, and health authorities had the power to commission beds in independent nursing homes.

The residential care system was largely funded by central government through social security benefits. Those placed in local authority Part III accommodation, or in sponsored beds elsewhere, had to be charged for their accommodation, under s 22 of the NAA 1948. Those with means would be asked to pay a standard charge which was related to the economic cost of providing the bed. The local authority's responsibility was always in the nature of a safety net, however, so that most people placed were at poverty level. A means test was prescribed by charging regulations, and a minimum contribution was payable which could be met either by paying over the basic retirement pension, or by claiming income support (previously supplementary benefit) which was available at a special 'Part III' rate.

Establishments in the independent sector would set their own fees. Residents who had insufficient income to pay the fees, and whose capital was limited, could claim income support at the enhanced level. During the early 1980s, rates for income support matched home fees. In 1986, the link was broken and

---

1   The capital thresholds are still different: £8,000 for claimants living in the community and £16,000 for claimants in residential accommodation; see **14.2.3**. These thresholds will remain in place after April 2001, although the corresponding thresholds for the local authority means test will rise. See Appendix 3 for benefit levels from April 2001.

regulations set maximum fees for different categories of residential home accommodation. In March 1993, the benefit payments ranged from £175 (outside Greater London) per week for residential care homes for elderly people with a physical disability to £280 per week for nursing homes for elderly people with mental health problems. Residents were not asked to establish need for a particular type of residential care, or indeed for care at all. This created a 'perverse incentive' so far as the Audit Commission was concerned.[1]

Thus, the benefits system funded independent sector beds in both residential care homes and nursing homes. In particular, it allowed health authorities to camouflage the gradual reduction in continuing care provision within the NHS by discharging elderly patients from hospital into nursing homes, where their care could be paid for by the DSS rather than the NHS.

In 1993, this convenient practice was questioned by the Court of Appeal in *White v Chief Adjudication Officer and Another*,[2] when it ruled that an arrangement to place former long-stay hospital patients in a nursing home was nothing more than an extension of hospital care, and could not be funded through income support.[3]

7.3 PAYING FOR SERVICES DELIVERED AT HOME BEFORE 1 APRIL 1993

For many years local authorities have been empowered, not required, to charge users for non-residential social services. The present power emanates from s 17 of the Health and Social Services and Social Security Adjudications Act 1983 (HASSASSAA 1983). The scope of the power to charge, and the practice of charging are discussed in Chapter 8.

By comparison with residential care, regulation in this sector was minimal before April 1993. Section 17 of the HASSASSAA 1983 permits the imposition of 'reasonable' charges, but without direct reference either to the economic cost of providing services or to users' ability to pay. It was left open to local authorities to impose flat rate charges, adopt means tests and/or establish hardship policies. Some authorities made no charges at all, and generally speaking there were considerable variations in charging practice up and down the country.

---

1   See **1.6**.
2   (1993) *The Times*, 2 August. See also *Botchett v Chief Adjudication Officer* (1999) 2 CCL Rep 121.
3   This decision underpins the present rule that it is unlawful for the NHS to meet only part of the cost of care for someone in a nursing home who has health care needs. HSG (95) 45, para 3.2. In *R v North and East Devon Health Authority ex parte Coughlan* the Court of Appeal endorsed this rule.

7.4   CHARGING POLICIES FROM 1 APRIL 1993

For the residential sector, a new statutory means test now determines an individual's ability to contribute towards the cost of accommodation and care, and it is clear that the principle of means testing will eventually be extended across almost the whole range of social services. This fits in with the perception that all local authority provision is a safety net extended to those who are vulnerable and in need. As regards frail or disabled service users, the rationale is that the poorest should have free services, and those with modest resources should make a contribution towards the cost of their care. In practice, this means that social security benefits available to the poorest and most in need are effectively appropriated by the local authority to help make its resources stretch further.[1]

The 1989 White Paper on Community Care emphasised that the ability to pay for services in full or to make a contribution towards the costs should not in any way influence provision itself. This is also clear as a matter of law; there is no rule which makes the duty to provide services conditional upon payment of charges. However, the duty to assess need under s 47 of the NHSCCA 1990 raises a very obvious conflict for local authority care managers, in that where needs are bound to exceed budgets, awareness of means inevitably affects decisions about provision. The Policy Guidance[2] acknowledges this dilemma and takes a firm line:

> 'Assessment of financial means ... should ... follow the assessment of need and decisions about service provision.'

> 'The provision of services, whether or not the local authority is under a statutory duty to make provision, should not be related to the ability of the users or their families to meet the cost.'

According to the guidance, therefore, best practice requires the assessment of need to be finalised and communicated before any financial investigation is undertaken. However, as far as residential services are concerned, the law has moved on. In *R v Sefton Metropolitan Borough Council ex parte Help the Aged*,[3] the Court of Appeal acknowledged that having resources above £16,000 might make an older person ineligible for residential care arrangements under the NAA 1948. The legal position is now that financial assessments are authorised to be made even before an assessment of needs takes place, and certainly before any decision about provision.[4] It is accepted, therefore, that a prospective resident's own resources will be a crucial determinant of his or her need for residential services.

---

1   This is one reason why the real costs of publicly funded long-term care are so difficult to determine.

2   Paragraph 3.31.

3   (1997) 1 CCL Rep 57. See **6.9**.

4   Community Care (Residential Accommodation) Act 1998, and NA(AR) (Amendment) Regulations 1998, SI 1998/497 – amending the NA(AR) Regs 1992.

For non-residential services, the guidance applies and will be important where services are needed which cannot easily be purchased in the open market. In addition, it should be noted that s 47 of the NHSCCA 1990 creates a general entitlement to assessment, as a specific service, so that a refusal to assess, on financial grounds alone, will be unlawful.

7.5   PAYING FOR RESIDENTIAL CARE AFTER 1 APRIL 1993

For anyone requiring financial support, entry to all residential care homes and nursing homes is subject first to an assessment of need under s 47 of the NHSCCA 1990, and secondly to a means test conducted by the local authority and determined by assessment regulations made under s 22 of the NAA 1948. Chapters 8 and 9 consider the law in some detail.

Local authorities use their transferred funding either to purchase care beds in the independent sector or, to a much lesser extent, to maintain beds in what is left of their own Part III accommodation, but, either way, they are required to seek contributions from residents. 'Sponsorship' by local authorities of independent sector beds is no longer possible. Private arrangements are, of course, still available to individuals with substantial means. Those with modest means, whose funds may in time become exhausted, will need advice on when to seek a s 47 assessment.

Decisions about residential care funding are highly complex and are often taken in haste when there is pressure to discharge an older person from hospital into a home. Skilled advice may be crucial to a good outcome for the client, but unfortunately is seldom requested. The following section outlines the issues and the available options.

7.6   FUNDING OPTIONS FOR RESIDENTIAL CARE

(a)   Fully funded NHS continuing care which may be provided in an NHS unit or an independent nursing home. The *Coughlan* decision suggests that many older people should qualify for NHS care. Certainly, where an older person has had a stroke, suffers from a severe and chronic degenerative condition, or has dementia, the possibility of NHS funding ought to be explored.[1]

(b)   Care which is arranged and part funded by social services and is provided in the local authority's own Part III accommodation or in an independent care home or nursing home. This option is available for older people

---

1   See Chapters 2 and 3.

whose capital is below £16,000[1] and whose income from any source, including the state pension, falls below the weekly cost of the accommodation. Where the resident's income is low enough to entitle him or her to income support, the local authority is likely to insist that a claim is made, and the benefit will go to reduce the local authority's contribution.[2]

(c)   Care which is arranged by social services as in (b), above, but where the resident is self-funding, ie is able to pay the residential home or nursing home fees in full. The possible advantages of such an arrangement, as compared to option (d), below, are considered at **6.11**. In particular, whenever the resident is self funding, attendance allowance may be claimed.[3]

(d)   Care which is arranged privately by the resident with the home and where the local authority is not involved. The resident will meet his or her own care fees out of available capital and income, but may also claim attendance allowance.[4]

(e)   Care which is arranged privately, but which is largely funded by benefits (usually income support and attendance allowance). There is no local authority contribution. This is known as the 'loophole option' and exists, apparently, because of a failure to make legally watertight the policy that the local authority should control public funding for all residential care arrangements made post April 1993. The advantages and disadvantages of the loophole are considered at **12.4.6** and **12.6**.

7.7   PRESERVED RIGHTS

The new legislation is not retrospective in its effect. Elderly people already resident in independent sector care homes or nursing homes before 1 April 1993 now have 'preserved rights' which enable them to continue claiming income support at the old enhanced rates. Those who do not yet qualify for income support will be able to claim benefit, again at the enhanced rates, once their capital has been depleted beneath the £16,000 threshold.

This means that, at present, three separate financial regimes (two of them based on different forms of state subsidy) may co-exist in the same residential establishments:

---

1   From April 2001, the upper capital limit for local authority financial assistance will rise to £18,500 and the lower limit to £11,500.

2   The local authority's means test is explained in detail in Chapter 8, and details of benefit entitlement are in Chapter 14.

3   See **14.4**. From October 2001, a 'nursing care' element of the fees charged in nursing homes is to be funded by the NHS. It is not yet clear how this element of public funding will affect payability of the attendance allowance.

4   Ibid.

— residents with preserved rights, who entered residential care before or on 31 March 1993;
— new residents who are being funded by the local authority and who are making an assessed contribution towards the overheads; and
— new residents who are funding themselves and who have made their own arrangements with the establishments concerned.

In addition, as noted above, a small, but possibly growing number of people will occupy beds contracted by the NHS.

Before 1 April 1993, preserved rights status was perceived as potentially favourable, and there was pressure to place elderly people in residential care beds before the new legislation took effect. Local authorities, for obvious reasons, set out to mitigate their financial responsibilities by making placements before the implementation date. Now, however, it is apparent that preserved rights are creating very serious problems for some elderly clients and their families and proposals are now afoot for amending the rules which, at present, prevent local authorities from taking over funding responsibility are to be amended from April 2002. The legal position is analysed in Chapter 13.

7.8 PAYING FOR HOME CARE SERVICES AFTER 1 APRIL 1993

The law has not changed, but practice has changed considerably. The expectation has grown that users should pay for domiciliary services, subject to their ability to do so. Guidance issued by the Association of County Councils recommends that authorities adopt flexible charging policies which are not seen as a deterrent to the take-up of services or as causing hardship to those in need. On the other hand, increasing financial pressures on local authorities have quite evidently forced up charges over the past few years, and community care policies themselves expressly encourage the provision of more elaborate and more expensive domiciliary services. Clearly, regulation is needed in order to ensure equality of treatment across the country and to bring practice into line with residential care, where the charging process is standardised and highly regulated. Various pieces of research have identified the 'unacceptable disparities' between the charging policies of different local authorities,[1] and the Government has now committed itself to issuing new guidance aimed at ending what it calls 'the postcode lottery' in charging.

7.8.1 The direct payments scheme

Before 1996 local authorities did not have power to make cash payments to service users, even though there was a good deal of evidence that people prefer

---

1   See, for example, National Consumer Council *Charging Customers for Social Services* (1995), and Audit Commission *Charging with Care: How Councils Charge for Home Care* (2000). There is a more detailed discussion on current law and practice in Chapter 8.

to make their own care arrangements where funding is provided, and that this is an effective use of public resources. The Community Care (Direct Payments) Act 1996 enabled local authorities to make direct payments to disabled service users, but not to people over 65. However, new regulations which came into force on 1 February 2000[1] permit people aged 65 and over, who have been assessed as in need of community care services, to receive direct payments. A Policy and Practice Guide has been issued by the DoH.[2] It should be noted that all local authorities are required to consider setting up a direct payments scheme, but are not forced to do so, and provision is patchy. Direct payments are not available for residential care, and they may not be used to purchase services provided by partners or close relatives living in the same household. The Policy Guidance[3] also indicates that direct payments to any close relative will be permitted only exceptionally. The scheme is therefore likely to be of limited value to older people.

7.9   USEFUL REFERENCE MATERIALS FOR THE LEGAL ADVISER

Apart from the primary legislation and the various regulations referred to in Chapters 8 to 13, advisers on financial matters should have access to the following:

(a)   the *Charging for Residential Accommodation Guide* (CRAG) – produced by the Government for local authorities on the rules for the residential core means test set out in the NA(AR) Regs 1992 (copies of the CRAG may be obtained from Department of Health publications,[4] quoting reference LAC (99) 9;

(b)   the *Decision Makers' Guide* (DMG)[5] – this loose-leaf work from HMSO in ten volumes covers all social security benefits; vols 3 and 4, which deal with income-related benefits, will be particularly useful (the DMG is usually available in central reference libraries, university libraries or benefits agency offices, and is also available on the Internet, at www.open.gov.uk);

(c)   *Social Security Legislation 2000*, which is published by Sweet & Maxwell in three volumes, and will be updated annually. Volume 1 covers non income-tested benefits and Volume 2 covers income support. It contains annotated primary and secondary legislation and is used by the Appeals Service.[6]

---

1   Community Care (Direct Payments) Amendment Regulations 2000, SI 2000/11.
2   See DoH Circular LAC (2000) 1.
3   Ibid, at para 24.
4   The most recent update to the CRAG is DoH Circular LAC (2000) 11.
5   Adjudication officers were replaced by 'decision makers' following implementation of the Social Security Act 1998.
6   The Appeals Service was set up under the Social Security Act 1998, and has replaced the Independent Tribunal Service. It deals with (inter alia) appeals in respect of disability benefits, incapacity benefit and income support.

(d) a general guide to welfare benefits law and practice, for example *Welfare Benefits Handbook* (Child Poverty Action Group), *Rights Guide to Non-means Tested Benefits* (Child Poverty Action Group), and *Disability Rights Handbook* (Disability Alliance);

(e) *Paying for Care* (Child Poverty Action Group, 2001), a handbook which is updated annually, dealing with welfare benefits and local authority funding;

(f) decisions of the Social Security Commissioners, which may be downloaded from the Internet; see www.hywels.demon.co.uk/commrs/;

(g) Benefits Agency website, www.dss.gov.uk; and

(h) Age Concern Fact Sheets on charging and welfare benefits, numbers 11, 25 and 34.

Chapter 8

PAYING FOR NON-RESIDENTIAL SERVICES

'Local authorities are reminded of their long-standing powers to charge for some non-residential services for adults. Section 17 of the Health and Social Services and Social Security Adjudications Act 1983, which came into force in January 1984, gives authorities a discretionary power to charge recipients of day, domiciliary, respite care (such as holidays which have not been arranged under Part III of the National Assistance Act 1948) and other non-residential services. The Government's view, confirmed in the Community Care White Paper "Caring for People" of 1989 and in the subsequent policy guidance, has consistently been that users who can pay for such services should be expected to do so taking account of their ability to pay. The White Paper and Policy Guidance also make it clear that ability to pay should not influence decisions on the services to be provided, and the assessment of financial means should therefore follow the care assessment . . . any authority which recovers less revenue than its discretionary powers allow is placing an extra burden on the local population or is forgoing resources which could be used to the benefit of the service.'[1]

8.1 INTRODUCTION

Since April 1993, local authorities have reviewed their charging policies in respect of non-residential care services. As a result, there have been dramatic increases in fees and many recorded instances of users declining services which they need, but can no longer afford. The switch in focus from health to social care, described in Chapter 2, is part of this picture: as free services previously delivered by the NHS have been withdrawn, gaps in provision have been filled by local authority commissioned services, for which users are expected to pay.

A 1995 report prepared by the National Consumer Council highlights this change:

'For 30 years we have had care from the district nurses and doctors . . . . Now after all these years we have been put to home carers for bathing and nursing. The local council now demand payment for this service!! I have contested this as Mrs T requires total nursing. We now need more money, not less . . . .'[2]

The Policy Guidance on community care published in 1990 emphasised the expectation that users should be required to pay for services subject to their ability to do so[3] and, as outlined above, a more recent Circular reiterates that message. Since 1993, funding has been allocated by central government on the assumption that local authorities will raise a proportion of their revenue through charges. However, there has been no clear guidance as to the legal, practical or operational issues posed by the pressure to charge. Section 17 of the

---

1   DoH Circular LAC (94) 1, paras 17 and 18.
2   National Consumer Council *Charging Consumers for Social Services* (1995).
3   *Community Care in the Next Decade and Beyond*, Policy Guidance (HMSO, 1990), para 3.31.

HASSASSAA 1983 remains the enabling provision, but does not purport to regulate charging methods, or ways and means of promoting openness, equity or fairness in the practice of charging.

In its response to the Royal Commission on Long Term Care,[1] the Government has stated that it considers the variations in the charging system to be unacceptable. 'Mandatory' national guidance is to be issued early in 2001 to promote greater consistency and fairness.[2]

8.2   WHO CAN BE CHARGED?

The power to charge applies to the following community care services:

- services provided under s 29 of the NAA 1948 (welfare arrangements for the disabled);
- services provided under s 2 of the CSDPA 1970 (services for disabled people);
- services provided under s 45 of the HSPHA 1969 (welfare of old people);
- services provided under Sch 8 to the NHSA 1977 (prevention of illness, care and after-care, and home-help facilities).[3]

Local authorities are not empowered to impose charges in respect of social work support services, occupational therapy or advice and assessment in respect of client needs. Assessments carried out under s 47 of the NHSCCA 1990 will therefore be free of charge. In addition, there is no power to charge for services provided under s 117 of the MHA 1983, which requires social services and health authorities jointly to make after-care arrangements for people discharged from hospital after being detained under the Act.[4]

8.3   SECTION 17 OF THE HASSASSAA 1983

As noted above, local authorities derive their power to impose charges for non-residential services from s 17 of the HASSASSAA 1983. Section 17(1) states that 'an authority providing a service ... may recover such charge (if any) for it as they consider reasonable'.

The draftsman of the time clearly contemplated that local authorities might elect not to recover charges at all, and until April 1993 this was indeed the approach adopted in some areas.

Section 17(3) states:

---

1   *The NHS Plan 2000*, Cm 4818–I, para 15.18.
2   A new power to issue section 7 guidance was taken in the Care Standards Act 2000; draft guidance was issued for consultation in January 2001.
3   From sometime in 2001 local authorities will acquire power to change for carers' services provided under the CDCA 2000; see **5.14**.
4   *R v Richmond Upon Thames LBC ex parte Watson* (1999) 3 CCL Rep 276; see **4.2.4**.

'If a person—

(a)   avails himself of a service to which this section applies, and

(b)   satisfies the authority providing the service that his means are insufficient for it to be reasonably practicable for him to pay for it,

the local authority shall not require him to pay more for it than it appears to them that it is reasonably practicable for him to pay.'

Comparing s 17(1) with s 17(3), it appears that the section as a whole is purporting to impose two separate tests of reasonableness. Section 17(1) expects the local authority to make a judgment as to what is reasonable, based, presumably, on the overall needs and financial circumstances of its local population, coupled with the perceived need to recover costs as far as possible. Considerations of equity also have to be borne in mind. Is it, for example, appropriate or reasonable for local authorities to charge one client group and not another, or to charge for some services and not others?

Section 17(3) postulates a test of reasonableness which is focused on the individual, and which would indicate the need for procedures to review charging decisions on the basis of individual circumstances. It also carries the underlying implication that the application of a means test, as for residential care services, may commend itself to local authorities as a way of achieving reasonableness and equity across the population of service users.

8.4   CHARGING STRATEGIES

It seems that many local authorities interpret 'reasonableness' in s 17 of the HASSASSAA 1983 as meaning 'affordable',[1] and so will seek to match charges with users' ability to pay. Advice published by the Social Services Inspectorate emphasises that local authorities should 'take account both of the full cost of providing the service and within that of what recipients can reasonably be expected to pay. . .'.[2] Flat-rate charges which were commonly fixed before April 1993 are less favoured now because of their regressive nature. Means-tested schemes vary from authority to authority, but generally involve an assessment of a service user's available capital and income and of allowances to meet the costs of daily living. For each individual, the balance between these two figures is then regarded as a 'disposable' resource from which care fees can be met. In the absence of detailed regulation, however, there are considerable differences in approach to the basic calculation. Sometimes all 'disposable' resources are judged to be available to meet charges; sometimes a fixed percentage of such resources is taken; sometimes a sliding scale is adopted, relating disposable resources to the service provided. Approaches to the

1   *Charging Consumers for Social Services* (National Consumer Council, 1995) p 42.

2   Social Services Inspectorate Advice Note, 1994, para 5. This is not made under LASSA 1970, s 7(1) and, consequently, is not 'mandatory' guidance. The new draft guidance, published in January 2001, rejects flat-rate charges.

assessment of income and capital resources are variable. Inevitably, too, there are different perceptions as to what level of basic resources should be exempt from any charge, although it is clear that many local authorities relate their living allowances to income support, as a measure of the ability to pay.

A study commissioned by the Joseph Rowntree Foundation, published in 1996,[1] found 'enormous variations' in charging policies across local authorities as regards the levels of charge, the means test applied and the services charged for. It concluded:

> '. . . local discretion allows flexibility and makes it possible to respond to local circumstances and create local priorities. It also raises questions of territorial equity. Depending upon where they lived, service users experienced very different rules about: the treatment of income, including benefit income; the expenses which were disregarded in calculating the income "available" to put towards the cost of services; the amount of savings they could hold before paying the full cost of services; and how any income from savings was calculated.'[2]

A more recent study by the Audit Commission echoes this conclusion.[3]

It goes without saying that local authorities should have clear policies on financial assessment which include the criteria for assessing financial resources, and the information which will be required for the assessment. The local government ombudsman has found maladministration in several instances, where criteria have been irrelevant, arbitrary or absent.[4]

8.5   WELFARE BENEFITS AND CHARGING

Nothing in s 17 of the HASSASSAA 1983 prevents local authorities from charging recipients of social security benefits for community care services. Those dependent on income-related (means-tested) benefits are, however, already on the poverty line and to charge them is arguably objectionable in principle. This was acknowledged during the passage of the Health and Social Services and Social Security Adjudications Bill in 1982.

Nevertheless, Government policy has shifted over the years, and the latest opinion expressed through the Social Services Inspectorate is that:

> 'In assessing ability to pay authorities may take into account all types of income including social security benefits . . . . They should, however, have regard to not just the service user's income but his/her overall financial circumstances . . . . The

---

1   Baldwin, S and Lunt, N 'Charging Ahead' *The Development of Local Authority Charging Policies for Community Care* (Joseph Rowntree Foundation, 1996).

2   Ibid, p 83.

3   *Charging with Care: How Councils Charge for Home Care* (Audit Commission, 2000).

4   See, for example, Commissioners' Decisions 90/A2675 and 90/B1676. In *R v Coventry City Council ex parte Carton* (2000) unreported, November, the Divisional Court accepted that it is unlawful for a local authority to alter its charging policies without consultation.

government does not consider that there should be an automatic exemption from charges for people receiving social security benefits such as income support ... housing benefit, Social Fund payments ... or disability working allowance .... '[1]

All the benefits referred to above are means tested. On the ground, there is evidence that some income support claimants are expected to pay standard charges for services out of their benefit. The Audit Commission found that 30 per cent of local authorities charge against income support. Given that such claimants are not required to pay council tax, it may be argued that local authorities are now seeking to collect, by indirect means, local taxes which they are not permitted to levy directly.[2]

Other benefits, particularly those targeted at disability, and payable irrespective of claimants' financial circumstances, may invite recoupment. Within this category are the attendance allowance and the disability living allowance (care component). Both are payable to claimants who can establish a need for personal care. Neither is means tested. The maximum rate for both benefits is currently £53.55 per week (2000/2001 rates).

Most local authorities will now assume that attendance allowance and disability living allowance (care component) are available to pay for services and that it is reasonable to take them into account.[3] They see these benefits as designed to enable claimants to purchase additional care from the local authority or elsewhere. In practice, however, service users who are otherwise on low incomes spend this extra money on meeting the other unavoidable costs of disability, which will not be met by the local authority.[4]

Again, charging practice varies. Some authorities, for example, impose flat-rate charges on all users who are in receipt of attendance allowance or disability living allowance (care component). Others will include the value of the benefit, or a proportion of it, in their calculation of a user's income resources. In some areas, the charge is based on the percentage of assessed care needs met by the local authority.

---

1   Social Services Inspectorate Advice Note 1994, paras 13 and 21.
2   National Consumer Council (1995), para 52. The new draft guidance published in January 2001 seeks to protect basic levels of income support.
3   In some areas, up to 90 per cent of the attendance allowance is taken in charges (Audit Commission, 2000). In *R v Powys CC ex parte Hambidge (No 2)* (1999) 2 CCL Rep 460, the Divisional Court endorsed a charging policy which required service users in receipt of disability living allowance to pay substantially more than others for their home care services. The draft guidance provides that both attendance allowance and DLA may be taken into account, but benefit payable for night care should not be taken into account when considering charges for day services.
4   All the published research emphasises this point. A joint statement by the Association of Metropolitan Authorities and the Local Government Information Unit, published in 1994, emphasises that these benefits are intended to reflect additional living costs incurred through disability.

The disability living allowance (mobility component) is a linked benefit, which is payable to those who are unable or virtually unable to walk.[1] However, it may not be taken into account for charging purposes under any means test, discretionary or not.[2] Whether for this reason or because of the highly specific definition of 'need' for this benefit, there is no evidence that it is treated as available to pay local authority charges.

A common tactic amongst local authorities is to run benefit take-up campaigns and employ additional welfare rights workers. This cuts into the revenue gained from charging.

8.6　TREATMENT OF CAPITAL FOR CHARGING PURPOSES

In the absence of legal regulation in this area, it is nevertheless clear that, in practice, local authorities take account of users' capital assets in setting fees for non-residential services.[3] Given that capital is taken into account for means-tested social security benefits and in the means test for residential care (see Chapter 7), it is not surprising that local authorities seek to follow suit, but, once again, the fact that there are differences in approach to this very contentious issue may be seen as unfair or inequitable.

It seems that local authorities have regularly imposed a tariff income on capital in excess of £3,000 and have also expected service users with capital above a set threshold (often £8,000) to pay for their services in full. Such practices reflect the income support rules for people living in their own homes.[4] The capital threshold for the residential care means test is £16,000 (£18,500 from April 2001).

The report by the National Consumer Council gives examples of hardship caused by setting capital limits:

> 'I have been informed that I will be charged £56 a week (because our savings are more than £8,000). The help provided is 8 hours per week. Home help (cleaning) 1 hour per week. The position is going to be reviewed because I have refused to pay £56 a week, which is more than the weekly attendance allowance, and, quite frankly we cannot afford it.'[5]

1　SSCBA 1992, s 73.

2　Ibid, s 73(14), and see Social Services Inspectorate Advice Note, para 23. The same applies to payments received from the Independent Living Fund (1993).

3　The Audit Commission in *Charging with Care* (2000), reported that 62 per cent of local authorities take account of savings, in one way or another. The new draft guidance suggests that local authorities should consider adopting the same capital disregards as apply to residential care, but without taking into account the value of a service user's home.

4　Income Support (General) Regulations (ISG Regs 1987), SI 1987/1967, regs 44 and 53.

5　*Charging Consumers for Social Services*, p 62.

As regards the value of the user's own home, it has become the received wisdom that an elderly person needing care may decide to remain in the community in order to avoid having to use the value of his or her home to pay for residential care. At the same time, there is an incentive for local authorities to place such people in residential care because the NA(AR) Regs 1992 allow them to recover their costs from the value of a property. It can be argued that the only position which is consistent with community care policies is to take account of capital tied up in the house in all circumstances. Given the current intense debate as to how far the value of the home should be available to meet residential care fees, there is an urgent need to clarify how far it is lawful, or acceptable, for local authorities to seek to access the capital value of a service user's home whilst he or she continues to live there.

8.7   COUPLES AND NON-RESIDENTIAL CHARGES

As explained in Chapter 9, the charging regulations which apply to residential care permit local authorities to assess and charge only the individuals who are being provided with residential care and not their spouses or partners. Section 42 of the NAA 1948 (the 'liable relative' provision) also applies only where residential accommodation arrangements are made.

The legal position as regards non-residential charges is less clear cut. Section 17(3) of the HASSASSAA 1983 also refers only to the circumstances of the 'person who avails himself of the service', and the Social Services Inspectorate Advice Note states that authorities may charge only the person receiving the service and should have regard only to that individual's means in assessing his or her ability to pay.[1] However, it then goes on to say that this will 'normally' mean that family members cannot be required to pay the charges (unless they are managing the resources of the service user) and that their own resources should not be taken into account. Again,

> '. . . local authorities may, in *individual cases* wish to consider whether a client has *sufficient reliable access to resources beyond those held in his/her own name for them to be part of his/her means for the purposes of s 17(3). The most likely instances of this kind will arise in relation to married or unmarried couples.* It will be for the authority to consider each case in the light of their own legal advice.'[2]

It is to be hoped that legal advisers will have an eye on the fundamental point that there is *no clear power* to charge anyone but the service user.

In practice, there is a great deal of confusion amongst local authorities, and the research highlights a wide divergence of approach. Some authorities routinely assess couples, whilst others make it clear that they are concerned only with the financial circumstances of service users. Not uncommon are financial assess-

1   Social Services Inspectorate Advice Note, para 18.
2   Ibid, para 19.

ment forms which seek to elicit financial information about family members 'in case' they may have some entitlement to welfare benefits. Local authorities do not have powers to trawl for information in this way. They should be explicit as to why it is required, and may be challenged if it is clear that they are purporting to apply what is, effectively, a household means test.

8.8   INABILITY TO PAY

Section 17(3) of the HASSASSAA 1983 implies that service users who feel that it is not reasonably practicable to pay service charges should have a right of review or appeal against a decision to impose them. Once again, local authorities are left to their own devices in this area, but basic public law principles would require that service users should be made aware of their right to make representations about their ability to pay charges and that local authorities should lay down adequate criteria to enable them to consider 'reasonableness' in individual circumstances on a review. The local government ombudsman has ruled that local authorities must have proper appeals procedures, and clear reasons for decisions must be given.[1]

In *Avon County Council v Hooper*,[2] which concerned the recovery by the local authority of the costs of a child's care after the parents received agreed damages from the health authority in respect of medical negligence, the Court of Appeal observed:

> '... the person availing himself of the service has ... to satisfy the authority under s 3 that his means are insufficient for it to be reasonably practicable for him to pay the amount which he would otherwise to obliged to pay ... he must show that he has insufficient means. ... As a matter of the ordinary use of English, the word "means" refers to the financial resources of a person: his assets, his sources of income, his liabilities and expenses. If he has a reliable asset, that is part of his means, he has the means to pay ... '

These words suggest that, whatever the local authority's particular charging policy, service users may argue, for example, that they have particular debts or expenses which make it impracticable for them to pay charges. Conversely, the local authority may expect payment to be made out of, for example, capital resources which are not referred to in its charging policy. The problem with any non-statutory means test is that special pleading is never ruled out. Just as in the 1980s, the social security tribunals were overwhelmed with appeals based on 'exceptional circumstances', so now local authorities may expect to devote substantial resources to reviewing charges.

It is important to note that, as with residential care, the local authority has no power to withdraw a service which has been provided on the basis of need, if

---

1   Commissioners' Decision 91/A3782.
2   [1997] 1 All ER 532.

the user is unable or unwilling to pay the charges.[1] Best practice would also require local authorities to investigate circumstances where users decline services because they cannot afford to pay for them. If a request to review service charges is unsuccessful, or if the service user is unaware of the possibility of a review, the complaints procedure is still available in respect of any question connected with the provision of community care services. Unfortunately, it is not well adapted to handle financial questions.

8.9 COLLECTING CHARGES

Section 17 of the HASSASSAA 1983 empowers local authorities to recover charges in respect of non-residential services. Where, consistent with the new philosophies of care, the local authority commissions services from independent providers, difficulties may arise in terms of how charges are to be paid. Collection of fees by providers raises questions of confidentiality and it seems inappropriate that this should be done without sanction from service users. Direct billing by local authorities will be the most appropriate procedure. The Social Services Inspectorate Advice Note emphasises that 'it should be clear to the user that any collecting of charges is being done on behalf of the authority and any revenue is remitted to the authority'. Where service users do not have bank accounts or credit cards or where they live in isolated areas, cash payments to service providers will often be the only practicable option.

Section 17(4) states that charges may 'be recovered summarily' as a civil debt.[2] In *Avon County Council v Hooper*,[3] it was held that a local authority may impose charges retrospectively provided that it is reasonable to do so, and provided that charges have not previously been waived. This decision gives some support to local authorities who are having to cut costs and are now seeking to recover charges from groups of service users who have not hitherto been required to pay for their services. The question is, understandably, very contentious.[4]

8.10 PRACTICE POINTS

(a) Legal advisers should obtain information about their local authority's scale of charges for non-residential services. In some areas, services may be purchased more cheaply from friends, neighbours, voluntary agencies or independent commercial providers.[5]

---

1 Social Services Inspectorate Advice Note 1994, para 26.
2 This is in the magistrates' court. However, the words 'without prejudice to any other method of recovery', which appear in s 17(4), suggest that a claim could also be brought in the county court.
3 [1997] 1 All ER 532.
4 In the past, some authorities have not charged people with learning disabilities.
5 At present, most private care providers will charge VAT. Voluntary agencies do not. Sometime in 2001, VAT on care services will be lifted.

(b) Where clients may be entitled to welfare benefits, advisers must be prepared to assist them to claim, or to refer them to someone else who has the necessary skills. Where non–residential services are needed, it will be very important to maximise a client's entitlement to benefits.

(c) Advisers should ask the local authority for information about its charging procedures, how charges will be collected and whether the spouse's or partner's resources will be taken into account in any assessment.[1] If, given what is said in this chapter, the local authority's practice appears to be unfair, or possibly unlawful, it may be necessary to initiate the complaints procedure.

(d) Attempts by a local authority to take account of the value of a property in which a client is still living should be questioned. A local authority may also need to be reminded that service provision, based on assessed needs, may not be made conditional on the payment of fees. It may be argued that excessive charges are unlawful because any rationing of services should be based on levels of need, not on individual resources.[2]

(e) Respite care arrangements may cause problems, because although charges for permanent residential care arrangements are regulated, s 22(5A) of the NAA 1948 allows local authorities to charge 'reasonable' amounts for temporary stays of up to 8 weeks. In practice, there are wide variations in respite charging policies, and many authorities will assess the resources of carers in fixing charges. There are dangers in creating disincentives to use respite care, because non–residential arrangements may break down altogether as a result, and legal advisers should be prepared to challenge policies which appear to have this effect.

(f) Some clients may be interested in purchasing their own services under the direct payments scheme,[3] which may offer them more control over their own lives than directly provided services. Where direct payments schemes are in operation, users are likely to be charged for the service.

---

1   Policies should certainly not go beyond the provisions for taking savings into account which are set out in the new draft guidance.

2   DoH Circular LAC (96) 7, Policy Guidance, para 3.1. However, it is now clear that as far as residential care services are concerned, the resident's own resources, as well as his or her needs, will affect that resident's rights under NAA 1948, s 21; see **6.9**.

3   See **7.8.1**.

Chapter 9

THE LOCAL AUTHORITY'S MEANS TEST FOR RESIDENTIAL CARE

'The Government Actuary's Department calculated, based on our estimates of public cost, that in terms of people's earnings from employment, from pensions and from investments, the current state funding system of long-term care represents a tax of some 2.2 per cent.'[1]

9.1 WHAT IS THE LEGAL BASIS OF THE MEANS TEST?

Section 22 of the NAA 1948 remains the source of the local authority's legal obligation to recover the costs of residential accommodation. That provision must now be read alongside s 26 of the NAA 1948 (substantially amended by s 44 of the NHSCCA 1990). The effects are as follows.

(a) Local authorities must fix and recover charges in respect of placements which they provide directly in their own maintained Part III accommodation, and in respect of placements which they arrange with independent providers in either residential care homes or nursing homes.

(b) Section 22(5) of the NAA 1948 contains the power to make regulations prescribing a means test of the resident in question. The current charging regulations are the National Assistance (Assessment of Resources) Regulations 1992 (NA(AR) Regs 1992).[2] Where the means test applies, a local authority must assess the resident's contribution towards care fees, and will meet the balance out of its social services budget.

(c) The previous central government subsidy for residential care arrangements, paid through income support, is still available but is considerably reduced. Benefit may be claimed by residents entering Part III homes or independent residential care homes or nursing homes, and will be taken into account as income in the local authority's means test. Higher levels of benefit are payable to claimants placed in the independent sector. This means that there is a financial incentive for local authorities to purchase beds from the independent sector and a disincentive for them to assume the provider role.[3]

---

1 Royal Commission on Long Term Care *With Respect to Old Age*, Cm 4192-I (Stationery Office, 1999), para 4.17.

2 SI 1992/2977, reg 1.

3 See **14.2.3**.

The NA(AR) Regs 1992 are modelled on the Income Support (General) Regulations 1987 (ISG Regs 1987).[1] Many provisions of the ISG Regs 1987 are applied directly. Thus, the means test is complex, technical and difficult for clients to understand. It will generally be administered by local authority finance officers, who may have little grasp of legal concepts and certainly lack the long experience of the Benefits Agency in operating the income support rules. To help them, the Department of Health has issued the *Charging for Residential Accommodation Guide* (CRAG),[2] which provides an authoritative explanation of the regulations themselves. Apart from being the common currency, the CRAG is 'section 7 guidance',[3] and it is essential that legal advisers have access to it.

The legislation does not provide any direct means of appealing[4] against local authority financial assessments. The complaints procedure is available, but is not well suited to interpreting black letter law. The following two consequences flow from this.

(1) Older people needing residential care will benefit considerably from legal advice given at the time of the financial assessment. At this point, there may be scope for correcting errors and for discussion and even negotiation on difficult conceptual issues, such as beneficial entitlement under trusts.

(2) There will be no opportunity to develop case-law concerning the interpretation of the regulations. This means that, for guidance, advisers will have to rely on analogous decisions of the Social Security Commissioners interpreting the income support rules.[5]

Even though the means tests for residential accommodation and income support are substantially similar, there are no prescribed links between local authorities and the Benefits Agency. The CRAG emphasises, however, that the quality of liaison between social services departments and the Benefits Agency will play an important part in ensuring that benefits are claimed when there is entitlement and that there is no misuse of public funds. It recommends that local authorities should establish, at senior level, a main channel of communication with Benefits Agency offices. As yet, however, there is little evidence of

---

1   In *Yule v South Lanarkshire Council* (1998) 1 CCL Rep 571, the Scottish Court of Session referred to local authority contributions towards residential care fees as an 'income-related benefit', to be equated with, for example, income support.

2   DoH Circular LAC (99) 9. See **7.9**.

3   See **Introduction**.

4   It may be argued that the absence of an independent right of appeal in respect of decisions where a local authority has a clear financial interest will be a breach of Art 6 of the European Convention on Human Rights. This is likely to be tested out under the Human Rights Act 1998. Housing benefit reviews (previously dealt with by local authorities (the decision makers)) themselves will be handled by the Appeals Service from April 2001, for the same reason.

5   In *Yule v South Lanarkshire Council* (1998) 1 CCL Rep 571, the Scottish Court of Session confirmed that the local authority means test is part of benefits law.

harmonisation within the system. Where a prospective resident is likely to be eligible for income support, two financial assessments will have to be made and two bureaucratic processes endured. In addition, as will be described in detail later on, there are certain crucial distinctions between the two sets of regulations, which are likely to generate confusion for individuals and confront local authorities with some hard decisions. Throughout this chapter, reference will be made primarily to the NA(AR) Regs 1992. Wherever the ISG Regs 1987 differ, the respective provisions will be compared. Otherwise readers should assume that the two sets of regulations run in parallel, and that the rules are essentially the same.

9.2 HOW DOES THE MEANS TEST OPERATE?

Sections 22(2) and 26(3) of the NAA 1948 require people placed by local authorities in residential accommodation to repay the full economic cost of accommodation if they are capable of doing so. Technically, the onus is then on a resident with limited means to satisfy the local authority that he or she is unable to meet accommodation fees in full, and in such cases the authority will assess his or her ability to pay a lower rate. If a resident withholds necessary information, so that the means test cannot be carried out, the local authority may charge him or her for the full cost of the accommodation.[1]

The financial assessment is applied to both capital and income. Since April 1996, individuals with capital of more than £16,000 have been expected to pay for their own care in full, irrespective of the amount of their income.[2] As the cost of a residential care home or nursing home is probably between £15,000 and £20,000 per year (subject to considerable variations), few older people who are above the capital threshold will be able to pay for their care from income alone, and most will be forced to draw heavily on savings to fund their placements.[3]

Since August 1998, when the Community Care (Residential Accommodation) Act 1998 (CC(RA)A 1998) was implemented, it has become standard practice for local authorities to issue means test questionnaires even before undertaking assessments of need. Where, for instance, an older person is likely to be discharged from hospital into residential care, financial information will often be gathered in advance of the multidisciplinary assessment and the decision as to whether or not the patient meets the eligibility criteria for NHS continuing care.[4]

---

1   CRAG, para 1.009; NAA 1948, s 22(3).
2   Social Security (Contributions and Benefits) Act 1992, s 134(1) and NA(AR) Regs 1992, reg 20. The capital threshold will rise to £18,500 from April 2001.
3   A Family Resource Survey published by the DSS in 1997 indicated that 44 per cent of people aged 75 and over had assets below £16,000 and a mean income of £85 pw. See *With Respect To Old Age*, op cit, para 2.12.
4   See **6.9** and **6.9.1**.

As noted in Chapter 6, the combined effect of the Court of Appeal's decision in *R v Sefton Metropolitan Borough Council ex parte Help the Aged*, the CC(RA)A 1998 and the contemporaneous amendments to the charging regulations has been to make financial circumstances the main arbiter of whether or not a local authority provides assistance under ss 21 or 26 of the NAA 1948. Put simply, older people who have capital below £16,000 (£18,500), modest income and who are 'in need of care and attention' will be the responsibility of the local authority. Older people with capital above the threshold, modest income and equivalent or greater needs, will usually be expected to purchase their own residential care, quite probably at a higher price than would be paid by the local authority. Consequently, although ss 21 and 26 of the NAA 1948 clearly contemplate that the local authority may still make the accommodation arrangements, thereby using its superior purchasing power, and subsequently recover a full contribution to the costs from the resident, in practice, this seldom happens.

If the client's capital is less than £16,000 (£18,500) at the outset (or is later reduced below that threshold) the local authority must determine the resident's income resources under the charging regulations. If those resources do not meet the full cost of the placement, the local authority itself must nevertheless meet its contractual obligation to the provider to pay the full placement fee.[1] The authority must then calculate and recover the appropriate contributions from the resident.

When an assessment has been completed, the local authority should provide a resident with a written statement of his or her contribution and how it has been calculated.[2]

9.3   HOW IS CAPITAL ASSESSED?

9.3.1   The capital limits

Since April 1996, the upper capital limit under the charging regulations has been £16,000.[3] There is a lower capital limit of £10,000. Residents whose capital assets are valued at £16,000 or less are eligible for financial assistance from the local authority. Assets of between £10,000 and £16,000 are subject to a tariff income calculation.[4]

The income support capital limits in respect of claimants who are in residential care have been brought into line. This means that, whilst a claimant living at home is subject to upper and lower capital thresholds of £8,000 and £3,000,[5] if

---

1   NAA 1948, s 26(2).
2   CRAG, para 1.015.
3   NA(AR) Regs 1992, reg 20.
4   Ibid, reg 28.
5   ISG Regs 1987, regs 45 and 53(1A), (1B), (1C) and (4). These thresholds will rise to £12,000 and £6,000 from April 2001.

he or she moves into residential care the thresholds are raised to £16,000 and £10,000. Consequently, there is now a new 'perverse' incentive' towards residential care, in the sense that more of an older person's assets can be protected if he or she is cared for in a home rather than at home.[1]

From April 2001, the £16,000 threshold under the charging regulations will be raised to £18,500. The Government believes that it will be 'fair to restore the 1996 real terms value of these capital limits and to keep them under review.'[2] The lower capital threshold will be raised to £11,500 at the same time. The income support thresholds will not be increased.

9.3.2 Method of valuation

Neither the regulations nor the CRAG go into detail as to how the assessment of capital is to be conducted. There is no explicit duty for residents to disclose assets and no explicit powers for assessors to force disclosure. However, the rule that the onus is on a resident to show why he or she should not pay for care in full means that clients should be advised that it is in their interests to respond to requests to see bank books, building society passbooks and other relevant sources of financial information. Where residents are unable to handle their own affairs, the local authority should find out if anyone has a power of attorney or has been appointed receiver and, if so, should seek information from that person. The CRAG stipulates that the local authority should also identify any DSS appointees although, as a matter of law, their power to provide information is strictly limited to benefit matters.[3]

The regulations contain no definition of 'capital' or 'income'. Therefore, a common-sense approach has to be adopted, even in the face of arcane provisions which allow income to be treated as capital or capital as income.[4] The CRAG defines a capital 'payment' as one which is not made in respect of a specified period, and not intended to form part of a series of payments.[5] Where capital assets are held by a resident, they must be valued at current market or surrender value less 10 per cent of the valuation for the expenses of realisation, where that would be necessary, and less the value of mortgages or other encumbrances, but not ordinary unsecured debts.[6]

National Saving Certificates are to be valued at the purchase price, except that, where certificates were purchased from an issue which ceased before 1 July immediately before a person entered residential care, they are to be valued at the July price.[7]

---

1   Charges for non-residential services are considered in Chapter 8.
2   *The NHS Plan 2000* the Government's response to the Royal Commission on Long-Term Care.
3   CRAG, para 1.016.
4   NA(AR) Regs 1992, regs 16 and 22.
5   CRAG, para 6.001.
6   NA(AR) Regs 1992, reg 23.
7   CRAG, para 6.018.

The CRAG states that, once an asset has been sold, the capital to be taken into account is the actual amount realised from the sale, and that the 10 per cent discount does not apply.[1] If, hypothetically, a resident has a capital asset which has a discounted value of £15,000, the local authority will subsidise the care arrangements, disregarding £10,000 of the capital, applying the tariff income to capital between £10,000 and £16,000,[2] but not utilising the capital itself. If, subsequently, the asset is sold for £16,500 (its actual value at the time of the assessment), the surplus above £16,000 can be claimed back in full to meet the care fees. Where the asset appreciates in value after the assessment, and is then sold, the full proceeds of the sale will have to be taken into account, and if the profit is large, the local authority might consider terminating its contract with the home and requiring the resident to make private arrangements. The CRAG gives no insight, however, into the position where assets remain unsold until after the death of the resident.[3]

Current market value is considered to be the price a willing buyer would pay to a willing seller.[4]

The CRAG gives examples of capital assets which assessors will commonly have to deal with:[5]

- buildings;
- land;
- National Savings Certificates;
- premium bonds;
- stocks and shares;
- capital held by the Court of Protection or by a receiver;
- any savings held, for example in building society accounts;
- bank accounts;
- unit trusts;
- trust funds; and
- cash.

It is clear that, for the most part, an approximate valuation will be enough. The assessor merely needs to know whether the resident's total assets exceed £16,000 in value. However, the CRAG states that 'in the case of land, building or a house where it is necessary to obtain a precise valuation because of a dispute, a professional valuer should be instructed'.[6]

---

1   CRAG, para 6.011.
2   NA(AR) Regs 1992, reg 23(2). The principle will remain the same after the new capital thresholds are introduced in April 2001.
3   CRAG, para 6.015.
4   Ibid, para 6.012; see also **9.3**.
5   Ibid, para 6.002.
6   Ibid, para 6.014.

9.3.3 Ownership of assets

The charging regulations require the whole of a resident's capital to be taken into account.[1] This includes all property in which the resident has a beneficial interest. Sometimes difficult questions of trust law will be raised during an assessment where, for example, the nature of the beneficial interests subsisting in a particular asset are unclear.

In principle, where a resident has an interest under a fixed trust that will be assessed as actual capital. The same applies to interests under resulting or constructive trusts, although, in practice, these may not be easily identifiable or quantifiable.

The CRAG states that the local authority should seek written evidence of ownership where there is any dispute. On assessment, the current market value principle will apply, and written evidence of the value of the trust fund may be sought. Contingent interests in capital will be regarded as having a discounted market value, and will be taken into account as actual capital.

Sometimes, it is difficult to distinguish between an outright gift and one which is subject to an implied trust. In *Ellis v Chief Adjudication Officer*,[2] an old lady transferred her house to her daughter, on condition that her daughter cared for her. On an income support claim by the old lady, it was held that the gift had failed when the condition was not fulfilled and that the property was held on resulting trust for her.

Discretionary trusts cause some difficulties in practice. In principle, the discretionary beneficiary has no entitlement to capital before it is appointed, and, therefore, the assessor should take into account only payments out of the trust fund. If the trustees exercise their discretion not to make payments out, the beneficiary will have no actual capital which is capable of assessment. The CRAG states that where payments are made 'wholly at the discretion of the trustees, and there is no right to income or capital', only payments which are actually made should be taken into account.[3] Advisers must resist any argument that regular discretionary payments have created a quasi-entitlement to a proportion of the trust capital. Not only does such argument seek to go behind the discretionary trust principle, but also a potential interest under such a trust is unlikely to have a market value.

Where a fixed trust contains an express discretionary power to advance capital, or where s 32 of the Trustee Act 1925 applies, it may be argued that, until the discretion is exercised, no value can be attributed to a mere expectation. There seems to be no reason why para 10.020, quoted above, should not apply in this situation. However, some of the income support case-law suggests that, if a beneficiary with a contingent interest in a trust fund is also the object of a

---

1   NA(AR) Regs 1992, reg 21.
2   [1998] 1 FLR 184.
3   CRAG, para 10.020.

discretionary power to advance capital, the underlying interest may carry an enhanced value.[1] In practice, advisers must always seek to negotiate with finance officers where valuations are not straightforward.

9.3.4   Co-ownership of assets

Where a joint beneficial interest in personal property is being assessed, reg 27(1) requires normal equitable principles to be ignored. Instead, assessors must assume that the property in question is owned in equal shares. This method of treatment is said to avoid 'administrative difficulties'.[2]

Example
Mr and Mrs Scott have £9,000 in a joint building society account. According to equitable principles, the beneficial shares are:

Mrs Scott: £3,500
Mr Scott: £5,500

Mrs Scott is about to go into a nursing home. Regulation 27(1) applies and the local authority finance officer, when conducting the financial assessment, will conclude that the building society account is to be treated as owned in equal shares and that Mrs Scott has £4,500 capital available to her. Anticipating the decision, Mrs Scott's solicitor may advise that the joint account should be closed and two separate accounts opened, in one of which Mrs Scott has £3,500 in her sole name. This would not constitute a 'deprivation' of capital by either Mr or Mrs Scott, because each has received no more than his or her beneficial entitlement. The CRAG instructs: 'Once the resident is in sole possession of his *actual* share, treat him as owning that actual amount'.[3]

Regulation 27(1) does not, however, apply to land. Therefore, the precise extent of a beneficial interest in land must be established before it is given a market value. Resulting and constructive trust principles may be relevant, as will express declarations of trust. There will be difficulties in some cases because the Benefits Agency, when assessing capital for income support purposes, is required to assume that *all* jointly owned capital assets are held in equal shares, irrespective of actual agreements and ignoring actual documentation. This means that the Benefits Agency will adopt a different approach from the local authority when valuing an interest in a jointly owned house.

---

1   *Peters v Chief Adjudication Officer*, R(SB)3/89.
2   CRAG, para 10.020.
3   Ibid, para 6.050. A further example of the benefits of severance is as follows: Mr and Mrs Scott have a joint account of £50,000, in which the shares are equal. Mrs Scott goes into a nursing home. Once the joint capital is reduced to £32,000 she will be able to ask for financial support from the local authority – ie £18,000 capital will have to be spent (each spouse has the benefit of a separate £16,000 disregard). If, however, the account is severed, only £9,000 will have to be spent before Mrs Scott can access State support.

Regulation 27(2) provides that a resident's share in shared property must be valued at an amount:

> '... equal to the price which his interest in possession would realise if it was sold to a willing buyer (taking into account the likely effect on that price of any incumbrance secured on the whole beneficial interest), less 10% and the amount of any encumbrance solely on the resident's share of the whole beneficial interest.'

This is a gloss on the rule that assets are to be valued at market value and raises difficult questions about what sort of market might exist in these circumstances. It is clear that the value of a resident's interest will be very much influenced by, for example, whether the property in question is a commercial asset or whether it is a home, occupied by members of the resident's family. The assessment and valuation of a resident's own home are discussed more fully in Chapter 10.

9.3.5 Disregarded capital

Regulation 21(2) of the charging regulations states: 'There shall be disregarded in the calculation of a resident's capital ... any capital, where applicable, specified in Sch 4.' That schedule lists, in some detail, a number of capital assets which will be ignored in a financial assessment. Schedule 10 to the ISG Regs 1987 contains a similar list. Some assets are disregarded for a period of time; others are disregarded indefinitely. Schedule 4 repays detailed consideration because it offers significant opportunities for financial planning. Quite simply, residents whose assets are invested/tied up in certain ways, and who may indeed be relatively wealthy, may still take advantage of public funding for residential care for as long as their assessable capital does not exceed £16,000.

The Social Security Commissioner has recently stated that income support claimants should be advised by the Benefits Agency of the existence of relevant disregards so that they can take advantage of them.[1] By the same token, older people need to be made aware of the considerable potential of the disregards in the local authority means test. There is an argument that a prospective resident who has substantial disregarded assets has care and attention 'otherwise available' to him or her, and so does not qualify for local authority support under the NAA 1948. However, the amendments to s 21 of the NAA 1948, which were instigated by the CC(RA)A 1998 seem to make it quite clear that, when it is determining whether care and attention is 'otherwise available' to a person, the local authority must apply the charging regulations as a whole, including reg 21.[2]

The most important and best-known disregard applies to the capital value of a home, which is occupied by a third party (for example the resident's spouse),

---

1   Commissioners' Decision CIS 600/1995.
2   Sections 21(2A) and (2B); this is confirmed by CRAG, para 1.007A.

and will be considered separately.[1] The following list is not exhaustive, but includes the disregards which are most important in practice.

(a) Personal possessions[2] (except those purchased with the intention of reducing other capital and so mitigating charges for accommodation[3]). It may be assumed that anything which is not real property or a chose in action is personal property, and there is no limit on value. Paintings, jewellery, antiques and other collectables are all personal possessions unless, possibly, where the owner deals in such assets.

(b) Any future interest in property of any kind, other than land or premises in respect of which the resident has granted a subsisting lease or tenancy (including a sub-lease or sub-tenancy[4]). It should be noted that the CRAG's interpretation of this paragraph is unduly restrictive.[5] The income support case-law suggests that a 'future interest' (the CRAG refers to 'reversionary interest', which was the term used before para 4 was amended in 1995)[6] is 'something which does not afford any present enjoyment but carries a vested or contingent right to enjoyment in the future'.[7] A beneficiary with a contingent interest in a trust fund or a person entitled in remainder on termination of a life interest clearly has a future interest within para 4. However, the term is potentially broader than this. It has been suggested, for instance, that the disregard may apply where property is subject to a licence, with a subsequent right of re-entry. The exclusion in respect of the landlord's reversion on a lease or tenancy is specific in terms, and does not affect parallel situations. The Social Security Commissioner has held that where a claimant, on separating from his wife, agreed that she could live in the former matrimonial home (which was in his sole name) he had a reversionary (future) interest in the property which was therefore disregarded so that he was enabled to claim benefit.[8]

(c) The capital value of an annuity or an occupational pension.[9] In both cases, income payments will be assessable.

(d) The surrender value of any policy of life insurance.[10] An important decision of the Social Security Commissioner in R (IS) 7/98 indicates that the scope of para 13 is wider than might be expected. The claimant had taken out an 'investment bond' with the Equity and Law Life Assurance Society. She invested a lump sum of £10,000 in a contract written as a

---

1   See Chapter 10.
2   NA(AR) Regs 1992, Sch 4, para 8.
3   See Chapter 11.
4   NA(AR) Regs 1992, Sch 4, para 4.
5   CRAG, para 6.028.
6   NA(AR) (Amendment No 2) Regulations 1995, SI 1995/3054.
7   Commissioners' Decision R (SB) 3/86.
8   Commissioners' Decision R (IS) 1/97.
9   NA(AR) Regs 1992, Sch 4, paras 9 and 15.
10   NA(AR) Regs 1992, Sch 4, para 13.

cluster of single-premium life-assurance policies, which had no set maturity date, and could be encashed at any time. There was a low guaranteed minimum death benefit which would become payable if the investment had not been fully cashed in before the claimant died, but the real value was in the encashment options. The Commissioner held that the bond was a 'policy of life assurance'; that the death of the investor need not be the only contingency under which money became payable, and that the relative size of the death benefits as compared to the investment benefits was irrelevant. The bond fell to be disregarded even though its full investment value was obtainable on demand.[1]

(e) The value of funds held in trust or administered by a court which derive from any payment made in respect of a personal injury to the resident. This disregard also applies where the compensation is held and administered by the Court of Protection.[2] It is important to notice that the creation of a personal injury trust does not fall foul of the notional capital rule.[3] The courts have approved such arrangements on behalf of plaintiffs being cared for in nursing homes, where the agreed damages were put into trust and so protected against nursing home fees. Had trusts not been set up, the fees would have been payable out of capital. Advisers who fail to take up this option on their clients' behalf will certainly be negligent.

(f) The value of the right to receive any income under a life interest or from a life rent.[4] This means the value of the lifetime right to future income from the trust. The income actually derived from the trust fund is, of course, assessable like any other income.

(g) The assets of any business owned (or part-owned) by a resident and in which he or she is engaged as a self-employed earner. Here, Sch 4, para 5 refers directly to the ISG Regs 1987, but the CRAG does not mention this disregard at all. Business assets are the funds which are 'employed and risked in business'. Normally an older person who is living in residential accommodation will not at the same time be 'engaged' in a business, because a financial commitment alone is not sufficient.[5] However, in *Chief Adjudication Officer v Kathleen Knight*[6] the Court of Appeal suggested that where an income support claimant had in the past been practically engaged in a business but was subsequently precluded from making a contribution 'by infirmity', the disregard could continue, subject, presumably, to there being a realistic prospect of the claimant recovering and resuming work.

---

1   See Chapter 11 for a discussion on the application of the notional capital rule to the purchase of such investments.
2   NA(AR) Regs 1992, Sch 4, paras 10 and 19; and see CIS 368/94.
3   See **10.5**.
4   NA(AR) Regs 1992, Sch 4, para 11.
5   Commissioners' Decision CIS 841/94.
6   Reported as an appendix to the Commissioners' decision in CIS 841/94.

(h) In addition, where the resident has ceased to be engaged in the business, the value of his or her assets will be disregarded for a 'reasonable period' to allow for disposal. Again, the CRAG does not mention this provision.

(i) Where a resident was engaged in a business as a self-employed earner, but has stopped work due to some disease or disablement, his or her share of the business assets will be disregarded for up to 26 weeks from the date when he or she entered the home, or was assessed as a prospective resident.[1] That period may be extended for as long as is 'reasonable' to enable the resident to become re-engaged in the business. The resident must 'intend' to engage in the business again when circumstances permit. This disregard would often be applicable to an older person who has suffered a stroke or other catastrophe quite unexpectedly. The 'intention' to resume work may be entirely subjective, and the 26-week period may provide a useful period of respite to enable business matters to be sorted out.[2] Advisers who wish to argue for a longer period of disregard must of course do so without the benefit of a right of appeal.

(j) The value of the right to receive rent except where the resident has a reversionary interest in the property in respect of which the rent is due.[3] Where, therefore, the right to receive rent is detached from the reversionary interest it will be disregarded. Given that rent received is assessable (as capital rather than income) the most interesting aspect of this disregard is that its existence points up the fact that if a resident's reversionary interest in leasehold property is in fact shorn of the right to receive rent, its open market value, as assessable capital, will be substantially diminished.

Example

Mr West is being assessed by the local authority for a nursing home placement. He has the following assets:

(i) an occupational pension producing £120 per week;

(ii) a category A retirement pension of £67.50 per week;

(iii) a life interest in the house in which Mr West lives (the house was owned by his late wife, who left it in her will to Mr West for life, with remainder to their grandchildren);

(iv) some paintings and antique furniture, worth £200,000;

(v) an investment bond producing £500 per month, with a guaranteed minimum death benefit; and

(vi) £15,000 in a building society account.

---

1 ISG Regs 1987, Sch 4, para 5 and Sch 10, para 6.

2 Any gift of business assets during that period might, of course, be subject to the notional capital rule. See Chapter 10.

3 NA(AR) Regs 1992, Sch 4, para 15.

Mr West's only immediate assessable capital will be £15,000, and his income will fall short of the average fee for a nursing home bed. If he so chooses he will be entitled to have his care fees topped up by the local authority.

9.3.6 Notional capital

In some circumstances, a resident may be treated as possessing a capital asset where he or she does not actually possess it.[1] The local authority may include this notional capital as part of its assessment. A very similar rule applies to income support claimants.[2] There is an extensive discussion of the notional capital rules in Chapters 11–13.

Where a resident has been assessed as having notional capital, that capital will be notionally reduced by the difference between the resident's assessed contribution and the weekly amount he or she would have been paying if he or she had not been treated as possessing notional capital.[3]

Example
Mr Crane is assessed as having notional capital of £8,000, plus actual capital of £10,000. He has been placed by the local authority in a residential care home. The contracted fee is £300 per week. Without the notional capital, Mr Crane's assessed contribution towards the cost of his bed would be £200 per week. With notional capital added on, Mr Crane is above the £16,000 limit, and will be responsible for the full fees. As he cannot 'spend' notional capital, it is reduced, week by week, under the above formula as follows:

Assessed contribution without notional capital:	£200.00
Full residential home fee:	£300.00
Notional capital reduced by £300 – £200	= £100.00

Paragraphs 6.050 and 6.051 of the CRAG are contradictory. Paragraph 6.050 states that a resident's capital is the total of all capital, whether actual or notional. Paragraph 6.051 then says that where a person has actual and notional capital, if the actual capital exceeds the capital limit, it 'is not necessary to consider the question of notional capital'. The clear implication is that if Mr Crane, in the above example, had had £17,000 actual capital, the local authority would not have pursued the question of notional capital at all. If para 6.051 can be taken at its face value, it means that an older person may dispose of property before the financial assessment and provided that s/he retains at least £16,000 of assessable capital, the local authority will take no further steps. It may be tempting, but possibly unwise to rely on this provision, which does not reflect the income support rules, or indeed the NA(AR) Regs 1992 themselves.[4]

---

1   NA(AR) Regs 1992, reg 25.
2   ISG Regs 1987, reg 51.
3   NA(AR) Regs 1992, reg 26.
4   The increase in the capital threshold to £18,500 from April 2001 will affect the numbers in the above example, but not the principle.

9.4 HOW IS INCOME ASSESSED?

The NA(AR) Regs 1992 make detailed provision for different types of income to be taken into account in the financial assessment. With older people, the following are most commonly encountered:

– retirement pensions;
– other social security benefits, such as attendance allowance, disability living allowance (care component), severe disablement allowance and incapacity benefit;
– occupational pensions;
– annuity income;
– income from capital;
– trust income; and
– rental income.

In addition, capital below the £16,000 ceiling but above £10,000 is considered to give rise to a 'tariff income' of £1 per week for every complete £250 or part of £250 capital over £10,000.[1] Accordingly, capital of £12,000 would give rise to a tariff of £8 per week; capital of £12,005 would give £9 per week. Clearly, the chosen tariff represents a (currently) highly inflated hypothetical return on capital. The tariff is supposed to equate to an amount which a resident with some capital should be able to contribute towards accommodation costs, but as it is applied in exactly the same way to income support claimants, the rationale is obviously fluid. The resident's capital is deemed to produce income at the tariff rate; if it does produce actual income, the tariff will apply none the less and the actual income will be treated as an addition to the capital.[2]

9.4.1 What is income?

'Income' is not defined by the charging regulations, but the CRAG says that a payment of income is one which:

– is made in respect of a period; and
– which forms part of a series of payments (whether or not payments are received regularly).[3]

Payments are generally attributed to the periods which they represent, or equivalent periods, if received late. Payments due weekly are therefore taken into account for a week, and monthly payments for a month.

---

1   NA(AR) Regs 1992, reg 28. From April 2001, the same tariff will apply to capital above £11,500 but below £18,500.
2   Ibid, reg 22(4).
3   See para 8.001.

9.4.2   What income is taken into account?

The following income is taken into account in full:

—   most social security benefits (including attendance allowance and income support);
—   annuity income;
—   income from most insurance policies;
—   income from certain disregarded capital[1] (for example business assets which are being disposed of);
—   occupational pensions;
—   trust income; and
—   third-party payments to meet home fees above the local authority's standard rate.[2]

9.4.3   Disregarded income

The charging regulations list sources of income which will be wholly or partially disregarded in the assessment.[3] Fully disregarded income includes:

—   income in kind (for example food, clothing and personal items);
—   disability living allowance (mobility component);
—   dependency increases paid with benefits such as incapacity benefit, invalid care allowance and retirement pension (where the dependant does not live with the resident, the increase is to be paid over to the dependant);
—   any income support which is referable to a resident's home commitments; this can apply only during the first 52 weeks in residential care;
—   Christmas bonuses;
—   council tax benefit;
—   charitable payments which are intended for and used to top up home fees which are set at a higher level than the local authority would normally pay; and
—   voluntary payments or payments by charities which are intended for specific items not covered by the standard fee paid by the local authority to the homeowner (for example payments to enable a resident to have his or her own telephone or television set).[4]

Partially disregarded income includes:

—   income from a home income plan annuity, provided that one of the annuitants is still occupying the house which is the subject of the scheme, and subject to conditions specified in Sch 3, para 12;[5]
—   war disablement pension (£10 disregarded);

---

1   The general rule is that income from capital is treated as capital, not income. See **9.4.4**.
2   See CRAG, para 8.018.
3   NA(AR) Regs 1992, reg 15(2) and Sch 3.
4   Ibid, para 10(2).
5   CRAG, paras 8.025–8.030.

– war widow's pension (£10 disregarded); and
– charitable or voluntary payments made for unspecified purposes or intended and used for items which are already covered by the standard charge for the home (for example food or heating). The maximum disregard is £20. Payments are 'voluntary' when the payer gets nothing in return. They may or may not be legally enforceable.[1]

Both disregards in respect of voluntary payments or payments by charities offer relatives or friends the option of making benefit-efficient payments to or for an elderly resident.

Example
Mrs Wilson tops up her mother's care fees in respect of a local authority arranged placement. These are taken fully into account as income. However, monthly payments in respect of chiropody, hairdressing and her mother's mobile telephone are disregarded. Mr Wilson's father is an Abbeyfield resident. He has a tenancy agreement, and pays rent and a charge for board. He receives housing benefit and income support. Mr Wilson tops up the payments for board by £50 a week, £20 of which is disregarded.

9.4.4   Income from capital, including rental income

Regulation 22(4) of the NA(AR) Regs 1992 provides that most[2] income from capital is to be treated as capital from the date it is normally due to be paid. This includes building society interest, dividends from shares and rental income. If these receipts are substantial, they may of course push the resident's assessable capital above the upper threshold and will then become available to meet care costs. In many cases, however, the effect of this provision will be effectively to disregard such payments.

9.4.5   Notional income

In some circumstances, a resident will be treated as having an income which he or she does not actually receive. In a sense, the tariff income previously described falls into this category, but reg 17 refers specifically to several categories of notional income which the local authority is required to take into account in its financial assessment.

(a)   The first category is income of which the resident has deprived himself or herself for the purpose of decreasing the amount that he or she may be liable to pay for his or her accommodation. This paragraph would cover the conversion of income into capital, for example selling the right to receive annuity income. As receipt of such income will increase an

---

1   *R v Doncaster Metropolitan Borough Council ex parte Boulton* (1992) *The Times*, 31 December.
2   Income from certain types of disregarded capital is taken into account in full; Sch 3, para 14.

individual's contribution towards residential care fees, conversion may seem an attractive idea, particularly where a resident has no other capital.

Example
Mr Pearson sells the right to receive income of £10 per week under an annuity. He receives £2,000. He already has other capital of £10,100, which is, therefore, producing a tariff income of £1 per week. The £2,000 consideration for the sale of the annuity will increase the tariff income by £8, and in addition, a notional income will be attributed to Mr Pearson. He will not lose out both ways, however, as the notional annuity income will be offset by the increase in the tariff income. Nevertheless, the net effect will be to give him a notional income of £10 per week.[1]

(b) The second category is income which would become available to the resident upon application being made.[2] The scope of this category of notional income is very limited. Whilst the CRAG suggests that some welfare benefits, such as retirement pension may be regarded as available, it also acknowledges that where entitlement to benefit is subject to medical conditions (incapacity benefit) or where a benefit would be fully disregarded (DLA mobility) an assessment of notional income is not appropriate.[3] It is submitted that only where entitlement is absolutely straightforward, and there is no means test, can a benefit properly be treated as available to a potential claimant.

Income which may be payable under a discretionary trust or a personal injury trust is not 'available'. Working families' tax credit and disabled person's tax credit[4] are also expressly excluded from reg 17(2). In addition, income available on request from a personal pension scheme or under a retirement annuity contract is exempt from the notional income rule until a person reaches the age of 60. If, after attaining that age, the person does not draw down available income, he or she will be assumed to have notional income which will be determined as laid down in reg 42(2) of the ISG Regs 1987.[5]

(c) The third category is income which is due to be paid to the resident, but has not yet been paid. This could include unpaid superannuation or unpaid earnings. It would also include trust income to which a resident is entitled but which has not been applied by the trustees. The distinction between a fixed trust and a discretionary trust is important here; income which is

---

1   There is an extended discussion of 'deprivation' for 'the purpose of' decreasing accommodation fees in Chapter 11. The increase in the upper and lower capital thresholds in April 2001 will affect the numbers, but not the principle, in the above example.
2   NA(AR) Regs 1992, reg 17(2).
3   CRAG, paras 8.064–8.068; income support is discussed separately at **9.8**.
4   Formerly family credit and disability working allowance.
5   CRAG, para 8.069A.

payable at the trustees' discretion is not 'due'. However, income payable under a personal injury trust, fixed or discretionary, is likewise excluded.

If the local authority comes to the conclusion that reg 17 applies, it will assess the accommodation charge, taking account of the notional income. In some cases, the local authority may seek to transfer liability to a third party under s 21 of the HASSASSAA 1983.[1]

9.5   THE PERSONAL EXPENSES ALLOWANCE

Section 22(4) of the NAA 1948 requires local authorities to allow residents to retain specified amounts of their assessable resources for personal expenses. Regulations made in April each year[2] specify a minimum amount which, for 2000/2001 is £15.45 per week.

The allowance is supposed to be inalienable. It is intended that residents should spend it as they wish on stationery, toiletries, treats, presents and other personal items.

In the view of the Department of Health, it would be unlawful for a local authority to allow a resident to use the allowance, even on his or her own initiative, to help pay for more expensive accommodation than the local authority is prepared to subsidise.[3] Instances have been reported of homes seeking to charge residents separately for services which either ought to be covered by local authority contracts, or ought to be part of community health provision. Charges are not infrequently made for incontinence or chiropody services.

There is some evidence that home owners retain the personal allowances paid for individuals, and pool them to meet collective expenditure, thus depriving residents of control over their own money.[4] As a general rule, attempts to relieve residents of their personal expenses allowances should always be questioned, whatever explanation is offered.

Section 22(4) of the NAA 1948 allows local authorities to raise the personal expenses allowance above the annually prescribed figure where they consider it appropriate to do so. There is no upper limit. Advisers should be aware of this power, and should be prepared to ask the local authority to use it. The CRAG suggests that the allowance could be increased to help residents with learning disabilities to live more independently or to meet the needs of a dependent child.[5] A further example is discussed at **9.6.2**.

---

1   See **12.17**.

2   Currently the National Assistance (Sums for Personal Requirements) Regulations 2000, SI 2000/798. The allowance will rise to £16.05 for 2001/2002.

3   DoH Circular LAC (94) 1.

4   Office of Fair Trading *Older People as Consumers in Care Homes* (1998).

5   DoH Circular LAC (99) 9, para 5.005.

9.6 MARRIED OR UNMARRIED COUPLES

9.6.1 Assessing one partner

The local authority has no power under the NA(AR) Regs 1992 to take account of the combined resources of married or unmarried couples when assessing one partner for residential care. Income and capital have to be allocated to the individual being assessed either according to normal proprietary rules or as prescribed by the Regulations. The approach will be the same for both temporary[1] and permanent placements. When income support is being claimed, the Benefits Agency takes a rather different approach for temporary placements. Here, income support will be assessed for the couple, and will be paid to one partner in respect of both, as is normal when partners are living together in the same household. Usually, payments will be made to the partner who is still at home, in the community.

9.6.2 Pension splitting

One problem with the approach prescribed for the local authority will arise where the partner in residential accommodation is technically entitled to income which is really intended to meet the needs of both partners. Occupational or personal pensions, often payable to a husband, provide a good example. The husband's income may be so substantial that he will be required to pay the full cost of his care, whilst his wife, living at home, is impoverished. At one time, the only way of dealing with this problem was for the local authority to consider using its power under s 22(4) of the NAA 1948 to raise the husband's personal expenses allowance beyond the statutory minimum, so that he could then support his wife at home. This was a very convoluted way of dealing with a serious problem, and eventually, as a result of strenuous lobbying by the Alzheimer's Society, together with Age Concern, the Government agreed to a limited amendment to the charging regulations. Since 1996 local authorities have been required to disregard one half of a resident's occupational or personal pension where it is paid to a spouse who is not residing with him or her.[2]

The CRAG states:

> 'Where a resident is in receipt of an occupational pension, personal pension, or payment from a retirement annuity contract and has a spouse who is not living in the same residential care or nursing home, 50% of the occupational pension, personal pension, or retirement annuity contract payment should be disregarded providing the resident passes 50% on to his spouse. If the resident passes less than 50% of any of these payments mentioned above, or none of them, to his spouse, for whatever reason, then the disregard should not be applied and the full amount in payment to the resident should be taken into account. The only other time when

---

1   See **9.7**.
2   NA(AR) Regs 1992, Sch 3, para 10A.

50% of any of the payments [by] a married resident should cease to be disregarded is on the death of the spouse or divorce.'[1]

This amendment does not apply to unmarried partners, or to any other pension or quasi-pension arrangement, and in such cases advisers must resort to persuading the local authority to consider using its discretionary power to vary the personal expenses allowance (referred to above). Where a spouse is entitled to receive part of his or her spouse's pension, for example because of a court order, the 50 per cent disregard can be applied to the amount actually in payment to the resident.[2]

9.6.3   Assessing both partners

Where both partners are admitted to residential accommodation, the local authority will always assess them separately, according to their individual resources, and each will be entitled to £16,000 'protected' capital.

The income support position may be different. The basis of any income support assessment in respect of a couple, is that one partner claims benefit on behalf of both, and that if they are living together in the same household they will be treated as one unit for benefit purposes, with a couple's personal allowance and a joint capital threshold of £16,000. This is financially adverse. At 2000/2001 rates, an individual claimant will receive a personal allowance of £52.20 per week. The allowance for a married or unmarried couple is £81.95.[3]

Where spouses are admitted to the same residential accommodation, the Benefits Agency has adopted a rather uncertain approach, because the regulations themselves do not specifically cover this situation. The legal question is whether partners can be said to be living in the same 'household' in such circumstances. Generally speaking, with dual-registered accommodation, where one spouse lives in the residential wing and the other in the nursing wing, they will be regarded as separate households, so that each may make a separate claim for income support. Recently, however, a number of appeals have come before Social Security Commissioners concerning married couples who share rooms in residential homes.

In CIS 4935/97, the Commissioner came to the conclusion, in relation to all five couples who had pursued appeals, that they were not living together in the same household. He held that 'household' implies the existence of an identifiable domestic establishment, the members of which enjoy a reasonable degree of independence and self-sufficiency and also have some responsibility for management and decision-making. He commented: 'I fail to see how an elderly and infirm married couple, who are bedridden and unable to care for

---

1   DoH Circular LAC (99) 9, para 8.024A.

2   Ibid, para 8.024C.

3   See Appendix 3 for 2001/2002 benefit rates.

themselves, can be categorised as a household because they occupy adjoining beds in a double room . . .'.

The decision suggests that where married or unmarried partners are living in the same home, they should generally be entitled to make separate income support claims. However, advisers must be aware of the need to submit separate claims in the first instance. Where only one partner makes a claim, the Benefits Agency will not necessarily look beyond that document, and may just assume that both partners are living in the same household.

9.6.4　Liable relatives

Section 42 of the NAA 1948 makes spouses (but not cohabitants) liable to maintain one another. Section 43 permits enforcement via the magistrates' court. Whenever one spouse's accommodation in a registered care home or nursing home is provided wholly or partly at public expense, the local authority may seek reimbursement from the liable relative. There seems to be no authority as to the extent of this liability, but it must be presumed that it is to provide 'reasonable maintenance'. Anachronistically, however, the liability will be affected by matrimonial conduct.[1]

The liable relative rule does not allow local authorities to assess the means of anyone apart from the person for whom care arrangements are being made. Spouses of those being assessed can be asked to contribute to the cost of a residential placement, but they cannot be asked to disclose information about their own resources.

The CRAG states:[2]

> '. . . where it appears to be appropriate to pursue liability, local authorities may ask a spouse to refund part or all of the authority's expenditure in providing residential accommodation for his/her husband or wife. Local authorities should not use assessment forms for the resident which require information about the means of the spouse. Local authorities should use tact in explaining to residents and spouses the legal liability to maintain and point out that the extent of that liability is best considered in the light of the spouses' resources . . .'.

Residents should always be advised not to complete assessment forms which seek to elicit financial information about their spouses. A local authority has to make a judgment on what a spouse could be expected to contribute and must then seek to negotiate reasonable maintenance payments. An 'appropriate' figure will be determined by reference to the spouse's financial circumstances, his or her expenditure, and normal standard of living. It would not be appropriate to expect spouses to reduce their resources to income support levels

---

1　*National Assistance Board v Parkes* [1955] 3 WLR 347.
2　DoH Circular LAC (99) 9, para 11.005.

in order to pay maintenance.[1] Ultimately, the court can be asked to order appropriate payments, but, as always with enforcement measures, local authorities will have to weigh the adverse publicity which court proceedings may bring against the need to recoup expenditure.

Where a resident is receiving income support, the assessing local authority may draw the conclusion that the liable relative obligation has already been explored by the Benefits Agency, as social security law also requires spouses (and cohabitants) to maintain one another.[2] Any payments subsequently exacted from the liable relative, unless very substantial, will simply reduce income support and will not benefit the local authority. In such cases, it will not be worthwhile pursuing maintenance at all.

9.6.5 Treatment of liable relative payments

Both the NA(AR) Regs 1992 and the ISG Regs 1987 contain arcane and highly complex provisions for dealing with payments by liable relatives.[3] In principle, such payments are to be taken into account as additional income of the resident so as to reduce the local authority's contribution towards the cost of his or her residential care. Where one-off or irregular payments are made, the regulations require them to be 'spread' and treated as income for a period of time which is calculated by reference to a statutory formula.

Where a resident is receiving income support, the situation is further complicated by the fact that benefit will be reduced by the amount of any liable relative payment.

There is always a risk that lump sums paid to residents by liable relatives may be treated as income under the above rules when they are intended to be capital payments, which should not affect an assessed contribution. The regulations provide that certain payments made by liable relatives will not be treated as 'liable relative' payments. These include gifts of up to £250 per year, property settlements on divorce, and payments made to third parties, which it would not be reasonable to take into account. Such payments might include TV rental payments made direct, or mail-order payments.

---

1 DoH Circular LAC (99) 9, para 11.006. Recent research by the Age Concern Institute of Gerontology examined local authority practices and found that relatively few authorities have operational policies in this area. Of those that do, most flout the guidance regarding the collection of financial information from a spouse, and ask for joint statements of assets. Most spouses interviewed felt that the level of payments demanded (from £30 to £200 per week) was unreasonable. See Thompson, P and Wright, F *All My Worldly Goods*, 2000.

2 SSCBA 1992, s 106.

3 NA(AR) Regs 1992, regs 29–34. ISG Regs 1987, regs 54–60. See also DoH Circular LAC (99) 9, paras 11.007–11.024.

9.7 TEMPORARY RESIDENTS

Older people who are being cared for at home may be admitted to residential homes for a temporary period, usually to provide respite for their carers. Even where permanent residential care is needed, an older person will usually be admitted on a temporary basis until he or she is settled, and it is clear that the placement is appropriate.

Section 22(5A) of the NAA 1948 acknowledges temporary arrangements as follows:

> 'Where they think fit, an authority managing premises in which accommodation is provided for a person shall have power on each occasion when they provide accommodation for him, irrespective of his means, to limit to such amount as appears to them reasonable for him to pay the payments required from him for his accommodation during a period commencing when they begin to provide the accommodation for him and ending 8 weeks after that.'

This provision relieves local authorities of the requirement to carry out a full financial assessment in respect of a short stay, and empowers them to charge temporary residents a 'reasonable amount'. However, it would not be safe to assume that such an amount will necessarily be less than an assessed contribution. Section 22(5A) is primarily administrative, and enables authorities to charge flat rate fees, which they usually do.

In addition, it should not be assumed that if an older person is still in a home after 8 weeks he or she must be considered to be permanently resident. Regulation 2 of the NA(AR) Regs 1992 defines a 'temporary resident' as one whose stay is:

(a) unlikely to exceed 52 weeks; or
(b) in exceptional circumstances, unlikely substantially to exceed that period.

Clearly, therefore, the law envisages situations where residents who are still temporary will have to be assessed under the charging regulations. In doing so, however, local authorities are required to disregard the value of the temporary residents' former home, provided that he or she intends to return there and that it is available to him or her.[1] In practice, however, finance officers almost invariably confuse s 22(5A) and reg 2, by regarding residence as permanent after 8 weeks, and taking account of the value of the house at that point. The CRAG acknowledges that stays which are initially expected to be permanent may turn out to be temporary, and vice versa. It emphasises that the distinction between 'temporary' and 'permanent' must be recognised, and decisions reviewed if needs be. Assessment as a permanent resident should begin from the date it is

---

1   NA(AR) Regs 1992, Sch 4, para 1. As noted at **10.1**, the Government proposes that the value of a resident's former home should be subject to a three-month disregard from April 2001. However, the relationship between this new rule and the temporary residence rule outlined above is unclear.

agreed that the stay is to become permanent.[1] Advisers should always try to ensure that this guidance is followed.

Temporary residents are not entitled to income support if their capital exceeds £8,000. The £16,000 threshold does not apply until their residence becomes permanent. Consequently, local authorities will not benefit from cross-subsidies from the DSS in respect of some temporary residents, which may increase the pressure to regard them as permanent.

If income support is in payment it may include an additional amount in respect of the resident's housing costs in his or her own home.[2] The local authority must disregard this amount when assessing a resident's contribution.[3] Benefit for home commitments may be paid for as long as residence is 'temporary' within reg 2. The same applies to housing benefit payments in respect of a resident's rent.

Attendance allowance or disability living allowance (care component) may be paid to temporary residents, but only for up to 28 days. Permanent residents, who are in receipt of local authority funding are disentitled to either benefit.[4]

9.8 CLAIMING INCOME SUPPORT

Residents must contribute to the cost of their accommodation the whole of their assessed weekly income, as calculated in accordance with the regulations (ie including their actual and notional income, but ignoring any disregarded income). They are, however, permitted to retain a specified amount for personal expenses.[5]

Where the individual's weekly income is below income support level, the local authority will expect him to claim benefit. However, nothing in the regulations directly requires a resident to make a claim. If income support could be regarded as income which 'would be available' to a resident if application were made, it would then be notional income under reg 17 and the local authority's assessment could take it into account irrespective of the resident's willingness to claim it.

Bearing in mind the complexity of the means test for income support, however, it is doubtful whether reg 17 should apply to unclaimed benefit. In addition, the local authority will always be liable for the full cost of the residential care under its contractual arrangements with the provider, and by virtue of s 26(2) of the NAA 1948. From its own budget, it will have to meet whatever costs it is unable to recoup from the resident or from central government.

---

1   DoH Circular LAC (99) 9, paras 3.004 and 3.004A.
2   Income support covers only interest on mortgages or home improvement loans.
3   DoH Circular LAC (99) 9, para 3.009.
4   Ibid, para 3.014; and see **14.4**.
5   See **9.5**.

9.8.1 The residential allowance

Since April 1993 older people in independent residential care homes and nursing homes who are eligible for income support have been entitled to a residential allowance, as part of their applicable amount.[1] The allowance was introduced in order to reflect the housing element in independent sector care delivered in residential settings.

For the financial year 2000/2001, the allowance is set at £61.30 per week, or £68.20 for homes situated in the Greater London area. The home must be registered, or deemed to be registered, under the RHA 1984. (Abbeyfield homes only qualify if registered under the RHA 1984.)

The allowance is not, therefore, available to residents in Part III accommodation owned or managed by the local authority. This disentitlement extends to residents of former Part III homes which have been transferred to the independent sector after 12 August 1991.[2] Manifestly, therefore, the allowance provides a financial incentive towards independent sector placements. The Royal Commission on Long-term Care was critical of its existence, and recommended that the resources which underpin it should be reallocated to local authorities to use in a more carefully targeted way.[3] Following consultation, the Government has accepted the Royal Commission's arguments, and proposes to effect a transfer of resources from April 2002. The change will relate to 'new' cases only.[4]

The present rules do not require that the local authority should necessarily finance the care arrangements. Residents who, for example, elect to fund their own placements, using available benefits plus financial assistance from relatives may, therefore, take advantage of the residential allowance.[5]

However, residents with preserved rights do not benefit from the residential allowance. As noted in Chapter 13, their income support payments are differently prescribed.

The residential allowance stops if a resident is absent from the home for more than 21 days, or 6 weeks if he or she is admitted to hospital. Where the local authority has made the care arrangements, it will remain liable to the provider for the full contractual price and, therefore, is likely to impose terms in respect of temporary absences.

---

1   ISG Regs 1987, regs 17(1)(bb), 18(1)(cc) and Sch 2, para 2A.
2   Ibid, reg 21(3A).
3   *With Respect to Old Age*, op cit, para 4.28.
4   *The NHS Plan 2000*, op cit, para 15.18.
5   See Chapter 14. These arrangements will also be affected by the Government's proposed changes.

9.9 PLACEMENTS IN LOCAL AUTHORITY-MANAGED HOMES

The NA(AR) Regs 1992 apply to placements made in old-style Part III accommodation owned and managed by the local authority. As already explained, such placements carry financial disincentives and the decision of the House of Lords in *R v Wandsworth London Borough Council ex parte Beckwith*[1] has now given local authorities carte blanche to close or sell off all their own residential homes. Nevertheless, politics will ensure that some local authorities will continue to maintain the option of using their own accommodation to discharge their responsibilities under s 21 of the NAA 1948, rather than relying exclusively on contractual arrangements with the independent sector.

The local authority must purport to charge a resident the full economic cost of providing the placement.[2] Before April 1993, local authority beds were traditionally cheaper than beds in the independent sector, but the extension of the NAA 1948 regime to all residential placements has ensured that pricing in the different sectors has been brought into line.

Section 23 of the NAA 1948 allows local authorities to make rules regarding the management of their Part III accommodation. In particular, they may provide for accommodation charges to be waived in part where residents assist in running homes. This section does not apply to independent sector homes.

The financial regime for Part III accommodation now differs in one important respect from the (preferred) regime for independent sector placements. Income support is only available to top up a resident's resources to the basic state retirement level. No premiums and no residential allowance are available.

As the case studies below demonstrate, the effect is to diminish central government support for these placements, and to make them considerably more expensive for local authorities than contracted placements in the independent sector.[3]

9.10 CASE STUDIES: CALCULATING RESIDENTS' CONTRIBUTIONS

These case studies are based on 2000/2001 benefit rates. Appendix 3 contains details of the benefits uprating which takes effect from 7 April 2001.

---

1   [1996] 1 All ER 129; see **6.3**.
2   NAA 1948, s 22(3).
3   In areas where local authorities have retained substantial Part III provision, voluntary sector homes are often considerably cheaper. Homeowners argue that local authorities which try to direct older people towards their own Part III homes are engaging in unfair competition.

Example 1

The local authority has agreed to arrange a place in a private residential home for Mrs Anna Jones, aged 81. Her only sources of income are her state retirement pension and an occupational pension of £30 per week. She has £11,000 in savings. The contracted fee for the bed is £250 per week.

Cost to the local authority of providing the bed		£250.00
Mrs Jones's weekly income:		
retirement pension	£67.50	
occupational pension	£30.00	
tariff income	£4.00	
income support	£40.65	
personal allowance (£52.20)		
enhanced pensioner premium (£28.65)		
residential allowance (£61.30)		
less other income		
Total income (income support level)	£142.15	
Less personal expenses allowance	£15.45	
Mrs Jones's contribution		£126.70
Cost to the local authority		£123.30
Total fee		£250.00

Example 2

The local authority has agreed to arrange a place in a nursing home for Jim Craven, aged 75. The local authority would normally expect to pay £340 per week for someone with his care needs. Mr Craven has chosen, however, to enter a home with more facilities, which costs £400 per week, and his daughter has agreed to pay the extra £60 per week. Mr Craven transferred his house to his daughter some years ago, and she has been caring for him up to now. His assessable capital is £13,000.

Cost to the local authority of providing the bed		£400.00
What the local authority would normally have paid		£340.00
Mr Craven's weekly income:		
retirement pension	£67.50	
occupational pension	£250.00	
tariff income	£12.00	
daughter's contribution towards extra fees	£60.00	
Total income	£389.50	
Less personal expenses allowance	£15.45	
Mr Craven's contribution		£374.05
Cost to the local authority		£25.95
Total fee		£400.00

Note

(i)   The cost to the local authority of meeting the needs of a particular individual is always unpredictable because it depends on the extent of the individual's assessable resources.

(ii) Mr Craven's right to choose which nursing home he enters is discussed in some detail in Chapter 6. In this example, it must be assumed that the local authority is satisfied as to the financial standing and integrity of Mr Craven's daughter. The fact that Mr Craven's income is relatively high will doubtless have influenced this judgment. The family must be made aware, however, of the possible consequences of failure to meet the top-up payments.

(iii) It is unlikely that the local authority will seek to open up the possibility of assessing the value of Mr Craven's former house as notional capital. The ambit of the notional capital rules, together with possible planning options are explored, in detail, in Chapters 11–13.

Example 3

The local authority has agreed to arrange a place for Eva Stowe, aged 70, in one of its own homes. Her only income is the married woman's pension of £40.40. In addition, she has £1,000 savings.

Cost to the local authority of providing the bed		£250.00
Mrs Stowe's weekly income:		
pension	£40.40	
income support (up to full pension level)	£27.10	
Total income (income support level)	£67.50	
Less personal expenses allowance	£15.45	
Mrs Stowe's contribution		£52.05
Cost to the local authority		£197.95
Total fee		£250.00

Note

Income support level for Mrs Stowe is £67.50 per week. Compare Mrs Jones. The local authority's financial subsidy for Mrs Stowe is much higher than for Mrs Jones.

9.11   ENFORCING PAYMENT OF ASSESSED CONTRIBUTIONS

Although there is no contractual relationship between a local authority and residents in respect of whom it makes arrangements under ss 21 or 26 of the NAA 1948, s 56 of that Act provides that any sum due 'under this Act to a local authority (other than a sum due under an order made under s 43 of this Act) shall be recoverable summarily as a civil debt'.[1] Orders made under s 43 for contributions from liable relatives towards the cost of a spouse's care will be enforceable like any other maintenance orders made by the family proceedings court.

Section 56 allows the local authority to take the same steps as any commercial creditor to enforce payment of assessed contributions and, in some cases, the final outcome may be proceedings under the Insolvency Act 1986. How readily local authorities will take such steps is hard to predict. There is undoubtedly a cultural antipathy towards enforcement against service users who are frail and vulnerable, and the cost of recovery may also deflect local authorities in cases where the debt is small and prognosis for the resident perhaps limited.

Unpaid contributions are most likely when the value of a resident's home is taken into account in assessing a contribution. As the local authority has no power to waive its charges pending sale of the property, a debt will build up very quickly unless the resident has other sources from which to meet the care fees. In these circumstances, a further statutory remedy is available which carries attractions for local authorities and is now routinely used.[2]

---

1   The reference to summary recovery implies that proceedings may be brought in the magistrates' court, or, these days, under the small claims procedures in the county court. The limitation period is 3 years (s 56(2)).

2   See **10.8**.

Chapter 10

TREATMENT OF THE RESIDENT'S FORMER HOME

'If I was forced into a position where I was going into care and I'd got to sell my house, I'd say to somebody, "Give me a bottle of whisky, some tablets and go out that bloody door" – they'd never get their hands on mine [house].'[1]

10.1   THE POLICY

For many people entering residential care, their home will be their only substantial capital asset. The state – represented by the local authority or by the Benefits Agency in some cases – will have an interest in using its capital value to offset care fees, but this interest has to be balanced against the interests of other people who occupy, or have proprietary rights in, the property.

At present, as soon as an older person enters residential care on a permanent basis, the local authority's charging regulations require that the value of any property he or she may own or part own is taken into account, subject, however, to certain disregards on occupation (explained below) which in practice protect a significant number of properties.

There is no doubt that one of the most emotive images to be traded in debates about the funding of long-term care is that of a vulnerable older person being forced to sell the family home, which represents a lifetime's savings, in order to pay care fees. The Royal Commission on Long Term Care quoted as follows from one of the people who gave evidence: 'it is an iniquitous thing that an elderly person, at their most vulnerable time of life, should have their home sold from under them in order to pay for their care after a lifetime of work and service to the nation'. The Report of the Commission endorses this perspective, saying that 'a situation where the value of their home effectively dictates whether people are potentially entitled to state help for their care needs does not represent a form of effective pooling of risk'.[2]

The Commission also argued that the assessment rules should not force the premature disposal of property so as to exclude the possibility of a return from residential care, and it proposed that, for purposes of means testing, the value of the house should be completely disregarded for up to 3 months. This was put forward as a free-standing option which could be introduced separately from

---

1   *Meeting the Costs of Continuing Care, Public Views and Perceptions* (Joseph Rowntree Foundation, 1996), p 32.
2   *With Respect to Old Age* op cit, para 4.17. It has been estimated that about 40,000 elderly people a year are forced to sell their homes to enable them to meet care fees.

the main Commission proposals. The Government has indeed adopted this proposal, which will be implemented by an amendment to the charging regulations, in April 2001.[1]

Briefly, from 9 April 2001, the value of a resident's former home will be disregarded for 12 weeks from the moment when he or she is *permanently* admitted to residential accommodation. This may follow a temporary stay, during which there is also a disregard which may last for up to 52 weeks.[2] Advisers will need to consider how best to maximise these two disregards. A new local authority circular will be issued in March 2001.

10.2   DISREGARDING THE CAPITAL VALUE OF THE HOME

The NA(AR) Regs 1992 require the local authority to ignore the capital value of a resident's former home in the following circumstances.

(1)   Where the resident is only temporarily in residential accommodation (whether or not he or she is a 'prospective' resident or is simply receiving respite care) and:

   —   intends to return home; or
   —   is taking reasonable steps to dispose of the house in order to acquire another property to return to.[3]

   The house must still be 'available' to the resident. Here the parallel income support regulations are more prescriptive in specifying that the property must not be let.[4] Although the meaning of 'available' is not wholly clear, older people who enter residential care on a temporary basis should be advised against letting their homes, because loss of the capital disregard may have serious financial consequences.

(2)   Where the resident has entered a care home or nursing home on a permanent basis, but his or her house is still occupied by a spouse or partner (except an estranged or divorced spouse/partner) or by a specified relative of the resident or family member who:

   —   is aged 60 or over;
   —   is aged under 16, and is a child whom the resident is liable to maintain; or

---

1   *The NHS Plan 2000* (the Government's response to the Royal Commission on Long Term Care, Cm 4818–I), para 15.18 and now see clause 52 of the Health and Social Care Bill 2000. The Government suggests that 'around 30,000 people a year' will benefit from this disregard.

2   CRAG, paras 3.004 and 3.004A. See **9.7**.

3   NA(AR) Regs 1992, Sch 4, para 1. Note the more extensive discussion on 'temporary' arrangements at para 8.7.

4   ISG Regs 1987, Sch 10, para 1 and Sch 3, para 3(8).

—   is incapacitated.[1]

In those circumstances, the benefit of the disregard continues until the prescribed occupation ceases. The regulations do not define 'incapacitated', but the CRAG suggests that it should be taken to mean being in receipt of a social security benefit for incapacity (for example incapacity benefit, disability living allowance or attendance allowance), or having an equivalent level of incapacity. The same interpretation is used by the Benefits Agency for income support purposes.[2] Medical evidence of incapacity may be needed where a resident is not in receipt of a relevant benefit.

In addition, the local authority has discretion to ignore the capital value of premises owned by the resident if they are occupied by any other third party,[3] relative or not, and it is reasonable to do so. If, for example, an elderly person is admitted to a nursing home, leaving behind in his house a long-term carer or housekeeper, or a son or daughter, who has no other available accommodation, the local authority may decide to ignore the resident's ownership of the house in its financial assessment. The disregard will not be indefinite – the authority will review the situation from time to time, and will, of course, assess the capital interest when the carer dies or moves elsewhere.

The Benefits Agency has no such discretion. In equivalent circumstances, it *must* assess the resident's interest in premises as capital.

In applying its discretion, the local authority will have to balance a concern for the circumstances of the third-party occupant of the home against the need to ensure that residents with assets are not maintained at public expense. Where, for instance, an assessment would result in the house having to be sold to meet the cost of residential care, so that the occupant would become homeless and might become the responsibility of the housing authority, then it would seem reasonable for the social services authority to exercise its discretion in favour of continuing the capital disregard. It appears that practice varies between local authorities, and that discretion is being used less freely now than immediately following implementation of the charging regulations. Advisers should expect discretion to be exercised fairly and objectively, in accordance with declared criteria, and, where there is a dispute, should ask to see the local authority's policy statement on the potential scope of para 18. In *R v Somerset County Council ex parte Harcombe*[4] the local authority's policy that discretion should be exercised under para 18 only where the occupant of the property had been acting as carer was held not to be unreasonable.

---

1   NA(AR) Regs 1992, Sch 4, para 2. The term 'partner' refers to an unmarried partner. Same-sex partners are not covered by para 2 and must be considered under para 18.
2   DoH Circular LAC (99) 9, para 7.005. DMG para 30237.
3   NA(AR) Regs 1992, Sch 4, para 18.
4   (1997) 3 BMLR 1.

10.3 HOMES SUBJECT TO CO-OWNERSHIP

Where a resident has a joint beneficial interest in his or her former home, which the local authority is not prepared to disregard in the assessment, valuation is all important and good legal advice is likely to have a measurable effect on the outcome. In principle, a market valuation[1] depends on:

– there being a 'market', ie there exists a willing buyer; and
– the ability of the resident to transfer his or her interest to a willing buyer.

As co-ownership confers the right to occupy the property in question, any sale of his or her interest by one of the owners is subject to the occupation rights of the other(s). Therefore, it is likely that (notwithstanding the ultimate possibility of an application for sale), the only person(s) interested in acquiring such an interest will be the other co-owner(s).[2]

For these reasons, the value of a share in a jointly owned house could, effectively, be nil, as is conceded by the CRAG,[3] which states:

'Where an interest in a property is beneficially shared between relatives, the value of the resident's interest will be heavily influenced by the possibility of a market amongst his fellow beneficiaries. If no other relative is willing to buy the resident's interest, it is highly unlikely that any 'outsider' would be willing to buy into the property unless the financial advantages far outweighed the risks and limitations involved. The value of the interest, even to a willing buyer, could in such circumstances effectively be nil. If the local authority is unsure about the resident's share, again a professional valuation should be obtained.'

This approach has been derived from a decision by the Court of Appeal in an income support case, *Chief Adjudication Officer v Palfrey*.[4] Mr Palfrey, an elderly widower, and his daughter were beneficial joint tenants of a former council house. When Mr Palfrey's failing health forced him to go into a nursing home his half-share in the house was assessed by the district valuer, on behalf of the Benefits Agency, at £16,000, one-half of the net estimated selling price. Miss Palfrey made it clear that she had no intention of buying her father out, preferring to rely on her right of survivorship on his death, and it was also highly unlikely that any outsider would be willing to buy into a house where occupation would have to be shared. The Court of Appeal found that there was, therefore, no 'market' for Mr Palfrey's equitable interest.

Palfrey is now incorporated into Benefits Agency guidance and, as stated above, is endorsed by the CRAG. However, reg 52 of the ISG Regs 1987 prescribes that all shares in jointly owned property will be treated as equal shares,

---

1   NA(AR) Regs 1992, reg 23; see **9.3.2**.
2   Sections 14 and 15 of the Trusts of Land and Appointment of Trustees Act 1996 have re-enacted Law of Property Act 1925, s 30. Previous case-law is still relevant, but trustees no longer have a statutory duty to sell in cases of concurrent ownership.
3   Paragraph 7.014.
4   (1995) 92 (11) LSG 39.

irrespective of basic equitable principles or of specific agreement between the co-owners. For the Benefits Agency, therefore, the starting point in applying the market-value test is different from the local authority's starting point under reg 27(2) of the NA(AR) Regs 1992.[1] Nevertheless, *Palfrey* confirmed that a nil valuation will be appropriate in *some* cases,[2] and this represents the correct approach for both local authorities and the Benefits Agency.

However, the Court of Appeal has recently issued a reminder that the 'nil value' ruling in *Palfrey* derived from the facts of that case.[3] In different circumstances, where a brother and sister had inherited equal shares in their mother's house, the sister's share fell to be valued on the basis that an order for sale would give effect to the testator's purpose, and was achievable. In *Palfrey*, on the other hand, co-ownership had a collateral purpose which would be defeated if the property were sold.

The current approach to valuation of jointly owned capital has been helpfully summarised in a memorandum by the Adjudication Officer to the Benefits Agency.[4]

An expert opinion on the market value of the share in question should be obtained. The expert valuer should be asked to take into account the following points:

- that the claimant/resident is assumed to be a willing seller;
- whether the other co-owners would be willing and able to buy the share under valuation;
- whether the other co-owners would agree to the sale of the asset as a whole;
- whether the courts would be likely to order the sale or partition of the property;
- the rights of occupation of the other co-owners;
- whether any of the other co-owners are in occupation of the property, and whether they would be willing to leave;
- any rights enjoyed by occupants who are not owners but who are, for example, tenants;
- any incumbrances secured on the property;
- the legal protection available to a potential purchaser;

---

1   See **9.3.4**.
2   After *Palfrey*, reg 52 was amended to require the Benefits Agency to value a share in a property by taking the market value of the property as a whole and dividing that figure by the number of co-owners, irrespective of whether or not any of them were in occupation. The NA(AR) Regs 1992 were never similarly amended, and in October 1998 reg 52 was amended again, following a Commissioner's decision that the previous amendment was unlawful. (Social Security Amendment (Capital) Regulations 1998, SI 1998/2250, following CIS 3283/1997.)
3   *Wilkinson v Chief Adjudication Officer* LTL 24 March 2000.
4   AOG JSA/IS/35. Note that, since implementation of the Social Security Act 1998, 'decision makers' have replaced adjudication officers.

–   any risk that the legal owners may sell the property and appropriate the
    proceeds, lease the property, or encumber it with secured debts;
–   whether there are planning or other restrictions on the property.

The valuer should be asked to explain what would be the nature of the market
for the share in question and what (if any) comparables have been relied on. The
valuer should also be asked to state whether he or she has any experience or
knowledge of the sale of a share in property in similar circumstances.

As regards enforcing sale of a property, the legal position has changed little since
the implementation of the Trusts of Land and Appointment of Trustees Act
1996. If anything, an order for sale is now less likely than previously. The
case-law under s 30 of the LPA 1925, and based on the doctrine of conversion,
established that the courts would not order a sale so as to defeat the underlying
purpose of a trust for sale in respect of a family home. Since 1996 the doctrine of
conversion has been abolished and trusts of land are no longer underpinned by a
notional duty to sell. It is clear from ss 14 and 15 of the 1996 Act that, where a
sale is sought, the burden will lie on the applicant to show why the order should
be made. Section 15 states that, in determining an application, the court must
consider the intentions of those who set up the trust, and the purposes for which
the property is held.

The CRAG does not reproduce the Benefit Agency's memorandum, but
makes it clear that, wherever there is a dispute as to the valuation of property, or
an interest in property, a professional valuer should be asked to provide a
current market valuation. Paragraph 7.014 states: 'if the local authority is unsure
about the resident's share, or their valuation is disputed by the resident ... a
professional valuation should be obtained'. It is suggested that there should be a
clear requirement to seek valuation in every case, and advisers should always try
to ensure that, where a valuation is put forward, it is supported by expert
evidence. In principle, valuation evidence should be shared with residents, and
advisers should always seek to insist on disclosure.

10.4   BUYOUTS

Paragraph 7.014 of the CRAG sets out the following example:

> 'The resident has a beneficial interest in a property worth £60,000. He shares the
> interest with two relatives. After deductions for an outstanding mortgage, the
> residual value is £30,000. One relative would be willing to buy the resident's
> interest for £5,000. Although the value of the resident's share of the property may
> be £10,000, if the property as a whole had been sold, the value of just his share is
> £5,000 as this is the sum he could obtain from a willing buyer.
>
> The resident's actual capital would be £4,500 because a further 10 per cent would
> be deducted from the value of his share to cover the cost of transferring the interest
> to the buyer.'

As explained in **10.3**, above, the CRAG suggests that the 'market' for an interest in property shared between relatives is effectively confined to the other relatives/co-owners. It follows, therefore, that these people's willingness to purchase the resident's share will determine its value. The above example acknowledges this conclusion, but does not give any indication as to the possible parameters for a valuation. For instance, if the relative referred to above were to offer £2,000 rather than £5,000 for a share in a property which would convert into £10,000 cash on an eventual sale, would the local authority be bound to accept it as being the market value of that share? If the relative concerned is in occupation of the property (which para 7.014 does not make clear), it is difficult to see how the local authority could decline to accept £2,000 as the market value. However, common sense suggests that a buyout for a nominal sum would not be acceptable. Indeed, the local authority might seek to rely on the notional capital rule in such circumstances.[1]

It is suggested that the outcome of a buyout by a relative will be determined purely by negotiation, probably backed up by a valuer's opinion. Advisers should instruct valuers carefully; the AOG's memo provides a helpful model. In many cases, if the capital can be raised, a buyout will provide an effective resolution of a dispute over the valuation of a resident's interest in his or her former home, and may at the same time, ensure that the property remains in the family. It will also avoid any argument as to when the property should be sold, or how much of the proceeds of sale are due to the local authority.[2]

10.5 DISPUTES OVER BENEFICIAL OWNERSHIP

The principles outlined at **10.3** and **10.4**, above, apply whether co-ownership is express or implied. However, where the beneficial interests are not on the title, but depend on a resulting or constructive trust,[3] the local authority will need written evidence setting out the arrangements made between the purported owners of the property, and their intentions as to its use. It is worth noting that finance officers often have difficulty with some of the finer points of trust law, and legal advisers may best serve their clients' interests by offering detailed reasons (and authority) for the position they are taking. Council house purchases, where a son or daughter provides finance to top up a parent's discount, are notorious for raising difficulties on a financial assessment for residential care.

---

1   See Chapter 11.
2   See **10.7**.
3   CRAG, para 7.014A.

10.6 CONSEQUENCES OF TAKING THE VALUE OF THE HOME INTO ACCOUNT

Where the capital value of the resident's home is taken into account by the local authority, so that the £16,000 capital threshold is exceeded, the resident will be expected to pay the full cost of his or her care out of the capital, plus whatever income he or she has available.

Legal advisers should note the following points.

–   The resident will be expected to pay in full as soon as he or she enters residential care on a permanent basis. The local authority has no power to postpone levying its charges until, for example, a property is sold. However, from April 2001, there will be a new disregard on the value of a former home which will operate for 12 weeks from the date of a residents' *permanent* admission to residential care.[1]

–   The local authority has, however, no power to enforce the sale of the property, without taking further proceedings, nor may it withdraw services if its charges are not met. The duty to make residential provision where need exists is not conditional upon payment of an assessed contribution.[2]

–   Where a contribution based on the value of the property is unmet because the property remains unsold, the local authority may protect its position by placing a statutory charge on the property.

–   Where the house is occupied by a third party, the statutory charge will enable the local authority to secure fees which the resident is unable to meet without selling the house over the occupant's head.[3]

–   Income support will not be available where a resident's assessable capital exceeds £16,000. However, where the resident has been in receipt of benefit before entering residential care, the occupational disregard on the value of his or her former home will be extended for at least the first six months in care, provided that the property is put on the market. Once the disregard ceases, benefit will stop.[4]

–   A claim for attendance allowance should be made.[5] There is now strong persuasive authority that 'retrospective self funders' should be entitled to benefit.

---

1   This change is discussed more fully at **10.1**.
2   NAA 1948, ss 22(1) and 26(2).
3   HASSASSAA 1983, s 22; see **10.8**.
4   See **10.7** below.
5   See **14.4.8**.

– Exercise by the local authority of its discretion to disregard the value of a house which is occupied by a third party other than a prescribed family member[1] has important financial consequences. The placement is bound to be more expensive to the local authority than if the residents' capital assets are used to the full extent that the regulations allow. In addition, however, the Benefits Agency, having no discretion in such cases, will always refuse income support, so that there will be no central government subsidy to help the local authority meet its financial obligations.

– Where it is clear, in advance, that the value of the resident's house will be taken into account, and that the resident will have to fund his or her own placement, two options are available. The first option is for the resident to elect 'to go private', that is to make his or her own arrangements directly with the residential establishment, and to remain outside the local authority's sphere of influence. The advantages of this course of action are that the resident will have an unrestricted choice of home, and that attendance allowance may be available to help meet the home fees. Some residents who also qualify for income support may elect to take the 'loophole option'.[2] The disadvantages are that if the resident's capital is eventually exhausted, the local authority may have to take over the care responsibility and may then not be prepared to subsidise home fees which it regards as excessive.

– The second option is for the resident to elect to ask the local authority to assess his or her needs under s 47 of the NHSCCA 1990 with a view to making residential care arrangements under s 26 of the NAA 1948. If the local authority accepts responsibility, it will be able to negotiate a more competitive price with care providers than is likely to be available to a lone individual. The resident will also have the benefit of the quality standards imposed by the local authority on providers of residential accommo-dation.[3] However, it is possible that the local authority may take the view that care is 'otherwise available' to the resident and decline to make the provision.[4]

10.7   DEALING WITH SALE

Here the ISG Regs 1987 and the NAAR Regs 1992 diverge in one important respect. Where an older person who has entered residential care is taking reasonable steps to dispose of an empty property, the Benefits Agency will disregard its capital value for at least 26 weeks from when he or she first took those steps, and for such longer period as is 'reasonable' in the circumstances to

---

1   NA(AR) Regs 1992, Sch 4, para 18.
2   See **14.4.6**. Note the risks attached to loophole funding.
3   See Chapter 6.
4   See **6.9**. Implementation of the Health and Social Care Bill 2000 will prevent this.

enable him or her to dispose of the premises.[1] If no steps are taken, for instance by putting the property on the market, the capital disregard will immediately cease. It may, however, be revived if steps towards disposal are subsequently initiated. The resident may claim income support throughout the period allowed for sale of the property, unless his or her other capital or income resources are above the statutory limits. The net proceeds of sale will then be assessed as capital. The Benefits Agency is often willing to exercise its discretion to extend the initial 26-week period, especially if the property is difficult to sell.

A local authority has no equivalent powers under the NA(AR) Regs 1992. Once the decision is taken to include the value of a property within the financial assessment, so pushing the resident above the £16,000 capital threshold, he or she will immediately become responsible for the full weekly cost of the care bed. The availability of income support for at least 26 weeks (see above) may help to cushion this financial burden. There will, however, be pressure on the resident to realise the capital because he or she will be in debt to the local authority and, as time goes by, there will also be pressure to reduce the asking price of the property, particularly once the Benefits Agency takes its value into account. In recent months, however, there have been important developments in the law relating to attendance allowance, which mean that benefit is now likely to be available pending sale of a property. The position is considered, in detail, at **14.4.8**.[2] Attorneys dealing with sales in these circumstances should be aware that the local authority will almost certainly use its power to charge property[3] if payments fall into arrears. Nevertheless, the attorney may choose to sell the property when he or she judges the time is right.

Example 1
Bill Simpson, a 78-year-old widower, entered a nursing home six months ago following an assessment by the local authority. At that time, his wife was living alone in their home, which they bought as beneficial joint tenants 30 years ago. Mrs Simpson has just died. On her death, Mr Simpson became the sole beneficial owner of the house which is now worth £80,000 and is mortgage free. Mr Simpson's income consists of £67.50 state retirement pension and £50 occupational pension. He has capital of £2,500.

(a) While Mrs Simpson was alive, the local authority properly disregarded Mr Simpson's interest in the house. Now, however, the local authority must take it into account, and must re-assess his capital resources. The local authority will base its assessment on the price quoted by an estate agent for a quick sale. From the date of the assessment, the local authority will require Mr Simpson to pay his own nursing home fees in full.

---

1   ISG Regs 1987, Sch 10, para 26.
2   See Chapter 14. In *Chief Adjudication Officer v Creighton and Others*, the Court of Appeal in Northern Ireland held that attendance allowance is payable where a placement is retrospectively self-funded.
3   See **10.8**.

(b) The local authority will have insisted that Mr Simpson claimed income support before his wife's death because his other income is relatively low. The Benefits Agency will allow at least 26 weeks for the sale of the property before taking its capital value into account. After 26 weeks, or whatever reasonable period the Benefits Agency allows for sale of the house, Mr Simpson's capital will increase by the net proceeds of sale of the house, or by its estimated market value if still unsold, and he will no longer be entitled to income support.

(c) Neither the local authority nor the Benefits Agency can enforce the sale of the house directly. If, however, Mr Simpson is unable to meet his assessed payments to the nursing home, the local authority will seek to secure its position by imposing a charge on his house pending sale, under s 22 of the HASSASSAA 1983.[1]

(d) Had the beneficial joint tenancy been severed before Mrs Simpson died, only a half share in the house would have been available for nursing home fees, unless Mrs Simpson left her estate to her husband. Valuation of that half share would have been governed by reg 27 of the charging regulations.

Example 2
The facts are as in example 1, above, except that Mr Simpson has been a patient in a private nursing home since January 1993.

(a) Mr Simpson will have preserved rights to income support at an enhanced level because he was in residential care before 1 April 1993 (see Chapter 13).

(b) On his wife's death, the Benefits Agency will take into account the value of his interest in the house, but will allow 26 weeks for the sale to take place. If the sale proves difficult, the Benefits Agency may be prevailed upon to exercise its discretion to extend the 26-week period.

(c) Once 26 weeks (or an extended period) have elapsed, the capital disregard will cease and Mr Simpson's income support payments will stop because his capital will exceed the £16,000 threshold. There will then be considerable pressure to undersell the house.

(d) In cases like this, proprietors of residential accommodation are in a difficult position. If the house is not sold within the time allowed by the Benefits Agency, and benefit is stopped, their fees may not be met. They will, however, be reluctant to take steps to evict frail elderly residents. The local authority will have no power to assist in this situation by taking over the arrangements for Mr Simpson's nursing home care, and those advising him may have to consider other possible sources of financial support. This issue

---

1   See **10.8**.

is discussed in some detail in Chapter 13. Readers are reminded that the 'preserved rights regime' will cease to exist from April 2002.[1]

Example 3

John Wilson, a widower aged 79, has lived in the same council house for 30 years. Ten years ago, his 40-year-old daughter, who now lives with him, helped him to exercise his right to buy under the Housing Act 1985 and the house was conveyed to them as legal and equitable joint tenants. The house is now worth about £90,000 net.

Mr Wilson has been admitted to a nursing home following an assessment of his needs. His pension income is about £100 per week and his only savings are £6,000 in a building society account.

(a)   The local authority is not required to disregard Mr Wilson's capital interest in the house because his daughter is under 60 and, it seems, in good health.[2] It has discretion to disregard that interest, because Mr Wilson's daughter remains in occupation,[3] but is unlikely to do so in the given circumstances.

(b)   Both the local authority and the Benefits Agency would take the view that Mr Wilson has a 50 per cent interest in the house. A valuer for the local authority, setting out to quantify this interest, would have to express a view on the existence of a 'market'.

(c)   Mr Wilson's advisers should argue for a nil valuation by the local authority based on para 7.014 of the CRAG. Alternatively, Mr Wilson's daughter may wish to buy him out at a price which the local authority is prepared to accept as representing the value of his beneficial interest.

(d)   Mr Wilson will be able to claim income support, if his actual assessed capital does not exceed £16,000. However, he will not be entitled to the 26-week disregard referred to in Example 2, above, unless he puts the house up for sale.

(e)   If the local authority were to put a value of, say, £30,000 on Mr Wilson's half share in the house, he would then have to meet the cost of his care from total capital of £36,000 until this was reduced to £16,000 (£18,500 from April 2001), when the local authority would be able to assist with fees. A sum of £6,000 is at present free and available. Mr Wilson's daughter might consider helping with the care fees to avoid a sale of the house. Her father should be entitled to the attendance allowance.

(f)   A buyout by Mr Wilson's daughter looks like a better option unless Mr Wilson has a very limited prognosis. She should be advised to put forward a positive offer with support from a valuer if necessary. Taking the initiative is often an effective tactic in cases like this.

---

1   See **15.8**.
2   NA(AR) Regs 1992, Sch 4, para 2.
3   Ibid, para 18.

10.8 THE LOCAL AUTHORITY'S POWER TO CHARGE THE PROPERTY

Where a person fails to pay an assessed contribution and has a beneficial interest in land in England or Wales, s 22 of the HASSASSAA 1983 will apply, and the local authority may create a charge over that interest in order to protect its position.

This power is intended to assist local authorities which are reluctant to enforce debts in respect of accommodation fees. The charge covers the resident's indebtedness to the local authority at any one time, and 'crystallises' on the death of the resident. At that point, the local authority will normally expect the deceased resident's personal representatives to arrange for the property to be sold. If, however, a caring friend or relative is still in occupation, there may need to be a further postponement of sale, and the charge will remain in place. The local authority has no power to sell a property without first obtaining a charging order from the court.

Charges are very common in practice. Whenever a local authority makes arrangements under s 26 of the NAA 1948, and the resident has a house to sell, s 22 of the HASSASSAA 1983 is likely to be used unless the resident is able to pay the care fees in full, using available income and free capital. Advisers should note the following.

(1) Section 22(7) provides that a charge is to be created by a declaration in writing made by the local authority. No other formality is prescribed and the local authority is not required to give notice to the resident. However, the CRAG adds a gloss by stating that 'if the local authority is considering placing a charge on a resident's interest in land, the resident should be advised or assisted to consult a solicitor about this procedure'.[1]

(2) The local authority's interest is registrable as a class B land charge in the case of unregistered land, or as a registrable charge taking effect as a charge by way of legal mortgage in the case of registered land.[2]

(3) Interest runs on the amount charged from the date of the resident's death, but not before.[3] Annex D of the CRAG states:

'It is this Department's view that because a specific power to create a charge is contained in the HASSASSAA 1983, the general powers in s 111 of the Local Government Act [1972] cannot be used. Interest cannot be charged during the resident's lifetime on a debt which is covered by the creation of charge on property under s 22 . . . .'

---

1   CRAG, Annex D, para 3.4.
2   HASSASSAA 1983, s 22(8).
3   Ibid, s 24.

This paragraph makes it quite clear that the local authority should *not* purport to charge interest on the unpaid care fees until after the resident's death.

(4) Imposition of a charge does not sever a joint tenancy. On the death of the equitable joint tenant whose interest has been charged, the other joint tenant(s) takes the property by survivorship, subject to the charge. The amount of a charge cannot exceed the value of the deceased resident's interest in the property.[1]

(5) There is some uncertainty as to the mechanics of imposing a charge on co-owned property. At one time, s 22(3) of the HASSASSAA 1983 provided that the resident's interest under the statutory trust for sale imposed by the LPA 1925 was to be treated as an interest in land for the purpose of imposing the charge. This provision was repealed by the Trusts of Land and Appointment of Trustees Act 1996,[2] which also abolished the doctrine of conversion. However, the CRAG has not yet acknowledged this change. The current paragraph reads:[3]

'It is the Department's view that where one person owns land then his interest is in the land itself and a charge can be registered against that interest under s 22 of the HASSASSAA 1983. However where more than one person owns the same piece of land then their interest is technically in the proceeds of sale of that land and not in the land itself. In this case, s 22(8) of HASSASSAA 1983 has the effect of preventing the registration of an interest in the proceeds of sale of land. It would seem that registering a caution (which affords less protection than a registered charge) is the best step an authority can take in such circumstances.'

(6) A recent amendment to the CRAG states that where a local authority has placed a charge on a resident's property, it should establish the current market value of the property and calculate the resident's remaining interest by deducting the value of the charge and a further 10 per cent for the expenses of sale. Then:

'once the property has been sold, the amount of capital that should be taken into account from the sale of the property is the actual amount of money from the sale minus the actual expenses involved in selling and any debts secured on the property such as a mortgage. The 10% rule is only for the purposes of calculating the value of a property and should not be applied once the property has been sold.'[4]

This amendment does not refer to the fact that, where a property is jointly owned, the market value of the resident's share will have been agreed at the time of the financial assessment. As noted at **10.3**, that value may be considerably less than the resident's eventual share of the proceeds of sale.

---

1   HASSASSAA 1983, s 22(5) and (6).
2   Section 25(2) and Sch 4.
3   CRAG, Annex D, para 3.5.
4   Incorporated in paras 6.011A and 6.015; for further discussion of the '10% rule' see **8.3.2**.

The CRAG now implies that if a resident whose interest in the property has initially been subject to a nil or heavily discounted valuation nevertheless falls into arrears with care fees, so that a charge is registered, the local authority will seek to take up to the whole of his share of the proceeds of sale in satisfaction of the debt, and para 7.014 of the CRAG will no longer apply.[1] Certainly, there is anecdotal evidence that some local authorities are taking up this position. Even without a charge, local authorities may seek to recover care fees if the proceeds of sale substantially exceed the original valuation of the resident's share. This reinforces the view that the possibility of a buyout by relatives (see para 10.4) should always be actively considered.

Example 1
Robert Black owns a house valued at £90,000. He also has pension income amounting to £200 per week. The local authority arranges accommodation for him in a nursing home at a cost of £320 per week. There is no reason to disregard the value of the property, so Mr Black should pay the full cost of the bed because he has more than £16,000 capital.

He refuses to sell the house, with the result that he is only able to pay £200 per week, less his personal expenses allowance. The local authority places a charge on the property as soon as the first payment falls due, and, on Mr Black's death, six months later, the debt is paid.

Example 2
Henry Green, aged 65, enters a private nursing home under arrangements made by his local authority. He owns a house in which he has lived with his younger sister, Muriel, for the last 10 years. Muriel is aged 55. An estate agent has valued the house at between £50,000 and £60,000, and it is mortgage free. Mr Green's only income is his State retirement pension.

The local authority has assessed Mr Green as having capital of £55,000, and, therefore, he is expected to pay in full for his nursing home place.

(a) The CRAG indicates that if the local authority is considering placing a charge on a resident's interest in property, he or she should be advised/assisted to seek advice from a solicitor.

(b) Mr Green's solicitor should ask the local authority why it has not exercised its discretion to disregard his capital interest in the house, because his sister still lives there. The local authority should be prepared to state its reason and, if it has acted arbitrarily or without due consideration, Mr Green may challenge the decision.

(c) Otherwise, the imposition of the local authority's charge will be unavoidable.

---

1   See **10.3**.

(d) If Mr Green dies after 3 years, his sister will presumably inherit the house, subject to the charge, and interest will run from the date of Mr Green's death. The local authority's concern will then be whether to dispossess Mr Green's sister, or whether to postpone enforcement of the debt until after her death.

10.9 DOWNSIZING

Many older people move into smaller, purpose-built accommodation where some level of care is provided. Often this enables them to maintain their independence, notwithstanding ill-health or disability. Where couples are separated because one spouse or partner has gone into residential accommodation, a move into more manageable accommodation may become a high priority for the other.

Once a property is sold, the disregard based on occupation by a spouse or partner is lost. It resumes if another property is purchased within six months,[1] but any capital realised on the sale and not reinstated in the new property will be available to meet a co-owner's care fees.

Para 6.063 of the CRAG sets out a case study:

> 'A person moves into residential accommodation and has a 50% interest in property which continues to be occupied by his spouse. The LA ignore the value of the resident's share in property while the spouse lives there but the spouse decides to move to smaller accommodation and so sells the former home. At the time the property is sold, the resident's 50% share of the proceeds could be taken into account in the charging assessment but, in order to enable the spouse to purchase the smaller property, the resident makes part of his share of the proceeds from the sale available to the spouse. In these circumstances, in the Department's view, it would not be reasonable to treat the resident as having deprived himself of capital in order to reduce his accommodation charge.'

Deprivation of capital and the notional capital rule are discussed, in detail, in Chapters 11–13. This example presupposes that the new property is to be purchased in the sole name of the spouse who intends to occupy it. In those circumstances, a contribution by the resident out of *his* share of the proceeds of sale of the first property could amount to a 'deprivation' were it not for this dispensation. However, para 6.029 of the CRAG indicates that the six-month period of grace referred to above applies to 'capital received from the sale of a former home, where the capital is to be used by the resident to buy another home'. If this disregard is to have any application at all, it must be relevant to a new joint purchase by both partners. In such circumstances, there can be no place for the notional capital rule, and para 6.063 becomes superfluous.

---

1   NA(AR) Regs 1992, Sch 4, para 3; CRAG, para 6.029.

Chapter 11

PRESERVING ASSETS: GIFTS AND NOTIONAL CAPITAL

'The main thing we get correspondence on is people trying to preserve their property from being taken over by the local authority or being sold to defray the cost of care.'[1]

'The system at the moment helps people who are poor, demands that people of modest means make themselves poor before it will help, and affects people to a lesser degree the richer they are and better able to afford the sums required.'[2]

11.1 THE ISSUES

Although we have noted elsewhere that relatively few people over pensionable age are currently in a position to pay for their own care, it is nevertheless apparent that an increasing number of clients are seeking advice on how, if at all, they may be able to mitigate what are seen as the very onerous costs of residential care. As more of the over-60s become owners of their own homes and, consequently, of capital assets which may be available to meet care fees, it is likely that planning for residential and, ultimately, home-based care will become as commonplace as tax planning.

In both cases, the client may be seeking to preserve his or her assets from the State. For inheritance tax or capital gains tax, this means ordering his or her affairs in order to pay as little tax as possible. Planning for care has another dimension, however, which comes from expectations about the balance of expenditure as between the state and the individual.

There is much evidence that older people are experiencing a sense of betrayal by the welfare State, in which they invested such high hopes and expectations during their early years.

The commitment by the post-war State to care for its citizens from 'cradle to grave' sounds increasingly hollow in the new millennium, but for older clients that has been a fundamental expectation, on the strength of which National Insurance contributions will have been paid for many years.[3] Such clients find it unacceptable that, when they are frail and in need of care, modest wealth will quickly be exhausted by nursing home fees; that partners may suffer financial hardship; and that the younger generation may lose an inheritance in respect of which financial sacrifices have been made by their parents. In a study of financial decision-making by people over pensionable age commissioned recently by the DSS, most respondents expressed a predominant wish to have 'something to

---

1   *NOP* Survey, March 1994.

2   Royal Commission on Long Term Care *With Respect to Old Age*, Cm 4192-I (Stationery Office, 1999), para 4.16.

3   See Figure 2.

pass on' to future generations. This wish was often held despite contrary persuasion from children and others.[1]

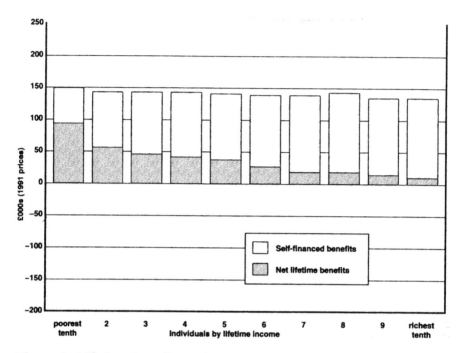

Figure 2. Lifetime benefits and taxes

People pay themselves for around three-quarters of the welfare benefits they receive over their lives; the 'lifetime rich' are net contributors to the system, the 'lifetime poor' are net gainers.[2]

Notes: 1 Individuals are ranked by lifetime equivalent net incomes.
　　　　　2 Calculations allow for share of tax bills necessary to pay for cost of welfare benefits (23% of gross incomes).
　　　　　3 Results use structure and relative generosity of 1991 tax and benefit systems.

Of course, the desire to leave an inheritance is linked to the fact that the vast bulk of care is provided within the family, not by the State.

> 'Rather than, as is sometimes suggested, occupying a monopoly or near monopoly position in the provision of care to older people, the public health and personal social services are, in fact, junior partners.'[3]

There is little evidence, for example, of extensive packages of care being provided for elderly people where they have relatives to care for them, and most of the research shows that family commitment to caring for elderly people is as

---

1   Finch and Elam *Managing Money in Later Life* (DSS, 1995).
2   Hills, J *The Future of Welfare: A guide to the debate* (Joseph Rowntree Foundation, 1993).
3   Walker, A 'The Future of Family for Older People', in Allen and Perkins (eds) *The Future of Family Care for Older People* (HMSO, 1995).

strong as it has ever been. Within this culture, it is clear that the expectation of inheritance may be an element of the inter-generational social contract upon which the family care system depends. 'Policy-makers tinkering with it should exercise extreme caution.'[1]

In addition, a national survey carried out between 1994 and 1997[2] by the Nuffield Community Care Studies Unit at the University of Leicester suggested that most people believe that the State should take primary responsibility for long-term care and that elderly people should not have to sell their homes to pay for residential or nursing home care.

It is clear from all the research that the home is always the main focus of concern in the debate about who should pay for long-term care. Parker and Clarke observe that:

> 'having capital tied up in one's *home* makes it both practically and emotionally difficult to use the asset to pay for care. In the UK context there is, in addition, the sense of betrayal for those who thought that they were buying a home in order to "cascade wealth down the generations" only to find that they will be asked to use it to pay for their own care.'[3]

The Royal Commission on Long Term Care explicitly accepted these findings, which were reflected in its own majority recommendations.[4]

It is not at all surprising, therefore, that older people should seek to protect their assets, rather than see them swallowed up in long-term care fees. The State has, of course, an interest in ensuring that people who are considered to be in a position to pay for their own care should not be permitted to throw the burden on to others. However, the basic freedom of any individual to dispose of his or her own property is fundamental to our system of private law and it follows that any purported inroads into this freedom must be explicit.

A discussion of the means by which the State seeks to limit dispositions whose outcome may be to enhance an individual's entitlements to public funding needs to take this principle as the starting point.

11.2 PROFESSIONAL ISSUES

Protection of assets is a concept which has caught the attention of the media in recent years and, in consequence, has become overlaid with emotional and ethical concerns which legal practitioners find extremely taxing. The fact that The Law Society has seen fit to issue guidelines entitled *Gifts of Property:*

---

1 Walker, A 'The Future of Family for Older People', in Allen and Perkins (eds) *The Future of Family Care for Older People* (HMSO, 1995).

2 Parker, G and Clarke, H *Attitudes and Behaviour towards Financial Planning for Care in Old Age* (University of Leicester, 1997).

3 Ibid, p 26.

4 *With Respect to Old Age*, op cit, paras 4.17 and 4.34.

Implications for Future Liability to Pay for Long-term Care[1] is evidence enough that advice-giving is considered to be a professional minefield. Given the level of client demand for advice, this is an unfortunate situation.

In fact, to a large extent, the debate is about nothing more than sensible financial husbandry. Advice about making wills, creating enduring powers of attorney, equalising assets between spouses or partners, and severing joint tenancies should enable clients to put their affairs in order and, in some cases, to mitigate possible care fees. There is also a growing market in financial services[2] packages designed to help clients to plan for care fees in a tax-effective way, and the needs of many clients will be met by sound advice in this area. Finally, there is no doubt that clients may benefit very considerably from simple advice and information about long-term care and, in particular, about the financial assessment for residential care. Such advice, in itself, may alleviate concerns which frequently arise from reading inaccurate press reports or listening to gossip.

11.2.1   The Law Society's Guidelines on Gifts[3]

The guidelines highlight, in general terms:

- the need for good legal advice;
- the need to be realistic in terms of what advice is put forward;
- the need to identify conflicts of interest; *who* is the client? Paragraph 30 states:

  'Solicitors must also be aware of the possible conflict of interest, or significant risk of such a conflict, between the donor and recipient of a gift ... given the potentially vulnerable position of an elderly client, the solicitor will have to consider carefully whether he can act for the donor and the recipient or whether there is an actual or significant risk of conflict';

- the need to base advice on the particular needs of the client, and not on any 'blueprint'[4] approach.

The above guidelines are, of course, applicable to all legal practice. In addition, however, The Law Society emphasises the need to address particular issues around the gift transaction, viz:

- Does the client have mental capacity?

---

1   These were first published in 1995, and revised in March 2000. They are available from the Policy Directorate at The Law Society, 113 Chancery Lane, London WC2A 1PL.

2   In the Government's response to the Royal Commission on Long Term Care, there is a commitment to consult on the regulation of long-term care insurance (Appendix to *The NHS Plan 2000*, Cm 4818–I, paras 2.38 to 2.40).

3   The Law Society *Gifts of Property: Implications for Future Liability to Pay for Long-Term Care* (1995).

4   This is a reference to various schemes which have been marketed as local authority-proof.

- Has there been undue influence?
- What are the client's financial resources, apart from the subject matter of the gift?
- Does the client appreciate the risk that the gifted property may still be taken into account under the residential care means test?
- Does the client understand that donees may fail to support the donor; die without making provision for the donor; become divorced or insolvent or unable to assist the donor?

11.2.2 Ethical issues

In some cases, a client's instructions will be that he or she wishes to dispose of assets in order to put them beyond the reach of the State in the event of residential care becoming necessary.

Some legal practitioners maintain that such instructions pose ethical questions for them as professionals.

> 'There is of course a moral question about whether it is right that an individual should be able to dispose of assets which would otherwise be used to pay for care and thereby load the cost on to tax payers generally.'[1]

However, most private client advisers engage without embarrassment in inheritance tax planning or advise clients on how to manipulate the tax exemptions available through the middle-class welfare state, and it is difficult to see why the ethical position here should be different. Provided that he or she is not being asked to endorse false accounting, failure to disclose assets or misrepresentation, is it really part of the legal adviser's job to pass judgment on where the balance should lie between the interests of the individual client and the interests of the State? The Law Society's Guidelines provide some reassurance when they state:

> 'The solicitor ... has a duty to ensure that the client fully understands the nature, effect, benefits, risks and foreseeable consequences of making the gift. The solicitor has no obligation to advise the client on the wisdom or morality of the transaction unless the client specifically requests this ...'[2]

It is worth emphasising that the legal provisions which will be the focus of the advisers' attention in these cases, are neutral in their terms. Both the ISG Regs 1987 and the NA(AR) Regs 1992 permit capital which has in fact been disposed of to be treated nevertheless as the notional capital of the donor and to be included in a financial assessment. The regulations are not penal in nature; they simply have to do with the definition of capital and how it is assessed. Even the the provisions in the Insolvency Act 1986 which permit certain gifts to be set aside when the donor becomes bankrupt and which may be invoked, exceptionally, by local authorities are similarly non-judgmental.

---

1   EAGLE, August 1994.
2   *Gifts of Property*, op cit, para 28, revised guidelines.

11.2.3 Risk assessment

A more serious concern focuses on how to assess risk where clients do decide to embark on schemes aimed at shedding capital. Unlike tax law, the relevant provisions in the social security legislation, and now in the assessment regulations made for local authorities, are still relatively undeveloped through case-law. It may be difficult, therefore, to advise with certainty on the likely outcome of proposals put forward by clients, and it is of the utmost importance that clients are made fully aware of this fact. Older clients often seek advice after there has been extensive media coverage of finanical hardship associated with residential care fees and advisers need to emphasise that they cannot always recommend watertight solutions.

Above all, the challenge for the legal adviser will be how to balance the client's wish to protect assets, particularly the home, against the possibility of residential care, and how to protect the client against possible hardship brought about by the misfortunes, or fecklessness or even the abusive behaviour of the younger generation. The Law Society's Guidelines emphasise the importance of enecouraging the clients to undertake a sensible risk assessment.

It is important, however, to maintain a sense of proportion. The Law Society highlights the possibility that donees of property may become involved in divorce or bankruptcy proceedings or may simply become estranged from the donor. When the subject of a gift is the donor's home, any of these eventualities may cause considerable problems. The guidelines do not, however, present the alternative perspective, which is that informal care by family members overwhelmingly outweighs state provision and that inheritance, or the disposal of assets inter vivos, is very much part of the network of intergenerational relationships and obligations on which this informal system is based. Disposal of assets by the older generation may well be perceived primarily as the recompense for family care-givers who have assumed, perhaps over many years, a responsibility which the State would otherwise have had to meet.

11.3 THE NOTIONAL CAPITAL RULE

Wherever direct or indirect State subsidies may be available to the individual citizen, he or she may seek to maximise or accelerate entitlement. If entitlement is based on a capital threshold – as with income support or local authority help with the costs of residential care – the State will have an interest in preventing individuals from disposing of resources prematurely in order to qualify. Therefore, the income support rules (and the supplementary benefit rules before 1988) have sought to control claimants who dispose of capital or income in order to maximise entitlement to benefit. The same is now true of the assessment regulations operated by local authorities when they arrange residential placements.

Such controls exist throughout the benefits and the tax systems. In all cases, the citizen is permitted to organise his or her affairs so as to mitigate tax liability or maximise benefit entitlement provided that he or she acts within the law. In considering the definition of notional capital and how to give appropriate advice, the following two points need to be borne in mind.

(1) As previously observed, all citizens are free to dispose of their assets either during their lifetimes or by will. Any legislation which cuts down such freedom must be explicit in its terms, and any public body or individual who relies on such legislation must carry the burden of proof.[1]

(2) It is not a foregone conclusion that all older people will end up in residential care. Even over the age of 95, the 'risk' factor is only 50 per cent. The average risk for an individual in their mid-70s is 1 per cent.[2]

In analysing the notional capital rules, the starting point must be reg 51 of the ISG Regs 1987. Regulation 25 of the NA(AR) Regs 1992 is directly modelled on reg 51, and the CRAG guidance on notional capital is derived mainly from decisions by the Social Security Commissioners on income support. Such judicial authority as exists relates to reg 51.

11.4 REGULATION 51 OF THE ISG REGULATIONS 1987

Unlike its predecessor in supplementary benefit law, reg 51 of the ISG Regs 1987 is now mandatory rather than permissive. Regulation 51(1) provides:

'. . . a claimant shall be treated as possessing capital of which he has deprived himself for the purpose of securing entitlement to income support or increasing the amount of that benefit except:

(a) where that capital is derived from a payment made in consequence of any personal injury and is placed on trust for the benefit of the claimant;[3] or

(b) to the extent that the capital which he is treated as possessing is reduced in accordance with reg 51A (diminishing notional capital rule).'[4]

Regulation 51(2) adds a gloss by prescribing that capital which would become *available* to the claimant upon application is to be treated as possessed by him or her. Here, as a matter of law, a distinction must be drawn between capital in which the claimant already has a beneficial interest but which he or she may have to take steps to realise (for example an interest under a trust, money held in

---

1   In the author's view, recent decisions by the Scottish Court of Session, for example *Yule v South Lanarkshire Council* (see further at **12.2** and **12.8**) are, quite simply, wrong.

2   *Older People in the United Kingdom* (Age Concern briefing, 1999).

3   The disregard on compensation payments held on trust is discussed at **9.3.5**; the disregard does not operate under a trust set up; reg 51(1)(a) prevents the notional capital rule from applying. Personal injury practitioners need to understand how to protect compensation payments in this way; failure to do so would be professional negligence.

4   The 'diminishing notional capital rule' is considered at **11.6**.

client account by his or her solicitor or money held by the court) and capital which is not regarded as owned by him or her until an application has been made (for example an unclaimed prize on the national lottery). The former is *actual* capital, and only the latter is covered by reg 51(2).

Regulation 51(3) goes still further in providing that, subject to some exceptions, payments made to third parties in respect of a claimant shall be treated as belonging to the claimant. This would catch, for example, household fuel bills or the costs of clothing paid by a relative in order to help out an elderly claimant. Lump sums paid to providers of residential accommodation to top up income support payments for residents with preserved rights also fall within reg 51(3). There is an important planning point here, in that such capital payments may pose problems for residents by taking them over the upper capital threshold or by triggering a tariff income.

In practice, it is reg 51(1) which provides the focus for those who seek to gain entitlement to income support. If it applies, its effect will be to cause capital of which a claimant has 'deprived' himself to be returned, notionally, to his ownership, even if he has no actual means of recovering it. For a long time, this was the ultimate 'Catch 22' in that claimants were denied benefit on the basis that they could be expected to rely for their subsistence on capital which either did not exist or was irrecoverable.[1]

Example

Ian Hamilton has been in a nursing home since 1992, and is claiming income support at the enhanced rate for residents with preserved rights. He has pension income of £160 per week and £5,000 free capital. The value of his house (which is in his sole name) was initially disregarded by the Benefits Agency, because his wife was living there. She has just died. Two years ago, Mr Hamilton put the property into his son's name.

(a) The death of Mr Hamilton's wife is a relevant change in circumstances, and the Benefits Agency will now expect to take the value of the house into account.

(b) If the Benefits Agency considers that the terms of reg 51(1) are met, Mr Hamilton will have notional capital in excess of £16,000, and, therefore, will lose his income support. Unless his son is prepared to meet the home fees, there will be considerable difficulties ahead. The Benefits Agency has no power to take any action against third parties, and no interest in doing so. The local authority is not empowered to take over the residential care arrangements because Mr Hamilton still has preserved rights to income support.[2]

---

1   Now see **11.5** which ameliorates the position, albeit slowly.
2   See **15.4**.

11.5 REDUCTION OF NOTIONAL CAPITAL

Notional capital can, however, be 'notionally' spent. Before 1990, the ISG Regs 1987 did not make explicit provision for this, but it was accepted that notional capital could be reduced over time by reasonable weekly living expenses. Now reg 51(1) lays down an express diminishing notional capital rule, which is linked to the income support that would have been available to the claimant had reg 51(1A) not been applied. Therefore, it is possible to calculate and advise as to the moment when notional capital will be deemed to have been reduced sufficiently to allow income support to be claimed.

11.6 REGULATION 25 OF THE NA(AR) REGULATIONS 1992

The local authority's approach to notional capital differs from that of the Benefits Agency in one important respect. Regulation 25(1) states that 'a resident *may* be treated as possessing actual capital of which he has deprived himself for the purpose of decreasing the amount that he may be liable to pay for his accommodation'. Otherwise reg 25(1) and (2) incorporates reg 51(1), (2) and (3) of the ISG Regs 1987, and reg 26 introduces a diminishing notional capital rule based on the difference between a contribution assessed to reflect notional capital, and an assessment which ignores notional capital.

Clearly, the substitution of the word 'may' in reg 25 for 'shall' in reg 51(1) has considerable significance. The local authority is given discretion as to whether or not to apply the notional capital rule. The same discretion also existed under the old supplementary benefits system, but was removed, as far as income support is concerned, after 1988. It makes sense for local authorities to have discretion because their duty to make arrangements for residential care is independent of their duty to charge for services and of the users' duty to pay assessed charges. If, for example, a frail, elderly resident effectively deprives him or herself of all capital, the local authority may take the view that, unless the capital is recoverable by the resident, applying reg 25 will serve no useful purpose. A mounting debt resulting from unpaid contributions may well not be enforceable even after the resident has died, and resources are therefore needlessly wasted on administration. It would be far better, perhaps, just to assess the resident's income and ignore the notional capital. In such cases, the local authority will have to take account of the Benefits Agency's lack of discretion and the fact that if income support is denied to the resident, the authority's own financial responsibility will increase.

Example
Joseph Bean, a pensioner, gives £20,000 (his life savings) to his son. He retains £2,000 only. He has a retirement pension of £67.50 (2000/2001 rate). The son

invests the capital in his own business. Soon afterwards, Mr Bean enters a nursing home.

(a) In carrying out its assessment of Mr Bean's resources, the local authority finds out about the gift. Mr Bean tells the social worker that he wanted his son to have the money, not the government.[1]

(b) The local authority decides not to seek to apply reg 25 of the NA(AR) Regs 1992. If it takes the £20,000 into account, Mr Bean will be required to pay for his care in full for a few months. As his resources, apart from notional capital, are very limited, a large debt will build up. There are no easy options for recovery open to the local authority and their responsibility to make care arrangements for Mr Bean persists regardless of the financial circumstances.

(c) The Benefits Agency would apply reg 51 of the ISG Regs 1987 and might well decide to take the £20,000 into account as Mr Bean's notional capital. In these circumstances, no income support will be payable until the notional capital is reduced to the £16,000 threshold through the operation of reg 51A.

11.7 WHAT DETERMINES THE APPLICATION OF THE NOTIONAL CAPITAL RULE?

Manifestly, one or other of the notional capital rules will inhibit individuals who may wish to distribute assets before claiming income support or entering residential care. On closer analysis, however, it becomes apparent that the precise scope of the rules is far from certain.

The *Adjudication Officers' Guide to Income Support* (AOG)[2] states that the following questions must be addressed when the State is considering the application of reg 51(1) of the ISG Regs 1987.

(1) Was the claimant the beneficial owner of the capital asset?

(2) Has deprivation occurred?

(3) What was the purpose of the deprivation? Was it in order to obtain entitlement to income support?

(4) Can the notional capital be disregarded?

The CRAG does not offer such a clear analysis of the relevant issues, but it should always be argued that an analogous approach by the local authority is

---

1   The possible implications of *Robertson v Fife Council* (2000) for the situation described in this example are considered at **11.8**.

2   Paragraph 30312. The Social Security Act 1998 abolished the post of Adjudication Officer. All benefit decisions are now taken by the Secretary of State for Social Security. The *Decision Makers Guide* (DMG) has replaced the AOG, but the substance is the same.

appropriate. It cannot be accepted that the approach of two public agencies to the interpretation of virtually identical regulations should diverge.

Issues arising from (1), above, are considered in Chapter 9. Those arising from (2), (3) and (4), above, will now be discussed in turn.

11.8 DEPRIVATION

Neither reg 51 of the ISG Regs 1987 nor reg 25 of the NA(AR) Regs 1992 offers a definition of 'deprive'. The Social Security Commissioners have adopted a 'natural' meaning, namely to bring about a situation where a capital asset previously possessed is no longer possessed. The AOG[1] gives the following as examples of deprivation:

— payment of a lump sum to a third party, either as a gift or in repayment of a debt;

— incurring substantial expenditure, for instance on an expensive holiday;

— creating a trust;

— pursuing an extravagant lifestyle;

— converting money into personal possessions, which would normally be disregarded capital;[2] and

— transferring a house to a third party when it has ceased, or will shortly cease, to be the claimant's home.

The CRAG cites the same examples.[3]

Given any one of these events, the State may take the view that the claimant or resident has deprived himself of actual capital. The specified purpose must then be established.

11.9 PURPOSE

The issue here is often presented, simplistically, as: did the claimant/resident *deliberately* give away assets in order to achieve the specified result? In fact, the analysis of 'purpose' is inevitably complex. Regulation 25 lays down a balancing test which depends, not on the timing of a transaction or its value, but on the establishment of a subjective intention to diminish possible care fees. The test in reg 51 is essentially the same, save for the fact that the Benefits Agency retains no discretion as to whether or not to apply it.

---

1   AOG, op cit, para 30317.
2   See **11.9**.
3   DoH Circular LAC (99) 9, para 6.061.

It is clear from the drafting of both regulations, first that the State must establish purpose, and secondly that this requirement is the only real constraint against wholly inappropriate interventions by public bodies seeking to limit a possible drain on public resources. As a matter of law, therefore, the State must be prepared to justify conclusions which are adverse to the interests of the individual. Experience shows, however, that local authority assessors, in particular, have great difficulty with the decision-making process involved, and with the 'reasonbable' expectations of them. The recent decision by the Scottish Court of Session in *Yule v South Lanarkshire Council*[1] has highlighted this issue.

A 'reasonable' local authority may be expected to explain, in detail, its conclusions as to purpose and the evidence on which they were based. The decisions which have been handed down by the Social Security Commissioners throw a good deal of light on the meaning of 'purpose', and local authority decision-making should be modelled on what is now well-established practice within the Benefits Agency. The Commissioners' conclusions are summarised at **11.9.1**, **11.9.2** and **11.9.3** below.

11.9.1   Possible reasons for deprivation

Where there is no direct evidence as to the purpose of deprivation, all the primary facts must be weighed one against the other before an influence as to purpose may properly be drawn. Hence, the fullest possible information should be obtained as to how the deprivation occurred. The Commissioners have mentioned a number of relevant factors: for example, whether the deprivation was made in return for a personal service; the state of the claimaint's health or personal needs; whether a loan is immediately repayable. The AOG emphasises that the Benefits Agency must look at what motivated the individual in the given circumstances, and at the choices open to him at that time. Were creditors pressing for repayment of a debt, for instance? Was the claimant in fact doing no more than satisfying his need for one of the 'necessities of life'? Did the claimant wish to offer something in return for personal care lovingly provided by family members?

11.9.2   Knowledge of capital limits

There must be evidence that the claimant or resident actually knew of the relevant capital limits at the time of the deprivation. The Commissioners have suggested that the existence of some time-limit might be said to be common knowledge,[2] but they have also made it clear that the individual's whole background must be considered, including experience of the relevant system, advice which is likely to have been received from the family or elsewhere, and his or her level of understanding. Research published in 1995 by the DSS

---

1   See **11.2** and **11.8**.
2   Commissioners' Decision R(SB)40/85.

indicated that older people had very considerable misconceptions about the capital limits for means-tested benefits. In particular, many were unclear about the precise threshold figure.[1] An opinion poll conducted in March 1994, one year after the community care changes, revealed that more than 60 per cent of respondents were unaware, or vague about the then £8,000 threshold for local authority assistance with long-term care fees. Although public awareness may have increased, these findings are nevertheless significant, given the importance for the State in establishing knowledge, and could be used on behalf of an older person to help rebut the suggestion that knowledge should be inferred.

11.9.3 Significant operative purpose

Reducing care fees or gaining entitlement to income support must have been a 'significant operative purpose' of the deprivation.[2] Paragraph 6.062 of the CRAG adopts the same approach for local authority assessments, stating: 'Avoiding the charge need not be the resident's main motive but it must be a *significant* one.' Where direct evidence of purpose is not available, the assessor must find primary facts from which to draw an appropriate inference as to purpose. There is an obvious temptation for the assessor to employ a 'but for' test: to say that, if obtaining benefit or mitigating care charges are objectively foreseeable consequences of deprivation, then it is reasonable to conclude that there was a significant operative purpose. However, both the AOG and the CRAG emphasise that the rest is subjective. The assessor must look at all the circumstances, and is not entitled to conclude that the significant purpose of a deprivation must have been to secure benefit solely because entitlement was a foreseeable consequence. Paragraph 6.063 of the CRAG provides a revealing example:

> 'A resident has £12,000 in a building society. Two weeks before entering the home, he bought a car for £10,000 which he gave to his son on entering the home. If the resident knew he was to be admitted permanently to a residential care home at the time he bought the car it would be *reasonable* to treat this as deliberate deprivation. However, all the circumstances must be taken into account. If he was admitted as an emergency and *had no reason to think he would not be in a position to drive the car at the time he bought it*, it would not be *reasonable* to treat it as deliberate deprivation.' [author's italics]

The 'deprivation' at issue in the above paragraph is the conversion of assessable cash into a personal asset, which would subsequently be disregarded under the regulations.[3] The example clearly supports the view that not only is the test of purpose subjective, but also the assessor must establish that the resident/donor had foresight of either residential care or the need to claim income support. It is

---

1 Finch and Elam *Managing Money in Later Life* (DSS, 1995). The forthcoming raising of the upper capital threshold to £18,500 in April 2001 may create further widespread uncertainty.

2 Commissioners' Decision R (SB) 40/85.

3 NA(AR) Regs 1992, Sch 4, para 8.

not acceptable to draw the inference that avoidance of care fees 'must' have been the donor's significant operative purpose where there is evidence that would point to a different conclusion.[1] There have been cases, for example, where it has been accepted that gifts were made in acknowledgement of the long-term care or support provided by family members for a resident, and not in order to reduce care fees or to gain entitlement to benefit.[2]

It is suggested that financial assessors must distinguish between two situations:

- where an elderly person has disposed of property directly foreseeing his or her own admission to residential care (perhaps because of increasing ill-health or frailty), and intending primarily to obtain entitlement to State support:[3]

- where an elderly person, being in good health, has weighed the possible risks of residential care alongside perceived obligations to family, long-term security and his or her own needs – and has then decided to make a disposition.

In the first situation, it would be reasonable to infer a significant operative purpose of gaining State support, especially if the disposition were made shortly before the claim. As already noted, however, that inference might be displaced by evidence of another paramount purpose in making the disposition (the repayment of a debt, for example) – or by evidence that the elderly person was unaware of the notional capital rule.

In the second case, the notional capital rules should not be applied. They are not intended to cover every act of pure benevolence or every cautious rearrangement of assets undertaken partly in order to minimise risks which may or may not materialise. It would, for example, be unreasonable effectively to reverse the burden of proof by inferring that, because older people do sometimes have to go into residential care, any disposition must carry an intention to avoid care fees.[4]

11.10 TIMING

Neither reg 51 of the ISG Regs 1987 nor reg 25 of the NA(AR) Regs 1992 specifies time-limits for the operation of the notional capital rule. Practitioners familiar with inheritance tax planning are sometimes surprised to find that there

---

1   An extreme example is Commissioners' Decision CIS 621/1991 where the claimant had been warned by the DSS about the notional capital rule, but nevertheless proceeded to make a gift; the Commissioner held that he could not have had, as any part of his purpose, securing entitlement to income support.

2   For example, Commissioners' Decision CIS 242/1993; see **11.11**.

3   DoH Circular LAC (99) 9, para 6.064.

4   See the discussion of *Yule v South Lanarkshire Council* at **12.9**.

is no 'safe period' within which disposals of assets may be made. Where there is a 'deprivation' immediately before a claim for benefit or entry into residential care, the facts may point to an inference that a significant purpose existed,[1] and the State is then entitled to ask whether that elderly person would have engaged in the transaction, at that moment, had he or she not intended to claim benefit or avoid care charges. In R(SB)9/91, for example, the Social Security Commissioner looked at an existing claimant's gift of her house to her two daughters just before she entered a nursing home. He held that the gift was caught by reg 51 because, although the claimant always intended that her daughters should have the house, since its capital value would remove her right to benefit once she became a permanent patient in a nursing home, the timing suggested that obtaining benefit was a significant operative purpose.

However, the facts of the individual case will still be crucial and it is not appropriate to draw inferences from the timing of a gift if there is evidence which points in a different direction. In CIS 242/1993, the Commissioner reached the opposite conclusion on the facts. Here, the claimant's son had cared for his mother for 15 years, and when she went into residential care she gave her share of the proceeds of sale of their jointly owned home to him to be used towards the purchase of a flat. It was accepted that the transfer had been made out of gratitude and not with a significant operative purpose of securing income support.

Where, on the other hand, a substantial period has elapsed between a deprivation and a claim for benefit or entry to residential care, it will be difficult for the State to discharge its burden of proof by making the necessary connection between the two events. Planning to cover an eventuality which may or may not arise is one thing; disposing of property with a significant operative purpose is something else. As both regulations suggest that the purpose of a deprivation must be directed at an event which is clearly foreseen and anticipated, timing must be extremely relevant. The CRAG underlines this approach, stating that it:

> 'would be unreasonable to decide that a resident had disposed of an asset in order to reduce his charge for accommodation when the disposal took place at a time when he was fit and healthy and could not have foreseen the need for a move to residential accommodation.'[2]

Nevertheless, advisers are still faced with a problem of quantifying the risks involved in disposing of assets at a particular moment, and this is not helped by the fact that the practice of the Benefits Agency and of local authorities up and down the country appears to lack consistency.

---

1   AOG, para 30329.

2   DoH Circular LAC (99) 9, para 6.064.

Chapter 12

PRESERVING ASSETS: ENFORCING THE ANTI-AVOIDANCE RULES

'Well-off people are increasingly resorting to various devices to get around means tests – for example giving property to their children. These are worthwhile when the sums involved are large.'[1]

12.1   THE OPTIONS

Application of the notional capital rule by a local authority or by the Benefits Agency is likely to have one of two outcomes:

(a)   it may prevent entitlement to income support – this will be particularly problematic for older people who have preserved rights to income support; or

(b)   it may trigger indebtedness to the local authority because the fee charged for residential accommodation will reflect notional capital.

For the Benefits Agency, the question of 'enforcement' does not arise. If notional capital is assessed and, as a result, the claimant's total capital is determined to be in excess of the £16,000 threshold, benefit stops. This may provoke a desperate situation for the claimant because he or she may be unable to recover the capital which was the subject matter of the gift, or to obtain support from the donee.[2]

Some important sections in the CRAG highlight the decision-making process that the local authority is required to adopt. Paragraph 6.06 states:

'If the local authority decides that the resident has disposed of capital *in order to* avoid a charge … the local authority will need to decide whether to treat the resident as having the capital *(notional capital)* and assess the charge payable accordingly; and then whether:

(a)   to recover the assessed charge from the resident, *or*

(b)   if the resident is unable to pay the assessed charge, to use the provision of the Health and Social Services and Social Security Adjudication Act to transfer the liability for the part of the charges assessed as a result of the notional capital.'

It is clear, therefore, that, having determined that they will assess notional capital, local authorities then have the options of either suing the residents for unpaid fees (and possibly invoking the anti-avoidance provisions in the

---

1   Royal Commission on Long Term Care *With Respect to Old Age*, Cm 4192-I (Stationery Office, 1999), Note of Dissent, para 74.

2   *Ellis v Chief Adjudication Officer* [1998] 1 FLR 184, CA.

Insolvency Act 1986) or of recovering the costs of care from third parties. These options are considered, in turn, below.

12.2   RECOVERY FROM THIRD PARTIES

Section 21 of the HASSASSAA 1983, which was brought into force on 1 April 1993, provides a potentially effective remedy for local authorities where dispositions of property are made with the intention of avoiding or reducing residential care fees.

Section 21(1) refers to a person who 'avails himself of Part III accommodation' and who 'knowingly and with the intention of avoiding charges for the accommodation' transfers an asset to a third party by way of gift, or for a consideration which is less than the value of the asset. In such circumstances, the transferee 'shall' be liable to pay to the local authority the 'difference between the amount assessed as due to be paid for the accommodation by the person availing himself of it and the amount which the local authority receives from him for it'.

This wording seems to imply that the local authority must make an initial decision to treat the subject matter of the gift as notional capital under reg 25 of the NA(AR) Regs 1992 in order to be able to make an assessment which includes the value of the property disposed of. The CRAG confirms this interpretation, emphasising that the local authority should only consider using its powers under s 21 if the asset disposed of is one which 'would have been taken into account for the purposes of assessing the charge'.[1] It would follow from this statement that local authorities may not use s 21 where the subject matter of a gift is disregarded under Sch 4 to the NA(AR) Regs 1992.[2]

Section 21 can be used only in respect of gifts which are made no more than 6 months before the donor begins to reside in Part III accommodation or after admission to such accommodation. In such circumstances, it will often be relatively easy for the local authority to show the deliberate intention required for both s 21 and reg 25.

It should be noted, however, that the drafting of s 21 creates a clear loophole for those seeking to avoid charges. The reference to 'Part III accommodation' links with s 21 of the NAA 1948, and must be taken to mean accommodation which is arranged by the local authority. Consequently, if a resident arranging his own residential care, makes a gift, waits for more than 6 months and then asks for an assessment with a view to the local authority making the care arrangements, s 21 is excluded.

The CRAG explains:

---

1   DoH Circular LAC (99) 9, Annex D, para 2.2.
2   See **9.3.5** and **13.2**.

'the 6 months before residing in Part III accommodation rule for disposing of assets can only be applied from the date a local authority has assessed a person as needing residential care under Part III of the National Assistance Act and has arranged a placement in a local authority home or independent sector home. The 6-month rule does not apply where a resident is self-funding in an independent sector home, has not been assessed, nor had their placement arranged by a local authority.'[1]

Various examples are given, including the following:

'A resident paid for his own accommodation for 2 years, then gave £20,000 to his daughter in March and continued to self-fund until December of that year. The resident then approached the local authority for support, therefore the 6-month rule does not apply. *Although s 21 of HASSASSAA 1983 does not apply in this case the local authority does still have recourse to reg 25(1) of the NA(AR) Regs 1992.*' [author's italics]

The reference in the above example to reg 25(1) underlines the fact that, unlike s 21, the notional capital rule itself carries no time-limit. A local authority can always consider notional capital, provided that it can demonstrate the 'significant operative purpose' required by reg 25. It is sometimes assumed that gifts made more than 6 months before entering residential care are 'safe'; this view is incorrect, as is explained below.

There is no express time-limit on the local authority's right to seek recovery under s 21, assuming that the gift itself is made within the statutory period. The extent of any liability is limited to the benefit accruing from the gift, and, where there are joint donees, the liability is proportionate to the benefit received. The value of any asset will be the amount which would have been realised on the open market at the time of the gift. The previous discussion of shared interests in property will be relevant here. Secured debts and reasonable expenses of sale will be allowable.

Section 21 appears to offer local authorities a realistic method of recovering costs where a deprivation of capital has taken place. It makes sense to recover care fees from those who have benefited from a gift rather than to bring proceedings against a vulnerable elderly person.[2] In fact, the evidence is that, up to now, local authorities have signally avoided using s 21. This position may change in the future if their auditors exert greater pressure to recover contributions.

Example
A year ago, Mr and Mrs Carruthers transferred their jointly owned home to their daughter, Margaret, by deed of gift, in consideration of their love and affection for her. Three months later, Mrs Carruthers, who suffers from Alzheimer's disease, entered a nursing home under a private arrangement.

---

1   DoH Circular LAC (99) 9, Annex D, para 2.1.
2   See **12.4**.

Seven months after that, her capital was reduced to £16,000, and Margaret asked the local authority to assess her mother's needs under s 47 of the NHSCCA 1990. There was no doubt that she needed nursing care. The local authority agreed to make arrangements under s 26 of the NAA 1948, but gave notice that it would be seeking clarification of the circumstances surrounding the gift to Margaret. Three months later, Mr Carruthers died.

(a) Given the relatively short time between the gift and Mrs Carruthers entering the nursing home, the local authority may draw the conclusion that the gift was made in order to avoid care fees. The onus is, however, on the local authority to show that this was Mrs Carruthers' significant operative purpose. It may be, for instance, that the transfer was initiated because Margaret had made financial sacrifices to care for her parents and they, in return, wished to offer her financial security.[1]

(b) Even if the local authority decides to pursue an assessment of notional capital, it will come up against the further problem that, were Mrs Carruthers' interest in the house still owned by her, it would have been disregarded for as long as Mr Carruthers remained in occupation of the house. By the same token, if the subject of the gift to Margaret were regarded as notional capital, it too would have been disregarded under the same rule.

(c) In practice, the local authority may not at first, pay too much attention to the gift, for the reasons stated in (b), above. However, its perspective is likely to change with the death of Mr Carruthers, because the house is unoccupied and appears to be available to meet the costs of Mrs Carruthers' care. The NA(AR) Regs 1992 are defective in that they do not require residents to notify the local authority of any change in circumstances, or give the local authority power to review an assessment on a change of circumstances. As yet, this very important issue has not been raised before the courts.

(d) As a matter of law, Mrs Carruthers no longer has an equitable interest in the house, so it will not be possible for the local authority to place a charge on it under s 22 of the HASSASSAA 1983 in respect of unpaid care fees.[2]

(e) Although the gift was made within 6 months of Mrs Carruthers entering the nursing home, it was not made within 6 months of her 'availing' herself of Part III accommodation as required by s 21 of the HASSASSAA 1983. Therefore, the local authority does not have the option of recovering care fees from Margaret.

---

1   See **12.8**.
2   See **10.8**.

12.3   THE DECISION IN *YULE v SOUTH LANARKSHIRE COUNCIL*[1]

This decision by the Scottish Court of Session provided the first authority on notional capital and local authority powers to enforce decisions based on notional capital.

At the age of 79, Mrs Yule transferred her house to her granddaughter for 'love, favour and affection'. She retained for herself a life rent (life interest) in the property. At the time of the transfer, she was in good health and living independently. Ten months later, she fell and broke her arm. She was admitted to hospital and subsequently her health deteriorated to the point at which she was unable to look after herself. She went to live with her son for a few weeks, but her condition deteriorated further, and she was admitted to a nursing home, some 16 months after the transfer of the property.

The Council's financial assessment form raised requisitions about gifts made within 6 months of entering the nursing home. This is (or was) normal practice in many authorities and the form was completed truthfully by Mrs Yule's son, acting as her attorney under an enduring power of attorney (EPA). Subsequently, the Council found out about the earlier gift and assessed the value of the house as Mrs Yule's notional capital, so bringing the total value of her capital above the £16,000 threshold. The Council then decided that Mrs Yule was not entitled to public funding for her care. Mrs Yule's placement should not have been at risk for the Council's decision that she was in need of care and attention meant that they had a duty to continue with the nursing home arrangements:[2] – payment is not a pre-condition for the service. However, it appears that the Council put pressure on Mrs Yule's attorney and her solicitors, who eventually issued judicial review proceedings on her behalf.

The first limb of the proceedings, which came to court in 1998, concerned vires. Recovery of care fees under s 21 of the HASSASSAA 1987 was clearly excluded because Mrs Yule's financial assessment took place more than 6 months after the transfer. Did the local authority, however, have power to make an assessment of notional capital? Manifestly yes, because there is no time-limit on the operation of reg 25 of the charging regulations. The argument on behalf of Mrs Yule was that s 21 provides the primary remedy for a local authority and is determinative of its enforcement powers. The Court of Session ruled, however, that s 21 creates *additional* anti-avoidance provision, supplementing but not superseding s 22 of the NAA 1948 (the primary charging rule) and the charging regulations. Any past gift can be reviewed with reference to reg 25, subject to proof of the necessary purpose.

---

1   (1998) 1 CCL Rep 571; (1999) 2 CCL Rep 394. The charging regulations apply in Scotland.

2   *R v Kensington and Chelsea RLBC ex parte Kujtim* (1999) CCL Rep 340; see **6.8.2**.

This ruling was in no way surprising; the law was quite clear. However, it highlighted the fact that there is no direct right of appeal against any decision made by a local authority under the charging regulations, however technical, however problematic. As will be seen, the second limb of the decision also highlights the inappropriateness of judicial review as a means of resolving significant financial issues.[1]

12.4   BRINGING PROCEEDINGS AGAINST THE RESIDENT

Section 56 of the NAA 1948 allows local authorities to recover residential care fees as civil debts.[2] As with liable relative contributions, summary proceedings may be used, but 'without prejudice to any other method of recovery'. The limitation period is three years. In addition, s 52 makes it a criminal offence knowingly to make a false statement or representation for the purpose of obtaining any benefit under Part III of the NAA 1948, or 'for the purpose of avoiding or reducing any liability under the Act'. False representations made in the course of the financial assessment would presumably be subject to prosecution, although, in practice, criminal proceedings are unheard of.

There is no reason why, in civil proceedings, a local authority should not recover disregarded capital – the £10,000 'free' capital or other disregarded assets. Ultimately, if the local authority obtains a judgment, which is not satisfied, it may resort to bankruptcy proceedings.

Where the debt to the local authority has arisen as a result of an assessment of notional capital, matters may not be wholly straightforward. The local authority will have to prove the debt by justifying its conclusions as to the debtor's purpose in depriving him or herself of the asset, and its consequent application of the notional capital rule. The authority will have to satisfy the burden of proof, and if its previous decision was arbitrary, or against the weight of the evidence, it should not stand. As has been noted elsewhere, the obstacles to recovery in bankruptcy are 'formidable'.[3]

12.5   SECTION 339 OF THE INSOLVENCY ACT 1986

In most cases, the only purpose in forcing a resident into bankruptcy will be to enable the trustee in bankruptcy to use his powers to set aside voluntary dispositions under s 339 of the Insolvency Act 1986.

---

1   See **12.9**.

2   HASSASSAA 1983, s 17(4) is in similar terms to NAA 1948, s 56 and it must, therefore, be concluded that local authorities also have that option in respect of unpaid home care fees.

3   *Older Client Law Service* (Butterworths), para 985.

Section 339 provides that a trustee in bankruptcy may apply to the court for an order to set aside a gift or other transaction entered into for a consideration, the value of which is significantly less than the value of the consideration provided. Dispositions made up to 5 years before presentation of the bankruptcy petition are open to attack in this way. Where, however, the transaction takes place within the 5-year period but more than 2 years before the petition is presented, the trustee has no powers unless the bankrupt was insolvent at the time of the transaction or became insolvent in consequence of it. Insolvency is presumed where the transaction is with an associate[1] (including spouse/partner or relative) and the contrary must then be proved in order to avoid s 339. If the trustee's challenge is upheld, the court may make such order as it thinks fit for restoring the position to what it would have been prior to the transaction. It may, but is not necessarily obliged to, set the transaction aside.

In its guidance on gifts of property, The Law Society[2] warns of the possibility that local authorities may seek to utilise s 339. In appraising this risk, it is important to reflect on the decision-making process which would lead to such action.

(1) The assessor identifies the fact that a gift has been made and raises requisitions. As a result, notional capital is included in the assessment.

(2) The resident's solicitor argues against the assessment. If the local authority will not change its position, the solicitor may invoke the complaints procedure. Given that the residential placement must be maintained in any event, the local authority is unlikely to take further steps until the complaint is resolved.

(3) The local authority may consider recovering care fees from third parties under s 21 of the HASSASSAA 1983 if the gift was made within the statutory time-limit.

(4) Otherwise, the local authority will proceed to seek an assessed contri-bution based on notional capital. If the resident owns any interest in land, this may be charged under s 22 of the HASSASSAA 1983, in order to secure payments.

(5) As a last resort, once the resident has fallen into debt to the extent of £750, the local authority may commence bankruptcy proceedings. The trustee in bankruptcy having been appointed, he or she may seek to set the gift aside under s 339. The resident is likely to have been solvent at the time of the gift, so that the trustee's powers will extend only 2 years back from the presentation of the bankruptcy petition. The resident may have taken the precaution of executing declarations of solvency. Even where the local authority acts with the utmost expedition, a bankruptcy petition is unlikely

---

1   Insolvency Act 1986, s 341(2).
2   See **11.2**.

to be presented until many months after the resident's admission to the home.

(6)   In the final analysis, too, the court has discretion and the local authority may not achieve the desired outcome. Costs may be substantial whatever the outcome.

(7)   In addition, public opinion is sensitive on this issue, and by adopting a stance which is seen as overly aggressive a local authority may incur criticism from the community which it serves. This, too, will be a factor in the decision on whether or not to use s 339.

12.6   SECTION 423 OF THE INSOLVENCY ACT 1986

This provision is often seen as the local authority's most effective option where use of s 21 of the HASSASSAA 1983 is barred. It allows the court to set aside, at any time, a gift or transaction at an undervalue, where it is satisfied that it was made for the purpose:

(a)   of putting assets beyond the reach of 'a person' who is making, or may at some time make, a claim against the donor; or

(b)   of otherwise prejudicing the interests of such a person in relation to a claim which he or she is making or may make.

Bankruptcy proceedings are not a pre-condition.

The High Court reviewed the law in *Midland Bank plc v Wyatt*[1] and made it clear that the meaning of 'purpose' in s 423 is much the same as for the notional capital rule: 'It is a question of proof of intention or purpose underlying the transaction'. The onus of proof is on the creditor, but, as with notional capital, it is enough if the 'dominant' purpose of the donor can be shown to have been the removal of assets from creditors in cases where there was also an intention to benefit a third party.

Nevertheless, it is not a foregone conclusion that s 423 is applicable to a disposition which has the effect of reducing or avoiding residential care fees. There has been little case-law on transactions taking place otherwise than in a pure business setting, but in *Midland Bank plc v Wyatt* the bank challenged a trust arrangement whereby the defendant gave the equity in the family home to his wife and daughters shortly before setting up a new business, in order to protect them from long-term commercial risk. The judge commented:[2]

> 'I consider that if the purpose of the transaction can be shown to be to put assets beyond the reach of future creditors, s 423 will apply whether or not the transferor was about to enter into a hazardous business or whether his business was as a sole

---

1   [1995] 1 FLR 696.
2   Ibid at 709.

practitioner or as a partner or as a participant in a limited liability company. It is a question of proof of intention or purpose underlying the transaction. Clearly, the more hazardous the business being contemplated is, the more readily the court will be satisfied of the intention of the settlor or transferor.'[1]

These words emphasise the business context of the transaction and the commercial nature of the risks which the defendant sought to avoid. It may be argued that s 423 is not appropriately used by a local authority which has acted under a public law duty in arranging residential care, and is seeking to recover fees under s 22 of the NAA 1948 from a resident with whom it has no contract at all, let alone a business relationship. Certainly, there appears to be no direct authority as to whether a local authority can even be 'a person' with locus standi within s 423.

In addition, the 'proof of intention or purpose' is always going to raise problems for a local authority. Advisers to elderly clients may take some comfort from the dicta of Millett LJ in *Tribe v Tribe*:[2]

> 'It is, of course, perfectly legitimate for a person who is solvent to make a gift of his property, particularly the matrimonial home, to his wife in order to protect her against the possibility of future business failure.'[3]

Can it not be assumed, therefore, that it would be equally legitimate to make a gift which seeks to protect the beneficiary against the *possibility* that the donor might have to go into residential care, and against the adverse financial consequences of such an eventuality? If so, then surely s 423, or indeed reg 25 of the NA(AR) Regs 1992, require evidence of more than the 'possibility' of residential care at the time of the disposition?

12.7 DISCOVERY OF THE SOLICITORS' FILE

The Law Society's guidance raises the possibility of discovery of the solicitors' file relating to a transfer of property, recording advice given and the 'true' purpose of the transaction. It has been held that the court may order discovery if there is existence of fraud and if public policy requires it.[4]

The risk of discovery has to be put into context.

(a) Discovery can only operate in the course of proceedings. In practice, these will be rare.

(b) Discovery, if ordered, would not necessarily reveal evidence of actual foresight of residential care or of the purpose which the local authority is required to demonstrate under reg 25 of the NA(AR) Regs 1992. It will

---

1   [1995] 1 FLR 696 at 709.
2   [1995] 2 FLR 966, CA.
3   Ibid at 987.
4   *Barclays Bank v Eustice* [1995] 1 WLR 1238.

not be enough if the file demonstrates, as it usually will, that the resident disposed of property in order to benefit family members, 'in case' he or she needed to go into residential care.

12.8   CARE AS CONSIDERATION FOR A TRANSFER OF PROPERTY

There is plenty of research evidence that, at the heart of the 'gift transaction' in many families, is the desire by parents to offer recompense to their children for care which has been received. It is not an easy thing for a parent to accept the reversal of accepted social and cultural roles and to receive care from his or her own child.

In view of the importance of informal, family care within the system as a whole there is, or ought to be, some pressure on local authorities to acknowledge reciprocity of family obligation as the main reason for a gift. Some authorities do in fact 'ignore' gifts made to a 'dutiful' son or daughter. Given also that care provided within families will often delay entry to residential care, and so relieve the state of the financial burden, there is an ethical dimension which needs to be addressed.

Legally, there is authority that care provided for a donor by a donee can be regarded as consideration in money's worth. In *Re Kumar (A Bankrupt) ex parte Lewis*,[1] for example, the court accepted that the compromise of a claim for family provision within matrimonial proceedings can be money or money's worth for the purposes of s 339 of the Insolvency Act 1986. Ferris J also accepted, implicitly, that the assumption of responsibility for children, within a marriage, is capable of forming the subject of a 'bargain' between husband and wife and so may provide consideration for a transfer of property.[2]

More recently, in *Ellis v Chief Adjudication Officer*,[3] where an elderly lady transferred her flat to her daughter, upon condition that her daughter looked after her, and paid off the mortgage, Staughton LJ suggested that, although such domestic agreements generally lack an intention to create legal relations and so are not contractually enforceable, there is no reason why they should not be regarded as binding and that the nature of the arrangement will be a question of fact in each case.

Clearly, therefore, there is legal as well as moral justification for the argument that care given may have provided some, if not total, consideration for a gift. *Re Kumar* suggests that, in this context, the fact that the consideration is technically 'past' should not prevent the court in Insolvency Act proceedings at least, from exercising its discretion so as to acknowledge and sanction the 'transaction'.

---

1   [1993] 2 FLR 382.
2   Ibid at 397.
3   [1998] 1 FLR 184, CA.

12.9   THE *YULE* CASE REVISTED

Chapters 10 and 11 demonstrate the complexities of the public law issues which are raised when older people give away their property. There remains, of course, a range of other issues which lie beyond the scope of this book: undue influence; when is a gift not a gift; inter-generational home-sharing arrangements; and proprietary estoppel – to name but a few.

As regards notional capital, there is little apart from anecdotal evidence of what local authorities actually *do*. No applications by a local authority under s 21 of the HASSASSAA 1983 appear to have come to court[1] and only one or two Insolvency Act applications have been recorded. There are obvious reasons why local authorities would wish to avoid such proceedings in terms of both costs and adverse publicity, but increasingly they are being pressed by their auditors to recover fees wherever possible. Therefore, it must be assumed that local authorities are now looking more carefully at the possibility of clawing back notional capital than they may have done in 1993.

The decision in *Yule v South Lanarkshire Council*, referred to earlier in this chapter, provides some important signposts for legal advisers. The facts are stated at **11.2**. Having come to the conclusion that the Council had acted lawfully in making its decision under reg 25 of the charging regulations, the Court of Session subsequently considered whether the Council had acted *reasonably* in so doing or whether, as was contended on behalf of Mrs Yule, there was no evidence to justify its decision. On this second issue, Lord Philip to justify reserved judgment for 6 months, finally ruling, in May 1999, that the Council's decision was not 'so unreasonable that no reasonable authority could ever have come to it'.

The evidence on which this ruling was based consisted solely of the correspondence between the South Lanarkshire Council and the solicitors acting for Miss Deborah Yule, the transferee of the property. By then, Mrs Yule herself was mentally incapable, and there was no documentary evidence signed by her or evidence of conversations with her. In particular, there was no evidence at all that, when the property was transferred, Mrs Yule contemplated going into a nursing home, or that she was in anything other than good physical health for her age. It is possible that she may have been beginning to show signs of dementia, but no diagnosis had been made, and there was a suggestion that she was, at that time, incapable of managing her affairs.[2]

In the course of correspondence, Mrs Yule's solicitors emphasised that she was in good health when she executed the transfer and that her subsequent accident was 'unanticipated'. She had a 'particular fondness' for her granddaughter, and

---

1   Indeed, there is an absence of received wisdom as to the exact nature of such proceedings.
2   The actuarial risk, for an 81-year-old, of needing residential care, is 5 per cent (Age Concern, 1999).

it was always her intention to gift the property to her. Mrs Yule did this in 1995, 'when she was putting her affairs in order'.

The Council acknowledged Mrs Yule's particular affection for her grand-daughter, but recorded that this could have been acknowledged by a testamentory gift rather than a gift inter vivos.[1] It then determined that 'no evidence' had been provided for a reason for the transfer of the property, 'other than with a view to the possibility of her requiring residential or nursing care in the future and attempting to avoid the value of the property being used for that purpose'.

Lord Philip rejected the argument put forward by counsel for Mrs Yule that the South Lanarkshire Council had not established that her purpose was to avoid care fees, as reg 25 requires. He also did not accept that the Council could only reasonably have made the decision it did if there was evidence that Mrs Yule knew of the existence of a capital limit, or that she had foreseen her need for nursing care. He ruled:

(1) it is a 'fact of life' which the Council was entitled to take into account, that people in their late 70s are 'increasingly likely to require nursing home accommodation';

(2) the avoidance of the requirement to meet the full cost of nursing home accommodation provided a *motive* for making the gift, and, in so far as any other motive or explanation was provided, the Council was entitled to reject it;

(3) given that there is no right of appeal under the NA(AR) Regs 1992, the weight given by the Council to particular pieces of evidence was entirely a matter for it and not open to challenge. It had no power to compel the provision of information and had to determine the purpose of the transfer from the information which had been provided. It was therefore entitled to infer the true purpose of the transfer without any specific finding of the state of knowledge or intention of Mrs Yule;

(4) there was no basis for a conclusion that the Council's decision was so unreasonable that no reasonable authority could have made such a decision.

12.9.1   Implications of *Yule*

Although the Scottish primary and secondary legislation is effectively the same as English law in respect of the issues raised in this case, the CRAG does not apply in Scotland, and at the relevant time, paras 6.063 and 6.064 of the CRAG, which have previously been discussed at some length[2] were not in issue in

---

1   This approach appears to deny people like Mrs Yule the right to decide between an inter vivos transfer of property, and a post-mortem gift of which the effective date is uncertain.

2   See **11.9**. The equivalent Scottish guidance did not have the same authority.

relation to Mrs Yule. Nevertheless, the suggestion by Lord Philip that the absence of a direct right of appeal meant that the Council's decision was administrative rather than judicial and so could be based on less rigorous enquiry than, say, a decision made by the Benefits Agency in identical circumstances, is deeply worrying.

As it stands, the *Yule* decision effectively reverses the burden of proof and encourages local authorities to become more assertive about clawing back gifts, without clearly laying down a minimum standard of reasonableness in making decisions effectively to expropriate property which has been lawfully transferred. The closely reasoned decisions of the Social Security Commissioners are sidelined by *Yule*, but the proceedings in that case demonstrate only too clearly the unsuitability of judicial review for determining complex issues of substantive law.[1]

12.9.2 *Robertson v Fife Council*

The Court of Session has now handed down a further decision on notional capital. In *Robertson v Fife Council*[2] the judge effectively reiterated Lord Philip's conclusions in circumstances where the Council had expressed the view that any transfer carried out for no consideration or legal obligation was prima facie to be treated as a 'deliberate deprivation' to avoid care fees, and where the transfer in question had been made some 2½ years before the need for residential care arose.

Obviously there is an urgent need for clarification of the law in this area. It is quite unacceptable that local authorities can be permitted so easily to curtail the fundamental right of disposition associated with ownership of property, without being put to the test, in circumstances where an individual's only real asset may be at stake, and where the Benefits Agency, dealing with an income support claim, would adopt an altogether different approach.

---

1   The Inner House of the Court of Session has now upheld an appeal brought on behalf of Mrs Yule (August 2000). The reasoning is very much the same as in the first instance decision. The court observed that the charging regulations have to be looked at in a different light from the regulations concerned with provision for income-related benefits, not least because the purpose of the individual may have been formed possibly some time ahead of the prospect that he or she might require to enter such residential accommodation. This part of the ruling is unacceptably vague, and appears to suggest that any gift made at any time may fall foul of the notional capital rule. It demonstrates only too clearly the human rights implications of the present decision-making process (see **12.9.3**). In addition, an inference was drawn that Mrs Yule may have lacked mental capacity when she transferred her house to her granddaughter, which raises serious questions as to whether the notional capital rule, relying as it does on 'purpose', should have been at issue in the first place (a transcript of the decision may be obtained from www.scotcourts.gov.uk/options).

2   See **6.9.1**.

12.9.3   Human rights implications

The implementation, in October 2000, of the Human Rights Act 1998 is likely to force significant change. It is difficult to see how a decision by any local authority on notional capital could comply with Article 6 of the European Convention on Human Rights when the authority has a financial interest in the outcome. There is already a good deal of European case-law under Article 6(1) which, in respect of the determination of an individual's 'civil rights and obligations', requires:

−   the right to an independent and impartial tribunal;
−   the right to disclosure;
−   the right to an 'adversarial hearing';
−   the right to reasons; and
−   the right to have decisions made within a reasonable period.

As a general rule, Article 6(1) will apply in welfare benefits cases and, by extension therefore, in decisions made under the NA(AR) Regs 1992. It is far from clear that the possibility of judicial review would satisfy the requirements of Article 6(1).[1] Significantly, the Government has already taken steps to comply with Article 6 in respect of housing benefit review boards, which are operated by local authorities to hear appeals against housing benefit decisions, made by local authorities. From April 2001, these appeals will be taken over by the (independent) Appeals Service.

---

1   See, recently, *Kingsley v UK* (Application No 35605/97) (2000) *The Times*, January 9, where the European Court of Human Rights held that the nature of judicial review proceedings which restricted the court to examining the quality of the decision-making process rather than the merits of the decision meant that the applicant had not received a fair hearing under Article 6(1).

Chapter 13

PRESERVING ASSETS: DISREGARDS AND TRUSTS

'You are always impartial as a solicitor. Your training is not to judge. Everyone is entitled to protect their assets and I don't blame them for maximising the possibilities, as long as it is legal and the older person is OK.'[1]

13.1 THE POSSIBILITIES

The NA(AR) Regs 1992 and the ISG Regs 1987 offer scope for dispositions which are, for one reason or another, 'protected' against the operation of the donor or settlor. The analysis offered in this chapter is supported by decisions of the Social Security Commissioners. Obviously it is important for advisers to be aware if the rules contain loopholes which may benefit their clients.

13.2 USING DISREGARDS

Regulation 46 of the ISG Regs 1987 and reg 21 of the NA(AR) Regs 1992 provide that specified assets will be disregarded by the State in assessing whether an individual has capital in excess of the prescribed threshold. Schedule 10 to the ISG Regs 1987 and Sch 4 to the NA(AR) Regs 1992 contain extended lists of such assets. Chapter 9 contains a detailed explanation of the range and scope of the disregards, but readers are reminded of the following, particularly important, examples:

(a) the capital value of a resident's interest in his or her home, or former home, which is occupied by a specified person;

(b) the value of the right to receive any income under a life interest and from a life rent;

(c) personal possessions, except those acquired with the intention of reducing capital for the purpose of claiming benefit or reducing residential care fees;

(d) future interests in property (except a landlord's reversion on a lease); and

(e) the surrender value of a life insurance policy (or a bond with an element of life insurance).[2]

The origins of the capital disregards are mysterious, and it is difficult to justify their existence in terms of any equity, as they allow certain people who may in no sense be 'in need' to access public funding whilst denying it to others who

---

1   *Ethical Dilemmas and Administrative Justice: perceptions of social and legal professionals towards charging for residential and nursing home care* (University of Hull, 2000) at p 10.

2   CRAG, para 6.028. As in Chapter 9, references in this chapter to specific regulations are to the NA(AR) Regs 1992, unless otherwise stated.

may have equal or indeed fewer assets. For example, resident A who has invested in fine art and investment bonds and is worth £250,000 may look to the State to subsidise his care if his assessable income will not meet the cost of a residential placement. Resident B, on the other hand, with £25,000 in investments, will be required to pay for his own care by disposing of his shares until the value of the portfolio is reduced to £16,000.[1]

The rules are arbitrary and lend weight to the Royal Commission's criticisms of the complexity and unfairness[2] of the present funding system. However, for as long as the present rules are in place some older people have the opportunity to benefit from them, and advisers must ensure that relevant information is made available to these clients. Schedules 4 and 10 offer opportunities for appropriate arrangements or rearrangements of assets, and should always be taken into consideration when clients are considering investing in long-term care insurance.

Given the above comments, what is the position if assessable capital is converted into disregarded capital? Are the converted assets sheltered from care fees? Schedule 4, para 8 disregards personal possessions 'except those which had or have been acquired by a resident with the intention of reducing his capital in order to satisfy a local authority that he was unable to pay for his accommodation at the standard rate or to reduce the rate at which he would otherwise be liable to pay for his accommodation'. Schedule 10, para 10 of the ISG Regs 1987 contains an equivalent provision.

Clearly, therefore, the acquisition of personal assets, with the relevant purpose, will attract the notional capital rule. The CRAG gives an example of a resident who draws £2,000 out of the building society, purchases a diamond ring and gives it to her daughter.[3] The act of 'deprivation' is the purchase of the ring, and the local authority may decide to assess as notional capital the cash of which the resident deprived herself. The ring itself is a disregarded asset, and is not assessable.

None of the other paragraphs of Sch 4 qualifies a disregard in the same way as para 8. However, the Social Security Commissioners seem to accept that whenever cash is converted into a disregarded asset, deprivation will be an issue, given the intention to avoid care fees. In Commissioners' Decision CIS 109/1994 and CIS 112/1994, purchases of an annuity and a life insurance policy (both disregarded assets) were in issue. These decisions make sense if 'deprive' is understood to mean 'cease to possess'. They emphasise that caution is needed when purchasing annuities or long-term care insurance in order to

---

1   This figure goes up to £18,500 in April 2001.
2   Royal Commission on Long Term Care *With Respect to Old Age*, CM 4192-I (Stationery Office, 1999), para 4.1.
3   DoH Circular LAC (99) 9, para 6.058.

generate income for care fees, because the price paid may be assessed as notional capital, with adverse consequences.[1]

13.3 DISREGARDING NOTIONAL CAPITAL

The regulations appear to encapsulate the principle that notional capital may be disregarded in the same way as actual capital.

Regulation 21 of the NA(AR) Regs 1992 states:

'(1) the capital of a resident to be taken into account shall, subject to paragraph (2), be the whole of his capital calculated in accordance with this Part [Part III: 'Treatment of Capital'] and any income treated as capital . . . .

(2) There shall be disregarded in the calculation of a resident's capital under paragraph (1) any capital, where applicable, specified in Schedule 4.'[2]

The CRAG clarifies this further by saying that 'The local authority should only consider questions of deprivation of capital when the resident ceases to possess capital which would otherwise have been taken into account'.[3]

It gives an example of the gift of a diamond ring by an elderly lady just before she enters a residential home, and advises that 'the local authority should not consider deprivation as, had the ring still been possessed, it would not be taken into account as capital'. There is, of course, an assumption that the ring had not been recently purchased.[4]

The AOG states unequivocally that notional capital is calculated in the same way as actual capital and that appropriate disregards should be applied.[5] A further example is given:

'A claimant gave away her interest in the property occupied as her home. She did this to retain entitlement to income support when she entered a nursing home. Although she was treated as having a sum of notional capital which represented the value of her former interest the notional capital was disregarded whilst she lived in the property.'

The conclusion must be that, for as long as capital which could legitimately be assessed as notional capital is held in disregarded form, its value cannot be taken into account. The Social Security Commissioner has confirmed this in a robust decision[6] where the appellant had transferred his former home to his parents in consideration of natural love and affection 3 months before claiming income

---

1   It should be noted that it is by no means certain that such transactions would be identified by the financial assessment. If sufficient income is generated, there will be no room for arguments about 'deprivation'.
2   ISG Regs 1987, reg 46 is in similar terms.
3   DoH Circular LAC (99) 9, para 6.058.
4   See **12.2**.
5   Paragraph 30337.
6   Commissioners' Decision CIS 231/1991.

support. By that time, he had moved to a new home which was disregarded in the assessment, but the value of the transferred property was taken into account by the adjudication officer as notional capital. The Commissioner held as follows.

(a) The capital disregards in Sch 10 apply to notional capital as well as to actual capital.

(b) Even if the appellant had transferred the property for the purpose of obtaining income support, its value was to be disregarded because it was occupied by close relatives of the appellant who were over the age of 60.[1] He added:

> 'It is not necessary that the disregard under Sch 10 should have been applicable before the claimant deprived himself of the capital . . . .'

The same principles must apply to the capital disregarded by under the charging regulations.

Example 1

Mr and Mrs Clark are legal and equitable joint tenants of their home. Mrs Clark has lived in a nursing home since February 1993 and has preserved rights to income support. She severs the equitable joint tenancy and transfers her interest in the house to her son.

(a) Mrs Clark's capital interest will be disregarded for income support purposes as long as her husband remains in occupation of the house.[2]

(b) Severing a joint tenancy does not constitute a 'deprivation'.[3]

(c) Mrs Clark's gift to her son is technically a 'deprivation' within reg 51(1) of the ISG Regs 1987. At present, however, the substance of the gift is in disregarded form and will remain so as long as Mr Clark is alive and is living in the house. It appears that Mrs Clark has no duty to disclose to the Benefits Agency the change in her circumstances as it will not affect her entitlement to benefit for the time being. If Mrs Clark predeceases her husband, the Benefits Agency will have no interest in the gift.

(d) If Mr Clark predeceases his wife, the Sch 10 disregard of her interest in the house will cease to operate unless another elderly or incapacitated member of the family continues to be in residence (Sch 10, para 4). Mrs Clark should notify the Benefits Agency of Mr Clark's death. At that point, her gift may be disclosed and the decision-maker may seek to apply the notional capital rule. Depending on how much time has passed, however, the case may not be clear cut. Can the officer establish, for example, that Mrs Clark had the necessary 'significant operative purpose' when she made

---

1　　See **10.2**.
2　　ISG Regs 1987, Sch 10, para 14.
3　　DoH Circular LAC (99) 9, para 6.010.

the gift, bearing in mind that it was by no means evident that she would outlive her husband?

Example 2

Anne Wright, who is 78 and a single parent, has a daughter with severe learning difficulties. Last year, she transferred her house to a voluntary organisation on the understanding that they would provide care for her daughter, at home, for the rest of her life. Mrs Wright has just had a stroke, and needs residential care.

(a) The transfer to the charity is a 'deprivation' within reg 25 of the NA(AR) Regs 1992.

(b) The local authority ought to ignore the transfer because the transaction effectively relieves it of responsibility for Mrs Wright's daughter. However, there is no guarantee that such a pragmatic view will be taken, although an intervention by Mrs Wright's adviser might assist in steering the local authority towards a sensible outcome.

(c) In any event, the situation is analogous to that in Commissioners' Decision CIS 231/1991. Mrs Wright's daughter is clearly incapacitated. Consequently, even if the local authority is inclined to treat the house as Mrs Wright's notional capital, the disregard based on occupation by a relative, who is also incapacitated,[1] will apply as it would if the house were still Mrs Wright's actual capital.

13.4 THE TREATMENT OF LIFE INTEREST TRUSTS AND POWERS OF ADVANCEMENT

Any reasonably sophisticated means test has to address the treatment of capital which is held on trust, and may produce income for a beneficiary. As has previously been explained,[2] a beneficial interest held under a fixed trust is assessable, unless it can be regarded as a 'future interest' which will be disregarded under the regulations.[3] Where a beneficiary is entitled to the income, that too is assessable, even if it is retained within the trust. Discretionary trusts raise different issues and will be considered at **13.5**.

As regards life interest (interest in possession) trusts, historically it has always proved difficult for legislators to devise:

– a means of assessing capital held under such trusts;[4] and
– an appropriate approach to trustees' powers to advance capital, which may exist either under the Trustee Act 1925, or under an express provision.

The present legal position may be summarised as follows.

---

1 NA(AR) Regs 1992, Sch 4, para 2; see **10.2**.
2 See **9.3.3**.
3 NA(AR) Regs 1992, Sch 4, para 5; ISG Regs 1987, Sch 10, para 5; see **13.2**.
4 See, for example, the mind-blowing discussions by a Tribunal of Commissioners in R(SB) 43/84.

(a) A simple (unprotected) life interest has two elements:

  –   the value of the lifetime right to future income from the trust fund, which is a saleable capital resource; and
  –   an income resource, which is the income actually derived from the trust fund.[1]

(b) The value of the lifetime right to receive income (the 'capital value') is disregarded under the regulations.[2]

(c) A discretionary power to advance/appoint capital to the lifetime benefici-ary should not, in principle, give rise to notional capital, on which the claimant might be assessed. The position should be the same whether or not the object of the power also has the life interest.

(d) Income derived from the trust is to be treated as capital.[3]

(e) The creation of a life interest trust may clearly be a 'deprivation' of property within regs 25 or 51 of the NA(AR) Regs 1992. If the settlor retains the life interest, the analysis must be that he has deprived himself only of part of the capital value of the property.

(f) However, it may be argued that the creation of the trust bypasses the notional capital rule because it creates interests which are to be disregarded under the assessment rules. The analogy is with Commissioners' Decision CIS 231/1991. The beneficial life interest is disregarded under the NA(AR) Regs 1992, Sch 4, para 11 and the reversionary interest under Sch 4, para 5.[4]

Example
Harry Brown, a widower, settles his house worth £120,000 on himself for life, with remainder to his two adult children. A year later, he has to go into a nursing home.

(a) For as long as Mr Brown remains in occupation of the house, its value will be disregarded if, for example, he claims income support.[5]

(b) In addition, his occupation will be protected against third parties (if, for example, he falls out with his children, or if one or both of them become bankrupt) by virtue of his equitable life interest.

(c) When Mr Brown is assessed by the local authority, the capital value of his life interest falls to be disregarded under Sch 4, para 11 of the charging regulations. The disregard is indefinite, and is not dependent on Mr Brown's occupation of the house.

---

1   See R (SB) 43/84 (op cit).
2   NA(AR) Regs 1992, Sch 4, para 11; ISG Regs 1987, Sch 10, para 13.
3   NA(AR) Regs 1992, reg 22(4).
4   ISG Regs 1987, Sch 10, paras 5 and 13. See the discussion at **13.3**.
5   Ibid, Sch 10, para 1.

(d) If the local authority assessor is considering an assessment of notional capital, he or she will have to contend with the fact that the subject of Mr Brown's 'deprivation' appears to be the interest in the property which is now owned by his children, and that this constitutes a reversionary or 'future' interest which is to be disregarded under para 5.

(e) Consequently, whatever the actual purpose of the trust, the two disregards protect the value of the property from assessment, so that reg 25 is excluded.

The life interest trust has practical advantages for the lifetime beneficiary and his or her family.[1] Occupation of the home is protected against all comers and the burden of upkeep can properly be passed on, or shared. The arrangement is straightforward and easy to comprehend, and the use or abuse of discretion by trustees is more limited than in a discretionary trust. The property may be let if the lifetime beneficiary goes into residential care, and the income used to meet care fees.[2]

There is one caveat. In *Yule v South Lanarkshire Council*, a recent ruling by the Scottish Court of Session, a gift of property with reservation of a life rent (life interest) was considered in the context of a decision by the local authority to assess the value of the property as notional capital. The decision, and its general implications, are discussed at **12.9**. The existence of the life rent was ignored by the Court of Session, but it ruled that the local authority had acted 'reasonably' in applying the notional capital rule. The decision cannot be regarded as providing any authority on the possible protective value of a life interest trust, but it will give confidence to local authorities and, in the absence of a direct right of appeal against a financial assessment, will no doubt encourage authorities to investigate trust arrangements more carefully than they may have done in the past.

13.5 DISCRETIONARY TRUSTS

Many practitioners[3] and local authority finance officers consider that discretionary trusts will be effective to shelter assets. Detailed analysis supports this view, subject, however, to an important proviso (see (2) below). The position is as follows.

The CRAG states:

'where payments are made wholly at the discretion of the trustees and there is no absolute entitlement either to capital or income, only take into account payments

---

1   Advisers must, of course, be mindful of the tax implications of any trust arrangement.
2   A local authority might require the property to be let on the basis that the resident is entitled to the income which is 'available' to him or her.
3   See, for example Neilson, W *Residential Care Fees, Defend the Assets!* (Spinning Acorn, 2000).

which are actually made. Do not assume notional capital or income from a discretionary trust'.[1]

(1) This advice reflects the fact that although capital or income which is 'available' to a resident would normally fall to be treated as her/his notional capital or income, assets held within a discretionary trust are expressly exempted.[2] Consequently, for as long as assets are held within a discretionary trust a beneficiary has no assessable resources. Payments out, whether of income or capital, are, of course, assessable.

(2) The transfer of the trust property to trustees upon discretionary trusts will be a 'deprivation' within reg 25 or reg 51 if the settlor ceases to have a beneficial interest in the property. From an assessor's point of view, the corpus of the trust property may be assessable as notional capital; the fact that individual beneficial interests are discretionary will be irrelevant. Where, however, the settlor is named as one of the beneficiaries of the trust the situation changes.[3] His interest, being discretionary, cannot be quantified and, consequently, it will also be impossible to quantify the extent to which he has deprived himself of capital. The notional capital rule is therefore excluded.

(3) Where the settlor's house is the major trust asset, it will be important to ensure that his continued occupation is wholly at the trustees' discretion.

(4) Payments made out of the discretionary trust are assessable, as explained above. The CRAG points out, however, that such payments are effectively 'voluntary' payments.[4] This means that they can be used to pay top-up fees in respect of beneficiaries who are in residential care or to purchase extra items for them. Provided that the payments are effective under reg 25(3), and are not taken into account as income of the resident, they offer a useful means of providing 'extras' for beneficiaries without causing them to forfeit public funding.

The discretionary trust model forms the basis of some of the off-the-shelf schemes which are being marketed by non-solicitor services. The Law Society is concerned that some of these schemes fail to take into account individual circumstances, and warns against them in its Guidelines on Gifts. Nevertheless, discretionary trusts are extremely flexible vehicles for protecting both individuals and assets, given appropriately skilled draftsmanship and proper management.

As with life interest trusts, advisers must always be mindful of possible tax consequences.

---

1   DoH Circular LAC (99) 9, para 10.020.
2   NA(AR) Regs 1992, regs 17 and 25 and ISG Regs 1987, regs 42 and 51. Strictly speaking, this exemption is unecessary if there can never be 'entitlement' or availability in respect of a discretionary trust. However, it avoids argument.
3   Possible tax consequences will need to be considered in relation to this model.
4   DoH Circular LAC (99) 9, para 10.021.

Chapter 14

USING WELFARE BENEFITS TO FUND
RESIDENTIAL CARE

'A proper assessment should be made of the amount of benefits, including disability benefits, which come back into the system to pay for care.'[1]

14.1 INTRODUCTION

The importance of identifying entitlement to certain welfare benefits for clients living in the community has already been noted (see Chapter 8). Once clients enter residential care homes or nursing homes, the interface between the rules for claiming certain benefits and the local authority's assessment regulations becomes very complex. Good and timely advice in this area will often result in measurable value for clients.

14.2 WHAT BENEFITS?

The benefits to be considered in this chapter are the attendance allowance; the disability living allowance (care component and mobility component) and, to a lesser extent, income support. A full discussion of eligibility for these benefits lies beyond the scope of this book, and readers are referred to the various benefit guides listed at the end of Chapter 7 for more detailed information. The relevant legal rules are to be found in ss 64–67 and 71–76 of the SSCBA 1992 and in the Social Security (Attendance Allowance) Regulations 1991 (AA Regs 1991) and the Social Security (Disability Living Allowance) Regulations 1991. The scope for entitlement, in brief, is as follows.

14.2.1 Attendance allowance and disability living allowance (care component)

Both these benefits are available for people who need personal care. The former can now be claimed only by older people over the age of 65, whilst the latter is available to any claimant below the age of 65[2] who meets the prescribed conditions. Once a successful claim has been made, both benefits may continue in payment for as long as the claimant lives, unless circumstances change. Most of the entitlement rules are identical for both benefits. In each case, the

---

1 Royal Commission on Long Term Care *With Respect to Old Age*, Cm 4192–I
    (Stationery Office, 1999), para 4.5.
2 From October 1997, disability living allowance cannot be claimed for the first time if
    the claimant has reached the age of 65. Social Security (Disability Living Allowance)
    Regulations 1991, SI 1991/2890, reg 3(1), (9).

maximum benefit payment will be £53.55 per week (2000/2001 rates).[1] The majority of older people who fall within the conditions of entitlement are in fact paid the highest rate of benefit.

Both attendance allowance and disability living allowance (care component) (DLA (care)) are non-contributory, and, therefore, are available irrespective of a claimant's other resources.

14.2.2   Disability living allowance (mobility component)

This benefit is available for people who are unable to walk or who have difficulty in walking. The present rules cover physical disability and also some types of mental incapacity. Older people with Alzheimer's disease may, for instance, establish entitlement to this benefit alongside entitlement to either attendance allowance or DLA (care).

The mobility component is non-contributory and non-means tested. Entitlement must now be established before the claimant's sixty-fifth[2] birthday, but may then continue until the claimant dies, assuming that the disability remains.

The higher rate of the mobility component is now £37.40 per week (2000/2001 rates).

14.2.3   Income support

Unlike the other benefits described in this chapter, income support is 'income related' or means tested. It is available for those whose resources fall short of their 'applicable amount' as determined by the legislation.

The applicable amount for a person entering a registered residential care home or nursing home after 1 April 1993 comprises the following three elements.

(1)   The first is a fixed personal allowance, which is currently £52.50 for an individual and £81.95 for a couple (2000/2001 rates).

(2)   The second is premiums, that is payments targeted at certain types of need. Older people are favoured above other groups in the system in that they are often eligible for several premiums which are capable of raising their applicable amount very significantly in some cases.

(3)   The third is relevant housing costs. There is a flat rate residential allowance of £61.30 per week (£68.20 per week for placements in the Greater London area).[3] This allowance is not available for people living in unregistered private sector homes or in local authority Part III accommodation.

---

1   New benefit rates, which will come into effect in April 2001, are set out in Appendix 3.
2   See DMG Memo Vol 10 1/100.
3   2000/2001 rates.

This model of entitlement closely resembles that for older people living in the community whose resources are limited (see Figure 3). For people with preserved rights, however, the applicable amount consists simply of a fixed allowance based on the type of residential accommodation plus a small personal expenses allowance.[1] There is a further prescribed variation of the applicable amount for people resident in Part III accommodation.[2] In all cases, the capital thresholds for claimants in residential care are £16,000 and £10,000 for 2000/2001 and will rise to £16,500 and £11,500 in April 2001. The equivalent thresholds for claimants living in the community are £8,000 and £3,000. This

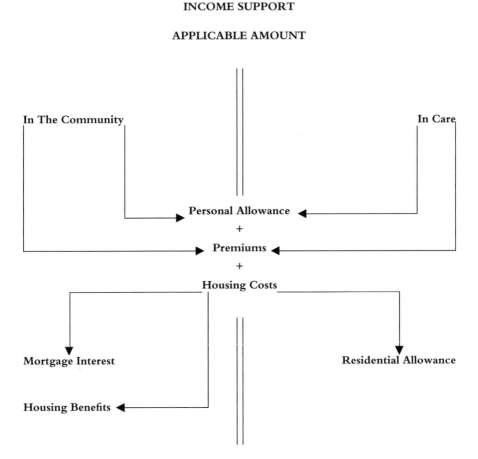

INCOME SUPPORT

APPLICABLE AMOUNT

In The Community

In Care

Personal Allowance

+

Premiums

+

Housing Costs

Mortgage Interest

Residential Allowance

Housing Benefits

Figure 3. Entitlement to income support.

1   See **15.1**.
2   Accommodation which is owned and/or managed by the local authority; see **9.9**.

imbalance can be represented as a revival of the pre-1993 'perverse incentive' towards residential care.[1]

14.2.4　The residential allowance

The residential allowance was intended to assist with accommodation costs incurred by people in residential care or nursing homes, and was originally set at a level that reflected the 'average' housing benefit payments for older people in sheltered housing. Residents placed under s 26 of the NAA 1948 do not benefit directly from the residential allowance, and it is recouped by local authorities, to mitigate their financial liability for care fees. Because the residential allowance is not available for council-run homes,[2] there is an obvious incentive for local authorities to favour independent sector accommodation, and an indirect but 'perverse' incentive to place older people in residential care rather than providing community support.

The Royal Commission on Long Term Care considered that the residential allowance serves no useful purpose and recommended that the resources which underpin it should be reallocated to local authorities to use in a way which better meets people's needs.[3]

The Government now proposes to implement this recommendation from April 2002.[4] The resources released will be available to 'promote independence and active rehabilitation for older people'. The change will be in respect of new cases only.

14.2.5　Income support premiums

The key to maximising income support entitlement on behalf of an elderly client lies in identifying premiums which may be available. These are as follows.

(a) The pensioner premium, which is available simply on the basis of age. There are two bands: age 60–74 and age 75–79.[5]

(b) Higher pensioner premium. The qualifying conditions are either advanced age (the claimant or his/her partner is aged 80 or over) *or* old age (age 60–79), together with disability signified by receipt of a qualifying benefit for disability.[6]

1　See **1.6**. However, the balance will change from April 2001, when income support thresholds for claimants in the community will rise to £12,000 or £6,000, whilst thresholds for residential care will remain the same. See Appendix 3.

2　See **14.2.3**.

3　*With Respect to Old Age*, op cit, para 4.28.

4　*The NHS Plan 2000*, op cit, para 15.18.

5　ISG Regs 1987, Sch 2, paras 9 and 9A.

6　Ibid, para 10.

(c) Severe disability premium. Here, the claimant must be in receipt of attendance allowance or one of the higher rates of disability living allowance (care component) and must not have an adult non-dependant residing with him or her. In addition, no one must be receiving invalid care allowance in respect of care given to the claimant.

Only *one* of the pensioner or higher pensioner premiums (whichever is the greater) can be claimed at the same time. Severe disability premium may, however, be paid in addition to either pensioner premium.[1]

In addition, a carer's premium[2] is available to those who are caring for elderly people and who are receiving the invalid care allowance, but need to top up their income with income support. It should be noted that where a carer lives with the person who is receiving care, a claim in respect of carer's premium will involve the loss of severe disability premium for the disabled person.

14.3 MAXIMISATION OF DISABILITY BENEFITS FOR OLDER PEOPLE LIVING AT HOME[3]

Advisers should bear in mind the following points.

(a) Attendance allowance and disability living allowance (care component) are paid on the basis of need to anyone who meets the qualifying conditions, irrespective of that person's other resources. Identifying entitlement and making a successful claim will always benefit clients financially.

(b) For clients who need personal care, and whose income and capital resources are low, attendance allowance does not reduce income support.

(c) Where a client is in receipt of attendance allowance or DLA (care), income support levels rise, because entitlement to either disability benefit triggers entitlement to the severe disability premium, which is added to the basic level of income support. At 2000/2001 rates, the income support threshold is raised by £14.20 per week for a single person. The Benefits Agency often overlooks entitlement to the severe disability premium, and advisers should always check that maximum benefit is being paid.

---

1   ISG Regs 1987, Sch 2, para 13.
2   Ibid, para 14ZA. A new premium, payable in respect of bereavement will become available in April 2001.
3   The same principles apply in respect of older people who are in residential care, who are self-funding, and who do not have preserved rights. See **14.4.4** and **15.3**.

14.4 AVAILABILITY OF DISABILITY BENEFITS TO THOSE IN RESIDENTIAL CARE

When a claimant or prospective claimant of attendance allowance, DLA (care) or DLA (mobility) enters a residential care home or nursing home, the conditions of entitlement and/or payability are affected. As regards the first two benefits, the legal position is complex.

14.4.1 Disability living allowance (mobility component)

For this benefit, the present legal position is relatively straightforward. A resident who meets the legislative requirements of being unable or virtually unable to walk, and who is within the prescribed age-limits, may claim benefit whilst in residential care and whilst in hospice care. However, most recipients of benefit who are admitted to hospital lose entitlement after 28 days.[1]

14.4.2 Attendance allowance and disability living allowance (care component)

The rules which affect claims made by residents in respect of either of these two benefits are far from straightforward. In principle, benefit may remain or become payable after a disabled person has entered a residential care home or nursing home. However, entitlement is based on a need for personal care, and given that provision of such care is the main function of residential accommodation, there is a policy objection to what amounts to double funding of the same need by local authorities and by the DSS. Consequently, the regulations seek to distinguish between claimants whose accommodation is publicly funded and those whose accommodation is not. Generally speaking, the former are disentitled to either the attendance allowance or the DLA (care), but the latter may claim benefit.

The regulations are complex, however, and there is still an element of uncertainty as to their precise implications. In the discussion that follows, for the sake of clarity reference in the text will be made only to attendance allowance and the AA Regs 1991.[2] The Social Security (Disability Living Allowance) Regulations 1991[3] are identical in all material aspects. In practice, most older clients will have entitlement, if at all, to attendance allowance rather than DLA (care).

Regulations 6–8 of the AA Regs 1991 apply to claimants who are in residential care.[4] Regulation 6 provides that any person who is maintained free of charge as an in-patient in hospital, or in a 'similar institution', is disentitled to attendance

---

1   Social Security (Disability Living Allowance) Regulations 1991, reg 12B. The rule was amended in July 1996.

2   SI 1991/2740.

3   SI 1991/2890.

4   Ibid, regs 8–10.

allowance.[1] In particular, this covers the situation where a health authority purchases a nursing home bed under s 23 of the NHSA 1977, in circumstances where the patient meets local criteria for entitlement to fully funded NHS continuing care.[2] Some patients who are severely physically disabled, or who are at an advanced stage of Alzheimer's disease are likely to fall into this category.

Regulation 7(1) goes on to state that attendance allowance is not payable to a person for whom accommodation is provided:

'(a) in pursuance of—

(i) Part III of the National Assistance Act 1948 ...

(b) in circumstances where the cost of the accommodation *is or may be* borne wholly or partly out of public or local funds ...'

14.4.3 Residents in Part III accommodation

Before June 2000, the effect of reg 7(1)(a) above was that, where a resident was placed under s 21 of the NAA 1948 in a home which was owned and/or managed by social services, attendance allowance was not available in any circumstances. Even residents who were fully self-funding were excluded from benefit.[3] This rule created a financial disincentive for local authorities to retain their own Part III accommodation, and tended to make such placements more expensive for residents who were funding themselves. New regulations[4] which came into force in June 2000 now permit payment of benefit to self-funding residents in local authority accommodation, thereby creating parity with the treatment of residents in private sector homes. However, residents in local authority homes who receive financial help with their fees remain excluded from benefit.

Where care arrangements are made by the local authority with an independent provider under s 26 of the NAA 1948, reg 7(1)(a) again applies, but only in circumstances where the local authority has accepted a financial responsibility for the placement, following an assessment of need under s 47 of the NHSCCA 1990 and an assessment of means. It should be noted that s 26 requires the local authority to enter into a contractual arrangement with the residential care

---

1   Benefit stops after 28 days as an in-patient. From 19 June 2000 the days of admission and discharge do not count as in-patient days, so are not included within the 28 days. This change in the law helps older people who have short periods of respite care (Social Security (Attendance Allowance and Disability Living Allowance) Regulations 2000, SI 2000/1401).

2   See Chapter 2. It is unclear at present what will be the consequences for attendance allowance of clause 48 of the Health and Social Care Bill 2000; see **2.4.11**.

3   Social Security (Attendance Allowance) Regulations 1991, reg 8(6).

4   Social Security (Attendance Allowance and Disability Living Allowance) (Amendment) Regulations 2000, SI 2000/1401, amending reg 8(6), ibid.

provider. If for any reason the local authority omits to do this, the arrangement is made 'otherwise' than under s 26.[1]

All residents covered by reg 7(1)(a) of the AA Regs 1991 are prevented from making first-time claims after they have entered residential care, and previous entitlement ceases, subject to dispensation in respect of the first 28 days in the residential establishment.[2]

14.4.4   Residents who make their own arrangements in independent homes

Where an older person purchases his or her own residential care directly from a provider, and the local authority is not directly involved, attendance allowance remains available to help defray the costs of care. As receipt of benefit will help to preserve the resident's capital, it is very important for advisers to identify entitlement, and to assist their clients in pursuing claims.

Sometimes the local authority may provide social work advice and assistance to help an older person to find a suitable residential placement. Provided, however, that such assistance falls short of making contractual arrangements with the provider,[3] s 26 of the NAA 1948 does not apply, and entitlement to attendance allowance is not excluded. This point will be of some importance where a resident has made his or her own care arrangements, but is or becomes unable to afford the fees without public assistance. If the local authority assumes financial responsibility for the fees, attendance allowance ceases to be payable. If, however, the resident elects to take the 'loophole option'[4] entitlement to benefit remains.

14.4.5   Accommodation where the cost 'is or may be borne' out of public funds

For older clients, publicly funded accommodation is, almost invariably, provided either by the local authority under Part III of the NAA 1948, or by the NHS under a s 23 arrangement.[5] As has been explained, in such cases residents are ineligible for attendance allowance wherever a public subsidy is involved. Other provisions under which the cost of care 'is borne' out of public funds are unlikely to affect older clients.

The application of the 'may be borne' provision is highly problematic. It is arguable, for example, that the fees of any older person needing residential care 'could' be borne by the local authority because its statutory responsibility under

1   *Steane v Chief Adjudication Officer* [1996] 4 All ER 83, HL; note the discussion of the 'loophole option' at **12.7**.

2   Social Security (Attendance Allowance) Regulations 1991, reg 8(1); the same rule applies to hospital patients.

3   *Steane v Chief Adjudication Officer*, op cit.

4   See **14.4.6**.

5   See **2.4**.

s 21 of the NAA is so broadly based. However, it was held in *Steane v Chief Adjudication Officer* that the s 21 responsibility is one of 'last resort', because it arises only where accommodation is 'not otherwise available' to the resident.[1] Consequently, if an older person can make and pay for his or her care arrangements, then the accommodation is 'otherwise available', and the local authority's statutory powers are excluded.[2] As a result, attendance allowance remains payable.

In *Steane*, an elderly lady had previously lived in a council-run home, paying her own fees. The home was transferred to a registered charity, set up by the council, and Mrs Steane was given the option of moving to another home, or staying where she was. She decided to stay and paid her fees to the charity. The House of Lords held that the council was no longer making provision for her under s 21 of the NAA 1948, and that s 26 did not apply either because the new arrangements did not provide for the council to make payments to the charity in respect of Mrs Steane.[3] Consequently, the cost of her accommodation was not borne out of public funds, nor 'could' it be so borne, because she was making her own arrangements. She was entitled to the attendance allowance.

At the time, Mrs Steane could not receive the attendance allowance when living in the council home. Now she would be able to do so for as long as she was self-funding.[4]

14.4.6   The 'loophole option' for funding

The view that arrangements under the NAA 1948 are a measure of last resort has also led to DSS acceptance of a funding option which clearly was not intended to be available to residents. The current regulations do not prevent a resident from making his or her own funding arrangements by claiming income support, and topping up with attendance allowance. The 'may be borne' rule does not apply to bar the claim to attendance allowance because residential care is available to the claimant otherwise than via the NAA 1948. Previously, the Benefits Agency's position was that those who are subsidised by central government funds through income support should be treated in the same way as those subsidised by local authorities. Thus, attendance allowance should not be available after the first 28 days in residential care. Since *Steane*, however, it has been accepted that an older person who enters residential care, without a local authority financial assessment, and claims income support to fund the placement, may also receive attendance allowance. Regulation 7 of the AA

---

1   [1996] 4 All ER 83, HL; see also Commissioners' Decision CA/2985/1997.
2   The same argument now justifies local authorities in declining to make care arrangements for older people in need of residential care who have capital in excess of £16,000; see **6.9**.
3   Section 26(2).
4   Social Security (Attendance Allowance and Disability Living Allowance) (Amendment) Regulations 2000. The Government is also considering abolishing the residential allowance, which will remove a further financial disincentive for local authorities to use their own residential accommodation.

Regs 1991 does not apply because the resident is making his or her own arrangements, and reg 8 is bypassed. Recent decisions by the Social Security Commissioners support this loophole, and it was incorporated into paras 7721–7723 of the former AOG.[1] The possible advantages of this option are outlined in **14.6**. For some residents, it offers a means of avoiding the local authority's assessment process and so of extending personal choice.

In *The NHS Plan 2000*, published in July 2000, the Government announced its intention to abolish the residential allowance and transfer the resources which support it to local authorities from April 2002. The effect of this change will probably make the loophole option unviable. In its response to the Royal Commission, the Government noted that:

> 'there is one group of people who self-fund their own residential care but benefit from the residential allowance while they are in the process of selling their own home. The changes which we are making to the capital disregard rules should mean that those people do not lose out overall in financial terms.'[2]

This is disingenuous, since the new capital disregard on property will operate only for the first three months after entry to residential care.[3] Disappearance of the loophole will, of course, place added financial pressure on local authorities.

14.4.7   Residents under s 26 arrangements who are nevertheless fully self-funding

The local authority's statutory responsibilities under Part III of the NAA 1948 are not restricted to older people of limited means. They are triggered by a need for care, not by financial needs, and s 22 makes it clear that residents will be expected to pay their way if they have sufficient means. The protection offered by a local authority contract is an advantage for a vulnerable person, wealthy or poor, and local authorities are able to negotiate keener prices with independent providers than can individuals acting alone.

Although the decision by the Court of Appeal in *R v Sefton Metropolitan Borough Council ex parte Help the Aged* and the Community Care (Residential Accommodation) Act 1998 have made it clear that local authorities may decline to make residential care arrangements for people with capital above £16,000 because care is 'otherwise available' to them, DoH Circular LAC (98) 19 emphasises their responsibility to make arrangements, irrespective of resources, for vulnerable elderly people who may lack mental capacity and who have no one to assist them or to make decisions for them.[4] Therefore, there will still be cases where the local authority will make care arrangements for a person under s 26, and will be able to recover the full economic cost of the placement. In such circumstances, attendance allowance will be available to the resident.

---

1   Now in the process of being re-published as the *Decision-Maker's Guide*.
2   Paragraph 2.37.
3   See **10.1**.
4   See **6.9**.

As has been seen, reg 8(6) of the AA Regs 1991 created an exception to reg 7 where the resident is in a home which is not owned and/or managed by social services (ie under a s 26 arrangement) and where the whole cost of the accommodation is met out of the resident's own resources, or wholly or partly with the assistance of another person or charity. That exception was extended in June 2000 to a placement made, in the same circumstances, in a local authority home.[1]

In *Steane v Chief Adjudication Officer*,[2] it was held that the whole cost is met if the resident pays the full fees charged by the home. Any additional contributions made by a local authority towards general running costs are irrelevant. A subsequent decision by the Social Security Commissioner[3] suggested that reg 8(6) applies only where the resident makes payments under a liability which is owed directly to the provider of the accommodation. His reasoning was that, if a resident in a local authority home is prevented from claiming the attendance allowance, even where he or she is meeting the full cost of the care, the same should apply to a s 26 arrangement, where the resident is protected by the local authority contract with the provider and cannot, for example, be evicted from the residential accommodation if he or she fails to pay the fees. At the time, there was some logic in the Commissioner's view, and his decision could (just) be read alongside *Steane*. However, the underlying rationale has fallen away since the change in the regulations relating to self-funding residents in local authority homes. In practice, it appears that the Benefits Agency is prepared to allow attendance allowance claims from all residents subject to s 26 arrangements who are self-funding. Nevertheless, there remains something to be said for arrangements (permitted under s 26(3)(A)), whereby with the agreement of all parties concerned, a resident pays the fee direct to the provider under the umbrella of a local authority contractual arrangement.[4]

14.4.8 Retrospective self-funding

Many older people enter residential care on the basis that their former home is to be sold to meet the fees. The local authority does not have the statutory power to force a sale, but will base its assessment of the resident's contribution towards the fees on the valuation of the property. Pending sale, the resident is likely to be in debt to the local authority, which may secure its position by registering a charge under HASSASSAA 1983, s 22.[5] As regards attendance allowance claims, it has been argued that benefit should be available retrospectively, from the date of placement, as, once the property is sold, the resident becomes self-funding and the local authority is able to recover the full care fees, from the commencement of the arrangements.

---

1   See **14.4.3**.
2   SI 2000/1401.
3   Commissioners' Decision CA/1185/1995.
4   See **6.10.2**.
5   Health and Social Services and Social Security Adjudication Act 1983; see **10.8**.

Until recently, there were conflicting decisions by the English Social Security Commissioners,[1] but the more generally accepted view was that residents were not entitled to receive the benefit during a period when a local authority was subsidising their care, notwithstanding that this outlay was subsequently repaid. However, in December 1999, the Court of Appeal in Northern Ireland[2] ruled that a group of residents, who received public assistance for varying periods but subsequently refunded care fees paid on their behalf, were entitled to receive attendance allowance throughout the period of care.

This ruling was considered to be persuasive rather than binding in England and Wales and, to date, the DSS has not amended the regulations. However, in November 2000, an English Commissioner[3] gave unequivocal support to the Northern Irish decision, stating that any other position is 'unjust and perverse' and is not to be regarded 'as being, or as ever having been, good law in Great Britain'. The Commissioner's decision implies:

(1) that attendance allowance should remain payable wherever a local authority is effectively 'bridging' a resident pending sale of his or her former home;

(2) that benefit awards which have been superseded in the past because local authorities were providing finance should be reinstated.

The Local Government Ombudsman recently awarded compensation against a local authority where the Benefits Agency had disallowed an attendance claim, and the local authority had not put to the resident's attorney the option of taking out a loan to cover care fees pending sale of the property, so that the full charges could be paid and attendance allowance claimed. Given the legal developments described above, such course of action should no longer be necessary, but, until the regulations themselves are amended, there may be difficulties at grass roots level, and this decision serves as a useful reminder that local authorities themselves are expected to be proactive in advising residents about the financial options which may be open to them.[4]

14.4.9 Respite care

Respite care arrangements can give rise to very complex problems with attendance allowance. Two or more short periods in a home and/or in hospital which are separated by less than 28 days are linked under the AA Regs 1991, and count as one period.[5] Once the linked periods exceed 28 days, attendance allowance is no longer available.[6] Therefore, it is important to try, where

---

1   Commissioners' Decisions CA/7126/95; CA/1185/95; CA/4723/95.
2   *Chief Adjudication Officer v Creighton (and Others)* [2000] NI 222, CA.
3   CA/2937/97.
4   Complaint No 98/C/1842.
5   Regulation 8(2).
6   Regulation 8(1). Note, however, the new provision that the day of admission and the day of discharge are not included within the 28 days; see **14.4.2**, fn 5.

possible, to leave more than 4 weeks between periods of respite. Failing this, an occasional period of more than 28 days without respite will allow the link to be broken and entitlement to start again.

14.5 MEANS TESTING OF BENEFITS FOR DISABILITY

It is also necessary to consider whether benefits for disability are ever subject to means testing where a resident is receiving income support.

14.5.1 Disability living allowance (mobility component)

In no circumstances will the mobility component be means tested.[1] Consequently, wherever a placement is wholly or partly publicly funded, whether through the local authority or the DSS, receipt of benefit will always leave the resident with a weekly sum (£37.40 maximum for 2000/2001) which cannot be recouped by the state. Where, on the other hand, a resident is privately funded, receipt of the mobility component will help to preserve his or her capital assets.

14.5.2 Attendance allowance and disability living allowance (care component)

It is a general rule that neither benefit is taken into account for the income support means test, although receipt of either benefit will usually affect the level of a local authority's charges for social services provided in the community.[2] For claimants who are in residential care, however, the rules are not consistent, but depend on the type of home occupied by the claimant.

(a) For temporary or respite placements of up to 4 weeks, either benefit may be claimed, and will not reduce the level of any income support which may be available to the resident.[3] Local authorities will, however, take either benefit into account when assessing a resident's contribution towards home fees.[4] Although local authorities are not required to carry out a full financial assessment during the first 8 weeks of a temporary placement in residential care, if they elect to do so the effect of the regulations will simply be to increase an individual's contribution during the first 4 weeks because the disability benefit will be taken into account.

(b) For permanent placements arranged and supported financially by a local authority in the independent sector after 1 April 1993, neither attendance allowance nor DLA (care) is available, and, means testing is not therefore

---

1   Social Security Contributions and Benefits Act 1992, s 73(14).
2   ISG Regs 1987, Sch 9, para 9; see the discussion at **11.5**.
3   AA Regs 1991, reg 8; Social Security (Disability Living Allowance) Regulations 1991, reg 10.
4   NA(AR) Regs 1992, reg 15(1).

an issue. The same is true of placements in Part III accommodation owned or managed by the local authority.

(c)   Where residents purchase their own residential care, and claim income support, both benefits are disregarded income under para 9 of Sch 9 to the ISG Regs 1987. In addition, the basic level of income support is likely to be raised in such cases because entitlement to either benefit will usually passport claimants on to the severe disability premium. Generally speaking, however, it will not be feasible for residents who are in a position to claim income support, and whose capital is, by definition, very modest, to take this option except on a short-term basis.[1]

(d)   Where residents have preserved rights, both attendance allowance and disability living allowance (care component) will be taken into account against the enhanced levels of income support which this legal status attracts. In other words, such residents will gain nothing financially from pursuing a claim to either benefit once they begin to claim income support.

(e)   Residents with substantial resources who make their own care arrangements, or are placed by the local authority but pay their fees in full may claim either benefit to help mitigate the loss to their estates.

14.6   AN EXAMPLE OF THE LOOPHOLE OPTION

Mrs Williams has a house worth £90,000, a few other assets and a modest income. She can no longer manage at home and is looking for a suitable residential care home. Mrs Williams has been advised that she will have to sell her house to fund the placement, but she is aware that this may take some time. She has also been advised that, if her local authority makes the care arrangements, it is likely to place a charge on the house immediately in order to secure payment of the home fees. The Benefits Agency, on the other hand, will continue to disregard the value of the house for at least 6 months and possibly for much longer after Mrs Williams enters residential care.[2] During that period, she may be able to fund the placement without involving the local authority, provided that her son agrees to pay a top-up.

---

1   See **14.4.6** and **14.6**.
2   ISG Regs 1987, Sch 10, para 26; see **10.7**.

Accommodation charge		£250.00
Mrs Williams' resources:		
Retirement pension		£67.50
Income support:		£120.05
Personal allowance	£52.20	
Higher pensioner premium	£33.85	
Severe disability premium	£40.20	
Residential allowance	£61.30	
Applicable amount	£187.55	
Attendance allowance		£53.55
Total available income		£241.10

14.6.1 Practice points

(a) The financial option demonstrated by the above example may be worth considering in respect of clients who have a limited prognosis and wish to preserve their house for their family. Benefits paid out pending sale are not recoverable by the State, and the arrangement, in effect, buys time before the State begins to encroach on the capital value of a property. There is a disadvantage, however, in that the resident becomes a private purchaser of residential care, without the protection of a local authority contract, and may be vulnerable to price increases which outpace the annual benefit increases.

(b) Mrs Williams will not have to sell her house for at least 6 months after entering the home, provided that it is put up for sale. The disregard is not indefinite, however, and once the value of the house is taken into account benefit will stop, whereupon Mrs Williams may find herself in a difficult financial position. She will then need to access local authority support straightaway.

(c) It is always worth identifying entitlement to attendance allowance or disability living allowance (care component) for clients who will be funding their own residential care. Over an extended period, the value to a client will be considerable, particularly if a claim for the disability living allowance (mobility component) is also indicated. The claiming process itself is not without difficulty, however, as the application forms are long and complicated and entitlement rests, to a large measure, on self-assessment. In addition, claims may not be backdated. Clients will benefit from hands-on assistance with claiming.

(d) It will be apparent that if attendance allowance is to be available to residents whose funding is being bridged by the local authority[1] pending sale of a property, the loophole option becomes less attractive. The 12-week disregard on properties which will be introduced into the local authority means test from April 2001 may also undermine the loophole.

---

1   See **14.4.8**.

Furthermore, once the income support residential allowance is no longer available (from April 2002),[1] such arrangements are unlikely to be financially viable.

14.7   USEFUL SOURCES OF INFORMATION ABOUT BENEFITS

(a)   *Paying for Care* (Child Poverty Action Group) is a handbook, updated annually, which deals with welfare benefits and local authority funding;

(b)   Age Concern factsheets on welfare benefits, numbers 11, 25 and 34;

(c)   *The Welfare Rights Bulletin*, published bi-monthly by Child Poverty Action Group; welfare benefits updates, published periodically by Legal Action;

(d)   *The Welfare Rights Handbook*, published annually by Child Poverty Action Group;

(e)   *The Disability Rights Handbook*, published annually by the Disability Alliance;

(f)   *Income-Related Benefits: The Legislation* (Sweet & Maxwell) and *Non-Means Tested Benefits: The Legislation* (Sweet & Maxwell) – primary and secondary legislation with detailed annotations;

(g)   Benefits Agency website: www.dss.gov.uk;

(h)   Social Security Commissioners' decisions: www.hywels.demon.co.uk/commrs/index.htm.

---

1   See **14.2.4**.

Chapter 15

PRESERVED RIGHTS TO INCOME SUPPORT

'A little-discussed legacy of the government's community care reforms is the provision of "preserved rights" to higher rates of income support for people resident in independent sector residential and nursing homes on or before 31 March 1993. For some, entitlement to "preserved rights" has protected their place in a care home; for others, the provision is like a sentence to worry and despair about how care home fees will be paid.'[1]

15.1 INTRODUCTION

As has been seen, the new rules for funding long-term care gave local authorities financial responsibility for making residential care arrangements from 1 April 1993. The old system of funding through DSS benefit payments continued to apply, however, to people who were living permanently in registered residential care homes or nursing homes on 31 March 1993.[2] It has been estimated that at that date there were 350,000 such people.[3] They have 'preserved rights' to income support[4] which is payable at the enhanced rates which were previously available to all residents in the independent sector who needed financial assistance with fees. The rates are nationally defined and vary according to age and disability.

In the 2000/2001 benefit year, the enhanced rates range from £221 weekly for a residential care home placement to £331 weekly for a bed in a nursing home offering care to patients with Alzheimer's disease. For homes in the Greater London area, there is a supplementary payment of £46 per week for residential care homes and £51 for nursing homes. The payments described are maximum payments and are not directly related to the fees charged for residential accommodation.

Two categories of people have preserved rights:

(1) those who were claiming income support before 1 April 1993 in order to maintain their residential placement; and

(2) those who were funding themselves on 1 April 1993, but who have subsequently claimed benefit, or may in the future claim benefit, once their

---

1   Age Concern, *Preserved and Protected? A Report and Recommendations about the Community Care Reforms and People with Preserved Rights to Income Support* (1994).

2   Including Abbeyfield homes, or 'small' homes, providing care for fewer than four people.

3   In 2000, 81,000 people in Great Britain were in receipt of income support at enhanced rates; 51,000 were over pension age; the remainder were younger people with disabilities (DoH Consultation Paper, April 2000).

4   ISG Regs 1987, reg 19(1ZB).

capital assets are reduced to £16,000[1] or less and they cannot sustain their placements out of their weekly income.[2]

All residents with preserved rights will have made their own arrangements with providers of residential or nursing home care. They will not have been assessed by the local authority, and the local authority will not have made care arrangements on their behalf.

Elderly people resident in local–authority–maintained accommodation ('Part III' accommodation) do not have preserved rights. As previously explained, the NHSCCA 1990 has not substantially altered their financial regime.

Example
Mrs Wainwright entered a nursing home in April 1992. At that time, she had substantial capital assets in excess of £150,000 and a small pension. In December 2000, her remaining capital amounts to £16,000, and she is entitled to claim income support. She has preserved rights.

Her benefit will be as follows:
Allowance for registered category:

Nursing home for people with a mental disorder	£331.00
Personal expenses allowance	£15.45
Income support available	£346.45

Mrs Wainwright's pension will be taken into account. It will reduce her income support, as will a notional tariff income on her remaining capital in excess of £10,000.[3]

Before implementation of the community care legislation, it was generally considered that preserved rights status would carry advantages. For this reason, considerable efforts were made to arrange residential placements before 1 April 1993. Certainly, assessments of need were avoided, and individual residents were able to exercise a free choice in respect of their accommodation because income support payments were then, and still are, based on categories of accommodation and not on an individual's actual needs. Local authorities, in particular, had a hidden agenda: to ensure that central government took over the ultimate financial responsibility for as many people as possible before the transferred funding became effective in April 1993. It is now apparent, however, that preserved rights status is giving rise to considerable individual hardship, and it is difficult to understand how legislators could have seen fit

---

1   The capital limit prescribed for the income support means test was raised to £16,000 from April 1996, to match the limits applied by local authority under the NA(AR) Regs 1992. This limit does not apply to claimants living in their own homes.

2   Residents in Abbeyfield homes or small homes have preserved rights only if they were actually in receipt of income support on 31 March 1993, not if they were then self-funding; ISG Regs 1987, reg 19.

3   ISG Regs 1987, reg 53. The same tariff is applied in the local authority means test, see **9.4**.

deliberately to create such a disadvantaged minority of vulnerable elderly people.

15.2 WHY DO 'PRESERVED RIGHTS' CAUSE PROBLEMS FOR CLIENTS?

(a) The main problem is that the income support payments, albeit enhanced, may not meet actual residential home fees in full. Historically, although enhanced income support has been available to subsidise residential care since the early 1980s, from 1986 onwards the DSS stopped matching benefit rates with actual fees charged, and by 1992/1993 there was nationally a gap between benefit payments and fees charged of, on average, £40 per week. Market forces allowed providers of care to raise their fees above benefit rates, either because there were plenty of resources to top up benefit payments (for example from residents' relatives, voluntary organisations or, in some instances, local authorities) or because they could sell their beds to well-off older people who could afford higher fees and would never need to claim income support. Since April 1993, the market has been further affected by the prices at which local authorities, now the major purchasers of residential care, have been prepared to buy from providers. It is clear, for example, that some providers are trying to increase fees charged to people with preserved rights in order to offset the downward pressure on fees exerted by local authority purchasers. A DoH consultation paper published in April 2000 suggested that about 45 per cent of residents with preserved rights may now be experiencing a shortfall between fees and benefit income.[1]

(b) Some residents also face unexpected increases in fees, either because their care needs have increased or because 'extras', such as incontinence supplies and chiropody services, which used to be provided by the NHS free of charge, now have to be paid for. Such extras often reflect on the adequacy of income support to cover the full economic costs of residential care. In contrast, residents who are the subject of post–1993 local authority contracts are protected against extra expenditure.[2]

(c) Residents whose health deteriorates and who need to upgrade their care, perhaps from a residential care home to a nursing home, may be prevented from moving because they are unable to meet the nursing home fees. Homes which have dual registration offer some advantages in these circumstances, but the rate of benefit payable depends on the type of care received by the resident, and there may be disputes with the Benefits Agency over this question.

---

1   See **15.8**.
2   See **6.10**.

15.3   ARE WELFARE BENEFITS AVAILABLE?

Residents with preserved rights may benefit from the attendance allowance or the disability living allowance (care component) provided that they are not yet claiming income support. The highest rate of either benefit (£53.55 in 2000/2001) makes a significant contribution to preserving dwindling capital. Once income support is in payment, however, benefit is subject to the means test and, from that point, the resident is no better off for claiming.[1]

The disability living allowance (mobility component) is immune from any means test.[2] It can always be used to top up fees or pay for extra services, but must be claimed, for the first time, before a resident's sixty-fifth birthday.[3]

15.4   CAN THE LOCAL AUTHORITY HELP?

Section 26A of the NAA 1948[4] expressly prevents local authorities from arranging residential care or nursing home accommodation for people who were ordinarily resident in private or voluntary homes on 1 April 1993. If, for example, an elderly person is evicted or threatened with eviction from a nursing home because relatives have failed to meet top-up payments, it will be ultra vires for the local authority to purport to intervene and support the placement. Similarly, where an elderly person in a residential care home now needs more specialised nursing home care, but has no access to top-up payments, the local authority cannot offer financial assistance.

However, s 26A(3) empowers the Secretary of State to exempt certain residents from this general exclusionary rule. The Residential Accommodation (Relevant Premises Ordinary Residence and Exemptions) Regulations 1993[5] have been made under s 26(A)(3) and offer limited relief. Regulations 8 and 9 provide that, notwithstanding the general prohibition in s 26(A), local authorities may nevertheless assist people over pensionable age who have been evicted or are about to be evicted from *residential care homes* (whether because the home is closing down or because the fees have not been paid), by finding them accommodation elsewhere, using their preserved rights and, if necessary, topping up the difference between income support and the new fees. They may not, however, move residents directly from residential care homes into nursing homes because the regulations permit the support of nursing home placements only where residents are under pensionable age. In order to avoid undue pressure on local authorities to take on such additional responsibility, reg 8(2) states that new placements may not be made in premises under the same

---

1   See **14.5.2**.
2   SSCBA 1992, s 73(14).
3   See **14.2.2**.
4   NHSCCA 1990, s 43.
5   SI 1993/3182.

ownership or management as the original home unless that home has been, or is about to be, closed down. This proviso hits at evictions which are 'contrived' in order to make the local authority financially responsible for a placement, but it means that elderly residents will have to be moved, even if that is not in their best interests, and even if higher fees have to be paid in a new placement.

15.5   DOES THE HEALTH AUTHORITY HAVE ANY RESPONSIBILITY?

As noted above, local authorities have no power to make arrangements in nursing homes for people over pensionable age who have preserved rights. Health authorities do have a general responsibility to meet continuing nursing care needs, which overlaps with the responsibility of local authorities to arrange nursing home care under s 21 of the NAA 1948.[1]

Health authorities may purchase beds in nursing homes for patients for whom they accept responsibility.[2] However, they have no specific power to protect people facing eviction from nursing homes or to top up inadequate levels of income support. If they do intervene, the complex income support rules force them to take over the funding of a placement, and preserved rights are lost.[3]

Department of Health guidance states that, where the health authority originally purchased the nursing home place, it should take responsibility for finding alternative accommodation for a resident threatened with eviction or home closure. It is not clear, however, whether the NHS is expected to fund the alternative placement. Where, however, a resident has entered a nursing home under private arrangements, as is usually the case, the guidance places the onus firmly on the resident, his or her relatives, and the home-owner to negotiate the placement or find alternative accommodation. Local authorities are expected to assist by providing 'advice and guidance' to help people in difficulty to find alternative accommodation using their preserved rights and 'any other resources available to them'.[4] Some local authorities are advising residents and their families to try to negotiate with home-owners wherever possible with a view to securing a reduction of fees, perhaps by virtue of an agreement to share rooms. Community care plans may be expected to lay down protocols for dealing with home closure or evictions, in order to minimise possible disruption and distress to residents.

---

1   For further discussion, see Chapter 2.
2   NHSA 1977, s 23.
3   *White v Adjudication Officer* (1993) *The Times*, 2 August (CA); note also *Botchett v Chief Adjudication Officer* (1999) 2 CCL Rep 121.
4   DoH Circular LAC (93) 6.

15.6   WHAT ARE THE OTHER OPTIONS?

The raising of the income support threshold from £8,000 to £16,000 in April 1996 (and to £18,500 in April 2001) helped the situation because residents now have more residual capital which they can use to top up their income support. The change did not, however, assist people who had relied on income support for some time and whose capital had been depleted or possibly exhausted before April 1996. Sometimes home-owners may agree to reduce fees, because giving notice to frail and often mentally incapacitated elderly residents is not easy to contemplate.

In addition, there are the following options.

15.6.1   Relative top-ups

Wherever there are difficulties in meeting the care fees, family members may top up an elderly relative's income support. Payments made are disregarded as income of the resident under the income support regulations.[1] The position is the same where a charity agrees to make top-up payments. Payments made by a spouse of the resident, however, are 'liable relative' payments under the income support rules and usually have to be taken into account as income of the resident.[2] Therefore, they are not effective in bridging the fees gap.

15.6.2   Termination of preserved rights status

Although the lifeline offered to residents with preserved rights by regs 8 and 9 of the Residential Accommodation (Relevant Ordinary Residence and Exemptions) Regulations 1993 is clearly very limited, reg 5 offers another approach. It states quite explicitly that s 26A(1) of the NAA 1948 shall not apply to any person who has ceased to have a preserved right by virtue of reg 19(IZF) of the ISG Regs 1987. Regulation 19 indicates that a resident will normally retain preserved rights for the rest of his or her life. Rights will persist, for example, if a resident moves from one independent-sector home to another, or from a care home to a nursing home. The same is true if ownership of the home itself changes. Short absences from registered accommodation have no effect on preserved rights. If, however, a resident is absent from a residential home or nursing home for a period exceeding 13 weeks (or 52 weeks where he or she has been in hospital) preserved rights will be lost, and s 26A(1) of the NAA 1948 will cease to apply. As a result, the local authority will be empowered to make new residential care arrangements.

Example
Jane Walsh, aged 55, has just retired early from her clerical job with the local authority, on account of ill health. She is unmarried and her only close relative is

---

1   ISG Regs 1987, Sch 9.
2   Ibid, reg 54.

her elderly mother, aged 83, who has been in a nursing home since 1992. Mrs Walsh has Alzheimer's disease.

Until her retirement, Jane was topping up her mother's income support payments to meet the nursing home fees. Currently, her mother's income support is £331 per week, plus £15.45 personal allowance (2000/2001 benefit rates). The nursing home fees have just been increased to £400 per week. Jane is now unable to afford the top-up payments. Her mother's capital is almost exhausted.

(a) It may be possible to obtain charitable assistance for Mrs Walsh, although this particular source of funds is now more limited than it once was. Charities, such as the Alzheimer's Society, should be contacted, together with local charities or benevolent associations with which Mrs Walsh may have had connections before she became ill. (For other sources of advice on funding, see the List of Useful Addresses.)

(b) If Jane fails to make the top-up payments, her mother could face eviction from the nursing home for non-payment of the fees. How soon this is likely to happen will depend on the financial pressures faced by the management of the home. The local authority should, at least, offer advice and general assistance, but it may not assist in paying the fees. The community care plan should be inspected, and approaches made to the health authority. It may be helpful to enlist support from the local media.

(c) If the old lady is 'evicted' from the nursing home and returns home to live with her daughter for at least 13 weeks, her preserved rights status will be lost.[1] Jane may then ask the local authority to assess her mother under s 47 of the NHSCCA 1990, and to arrange a nursing home placement for her. The local authority will be responsible for the home fees and will recover a contribution from Mrs Walsh, who will be in a position to claim income support at the reduced level which applies to all placements made after 31 March 1993. Jane will not be required to make a financial contribution. Subject to the fees charged being acceptable to the local authority, there is no reason in law why Mrs Walsh should not return to the previous nursing home.

15.7 PRACTICAL EXPERIENCE

The following case studies identified by Age Concern reveal the range of problems which may be encountered by elderly people with so-called 'preserved rights' and their advisers.[2]

---

1   Residential Accommodation (Relevant Premises Ordinary Residence and Exemptions) Regulations 1993, SI 1993/3182, reg 5.

2   Age Concern, *Preserved and Protected?* (1994).

(1) 'A 72-year-old pensioner in the southern counties. Mother, aged 94, has been in nursing home for 2 years. She receives no personal expenses allowance (presumably used to top up fees). When he went in to pay the latest bill, there was a charge for incontinence pads, which he knew nothing about. Referred to a charitable source.'

(2) 'Letter from a man in East Anglia regarding his father in a nursing home in Yorkshire. Fees have been increased from £76 a month to £165 a month over and above DSS limits (at that time). "I do not have the resources to keep it up."'

(3) 'Local authority social worker, very concerned about a person in residential care whom the home can no longer care for. There are no local nursing homes at income support rates. The local authority is prevented from stepping in on behalf of this person. They would do so if they had the power.'

It is clear from these and other well-documented examples that the community care changes have left behind a marginalised group of typically, very elderly, very dependent people, who have been made more financially vulnerable than they were before April 1993. Advisers need to be aware of their predicament and should be prepared to explore all possible options on their behalf.

15.8   FUTURE DEVELOPMENTS

The Royal Commission on Long Term Care recommended that the Government 'consider whether preserved rights cases should be brought within the post-April 1993 system or whether some other solution can be found to address the shortfall in funding experienced by this group.'[1] In response to this recommendation, the Government consulted recently with local authorities and other interested parties about possible changes to the system of preserved rights. The main areas of concern as regards older people were expressed to be:

- the shortfall between fees charged by homes and residents' weekly benefit income;
- the difficulty in moving from residential to nursing care when needs change;
- the limits on local authority powers to intervene.

Respondents indicated some ambivalence, expressing concerns about the current funding shortfall, whilst emphasising that preserved rights do provide security, independence and, in particular, choice through the guarantee of social security benefits. The Government has concluded that the preserved rights scheme should be wound-up, and intends that, from April 2002, local

---

1   Royal Commission on Long Term Care *With Respect to Old Age*, Cm 4192–I
     (Stationery Office, 1999), para 4.30.

authorities should be given responsibility for the assessment, care management and financial support of everyone who has preserved rights.[1]

An obvious concern about such a transfer of responsibility and, of course, resources, is that local authorities might, in future, seek to move residents into cheaper accommodation. To meet this concern, the Government says that it will issue guidance that residents must not be moved against their will unless there is a 'compelling reason' to do so. Pending the transition to local authority responsibility, the Residential Accommodation (Relevant Premises Ordinary Residence and Exemptions) Regulations 1993 will be amended to give authorities power to intervene to prevent residents from being evicted from residential care homes for failure to pay the fees.

---

1   *The NHS Plan 2000*, Cm 4818–I, para 15.18. Clause 49 of the Health and Social Care Bill 2000 makes provision for the transfer of responsibility. All residents who have preserved rights are to be assessed under s 47 of the NHSCCA 1990.

APPENDICES

Appendix 1

SUMMARY OF THE GOVERNMENT'S RESPONSE TO THE ROYAL COMMISSION ON LONG TERM CARE

Taken from *The NHS Plan 2000*, Cm 4818–I, July 2000

Recommendations	Government Response
1. Personal care should be available after an assessment, according to need and paid for from general taxation	The Government is making an unprecedented new investment over the next three years in improving older people's services making them more responsive and more fairly funded. The Government's investment would fund the cost of the Royal Commission's recommendation. However, the Government does not believe that making personal care universally free is the best use of these resources.
2. The Government should establish a National Care Commission	Broadly **accepted** in December 1999 with the announcement of a single National Care Standards Commission, now enshrined in the Care Standards Act 2000.
3. The Government should ascertain precisely how much money goes to supporting older people in residential settings and in people's homes	Any division between acute and long-term health care spending would be somewhat arbitrary. The Government believes that it is more important to get the right incentives in the system to promote older people's independence and to provide care closer to home. This is what the proposals in *The NHS Plan 2000* on intermediate care and associated services aim to do.
4. The value of the home should be disregarded for up to three months after admission to care in a residential setting and the opportunity for rehabilitation should be included as an integral and initial part of any care assessment	Both elements **accepted** in this response. Value of home will be disregarded for up to 3 months from April 2001, benefiting around 30,000 people a year.
5. Measures should be taken to bring about increased efficiency and improved quality in the system, including a more client centred approach	**Accepted**. Proposals in *The NHS Plan 2000* for personal care plans and closer working between health and social care. Quality Strategy for Social Care to be published next month.

Recommendations	Government Response
6. Other changes to the current system, such as changing the limits of the means-test, or making nursing care free (subsumed by recommendation 1)	Many suggestions **accepted** – free NHS nursing care from October 2001, benefitting around 35,000 people. Capital limits to be uprated to restore 1996 value from April 2001, benefiting around 20,000 people.
7. The resources which underpin the Residential Allowance in Income Support should be transferred to local authorities	**Accepted** – will be implemented from April 2002.
8. The Government should consider whether 'preserved rights' payments in social security should be brought within the post 1993 system of community care funding	**Accepted** – will be implemented from April 2002, benefiting up to 65,000 people.
9. The Government's proposals on pooled budgets should be taken further, with pooled budgets being implemented nationally	Boardly **accepted** in the NHS Plan, with proposals for strengthening partnerships between health and social care.
10. Budgets for aids and adaptations should be included in and accessible from a single budget pool and Local Authorities should be enabled to make loans for aids and adaptations for individuals with housing assets	**Accepted** in principle for aids and minor adaptations. Potential for use of pooled budgets using Health Act 1999 flexibilities.
11. The system for making direct payments should be extended to the over 65s	**Accepted** and implemented from February 2000.
12. Further research on the cost effectiveness of rehabilitation and the development of a national strategy on rehabilitation	**Accepted** in principle. Research is being undertaken on cost effectiveness of rehabilitation, and the National Beds Inquiry and NHS Plan proposals on intermediate care provide the context for developing a national framework for rehabilitation.
13 and **23.** Further longitudinal research is required to track the process and outcomes of preventive interventions	**Accepted** in principle. Work with the Office for National Statistics on proposal for a longitudinal survey of ageing.
14. It should be a priority for Government to improve cultural awareness in services offered to black and ethnic minority elders	**Accepted** as important in the NHS Plan and will be addressed as part of the National Service Framework for Older People. Reinforced for social care by project work with individual councils and inspection reports.
15. The role of advocacy should be developed locally, with backing from central Government	**Accepted** as important. Chapter 10 of the NHS Plan sets out our new proposals for patient advocacy services in the NHS.

Recommendations	Government Response
16. There should be wider consultation on the provision of aids and adaptations and on what should be free and subject to a charge	Broadly **accepted**. New powers in Care Standards Act 2000 will enable statutory guidance to cover fairer charging arrangements for services provided at home.
17. Better services should be offered to those people who currently have a carer	**Accepted** in principle. Additional resources for carers' services provided in the Spending Review.
18. The Government should consider a national carer support package	**Accepted**, as above, and through the Government's National Carers' Strategy.
19. The National Care Commission should be made responsible for making and publishing projections about the overall cost of long-term care	Agreed that this is an important task, but it is not central government's responsibility. The Department of Health has commissioned the Personal Social Services Research Unit at the LSE to make projections.
20. The Government should set up a national survey to provide reliable data to monitor trends in health expectancy	The Government **agrees** that a national longitudinal data may be valuable for measuring trends in health expectancy. Approval for this is being considered.
21. The Government should conduct a scrutiny of the shift in resources between various sectors since the early 1980s	The Government believes joint commissioning has developed significantly and that the new partnership arrangements (including pooled budgets) in the Health Act 1999 are also changing the allocation of resources and therefore remove the need for such scrutiny.
22. A more transparent grant and expenditure allocation system should be established	**Accepted**. The Government intends to issue a Green Paper in September 2000 on improving the way funding is allocated to local government.
24. The Government should consider how the provision of care according to need would relate to Independent Living Fund provision for the personal care needs of younger disabled people	This recommendation relates to recommendation 1.

Appendix 2

WHO'S WHO IN THE NEW NHS

A number of significant changes to the NHS have recently been introduced, including establishing primary care groups (PCGs). The roles and responsibilities of various statutory sector organisations are summarised below.

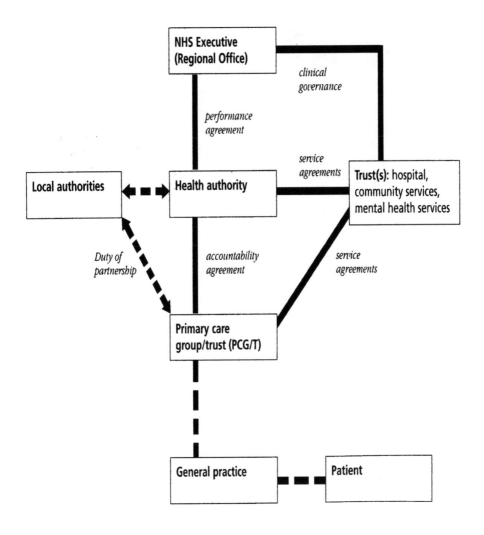

Appendix 3

WELFARE BENEFITS UPDATE – APRIL 2001

The (benefit) changes which will have most importance for older people are set out below.

	PREVIOUS RATES April 2000	NEW RATES April 2001
	£	£
Attendance Allowance		
higher rate	53.55	55.30
lower rate	35.80	37.00
Disability Living Allowance		
care component		
highest rate	53.55	55.30
middle rate	35.80	37.00
lowest rate	14.20	14.65
mobility component		
higher rate	37.40	38.65
lower rate	14.20	14.65
Earnings rules		
Invalid Care Allowance	50.00	72.00
adult dependant when claimant receiving retirement		
pension	52.20	53.05
Invalid Care Allowance	40.40	41.75
Retirement pension		
basic pension	67.50	72.50
married woman	40.40	43.40
couple on husband's insurance	107.90	115.90
over 80s pension (non-contributory)	40.40	43.40
Additional pension, and increments to pension increase by 3.3%		
Graduated pension (unit) (pence)	8.77	9.06
Addition at 80	0.25	0.25
Widow's benefits		
widow's payment (lump sum)	1,000.00	1,000.00
Bereavement Benefit (from April 2001)		2,000.00

	PREVIOUS RATES April 2000	**NEW RATES** April 2001
	£	£
Widow's pension (standard rate)	67.50	72.50
Bereavement Allowance (from April 2001)		72.50

Income Support, Housing Benefit, Council Tax Benefit and Income-based JobSeeker's Allowance

Personal allowances		
single person 25 or over	52.20	53.05
couple 18 or over	81.95	83.25
Premiums		
pensioner		
single	26.25	39.10
couple	40.00	57.30
pension (enhanced)		
single	28.65	39.10
couple	43.40	57.30
pensioner (higher)		
single	33.85	39.10
couple	49.10	57.30
disability		
single	22.25	22.60
couple	31.75	32.25
enhanced disability		
single		11.05
couple		16.00
severe disability		
single	40.20	41.55
couple (one qualifies)	40.20	41.55
couple (both qualify)	80.40	83.10
carer	14.15	24.40
bereavement		19.45
Residential allowance		
except Greater London	61.30	63.30
Greater London	68.20	70.45
Income Support – preserved rights		
a) Residential care homes		
old age	221.00	225.00
very dependent elderly	256.00	261.00
mental disorder (not handicap)	234.00	238.00
drug/alcohol dependence	234.00	238.00
mental handicap	266.00	271.00
physical disablement		
under pension age	303.00	308.00
over pension age	221.00	225.00
others	221.00	225.00
maximum Greater London increase	46.00	47.00

	PREVIOUS RATES April 2000	NEW RATES April 2001
	£	£
b) Nursing homes		
mental disorder (not handicap)	331.00	337.00
drug/alcohol dependence	331.00	337.00
mental handicap	337.00	343.00
terminal illness	330.00	336.00
physical disablement		
(under pension age)	373.00	379.00
(over pension age)	330.00	336.00
others (including elderly)	330.00	336.00
maximum Greater London increase	51.00	52.00
Allowance for personal expenses private and voluntary residential care and nursing homes	15.45	16.05

Note:

- There is an above-inflation increase in the basic retirement pension;

- From April 2001 the income levels for the minimum income guarantee will increase. They will be £92.15 for single older people and £140.55 for couples;

- The earnings limit for invalid care allowance will go up from £50 to £72 per week;

- Two new income support premiums are being introduced from April 2001. The *Bereavement Premium* is for people aged 55 and over who are widowed after 2001. It is intended to provide transitional protection for those affected by the changes to widows' benefits (see above). The *Enhanced Disability Premium* will provide enhanced support for people under 60 who receive the highest level of DLA (care component).

- Widows' benefits will change. A new Bereavement Allowance will replace the widow's pension, and a lump sum Bereavement Benefit will become payable.

Note particularly:

- The general capital thresholds for income support will rise from £8,000 to £12,000 and from £3,000 to £6,000 (Social Security Amendment (Capital Limits and Earnings Disregards) Regulations 2000). The Government will not increase the income support thresholds for income support in respect of older people who are in residential care. They will remain at £16,000 and £10,000. This will create further complexity in the means test for residential care.

BIBLIOGRAPHY

Age Concern *The Community Care Changes: Assessment and Care Management* (1992).

Age Concern *The Community Care Changes: Community Care Plans* (1992).

Age Concern *The Community Care Changes: Purchasing and Contracting* (1992).

Age Concern *The Community Care Changes: Quality and Inspection* (1992).

Age Concern *Gold Standards: Professional Targets for the Care of Elderly People* (1994).

Age Concern *The Law and Vulnerable Elderly People* (1986).

Age Concern *The Next Steps: Lessons for the Future of Community Care* (1994).

Age Concern *No Time to Lose: First Impressions of Community Care Reforms* (1993).

Age Concern *Preserved and Protected? A Report and Recommendations about the Community Care Reforms and People with Preserved Rights to Income Support* (1994).

Allen, I and Perkins, E *The Future of Family Care for Older People* (HMSO, 1995).

Alzheimer's Disease Society *NHS Psychogeriatric Continuing Care Beds* (1993).

Ashton, G *Elderly Client Handbook*, 2nd edn (Law Society Publishing, 1999).

Ashton, G *Elderly People and the Law* (Butterworths, 1995).

Ashton, G 'Elderly People and Residential Care' (1995) *Solicitor's Journal*, 27 October.

Ashton, G and Ward, A *Mental Handicap and the Law* (Sweet & Maxwell, 1992).

Association of Directors of Social Services *Towards Community Care: A DSS Review of the First Year* (1994).

Association of Metropolitan Authorities *Guidelines on Contracting for Domiciliary and Day Care Services* (1995).

Association of Metropolitan Authorities *Review of Issues Relating to Charging for Community Care Services* (1992).

Audit Commission *The Coming of Age: Improving Care Services for Older People* (1977).

Audit Commission *Community Care: Managing the Cascade of Change* (1992).

Audit Commission *Community Revolution: Personal Social Services and Community Care* (1992).

Audit Commission *Homeward Bound: A New Course for Community Health* (1992).

Audit Commission *Making A Reality of Community Care* (1986).

Audit Commission *Progress with Care in the Community Bulletin* (1993).

Audit Commission *Taking Stock: Progress With Community Care* (1994).

Baldwin, S, Parker, G and Walter, R (eds) *Social Security and Community Care* (Avebury, 1988).

Balloch, S *A Survey of Social Services Charging Policies 1992/1994* (1994).

Bewley and Glendinning *Involving Disabled People in Community Care Planning* (Joseph Rowntree Foundation, 1994).

Bonner, D, Hooker, I, White, R *Non-Means Tested Benefits: The Legislation* (Sweet & Maxwell, 1994).

Bull, J and Poole, L *Not Rich: Not Poor – A Study of Housing Options for Elderly People on Middle Incomes* (SHAC/Anchor Housing Trust, 1989).

Burchardt, T and Hills, J *Private Welfare Insurance and Social Security – Pushing the Boundaries* (Joseph Rowntree Foundation, 1997).

Carers National Association *Community Care: Just a Fairytale* (1994).

Cassidy, P 'Community Care and Benefits' (*Legal Action*, March 1993).

Centre for Policy on Ageing *Community Life: A Code of Practice for Community Care* (1990).

Centre for Policy on Ageing Home Life: A Code of Practice for Residential Care (1984).

Child Poverty Action Group *National Welfare Benefits Handbook* (1995/6).

Child Poverty Action Group *Paying for Care Handbook*, 2nd edn (2001).

Clapham, D and Franklin, B 'Housing Management, Community Care and CCT' *Housing Research Findings* 135 (Joseph Rowntree Foundation, 1995).

Clapham, D, Monro, M and Kay, H 'Financing User Choice in Housing and Community Care' *Housing Summary* 6 (Joseph Rowntree Foundation, 1994).

Clements, L *Community Care and the Law*, 2nd edn (Legal Action Group, 2000).

Clements, L 'Community Care: Definition of Need' (*Legal Action*, 1994).

Clements, L 'Community Care: Legal Structure' (*Legal Action*, July 1993).

Clements, L 'Duty of Social Services Departments' (*Legal Action*, September 1992).

Clements, L 'Shifting Sands' (*Community Care*, 29 September 1994).

College of Law *Law and the Elderly Client* (1992).

Commission for Local Administration in England *How to Complain to the Local Government Ombudsman* (CLAE, 1993).

Commission for Local Administration in England *Annual Report* (CLAE, 1993/4).

Commission for Local Administration in England *Local Government Ombudsmen Annual Report* (CLAE, 1993/4).

Common, R and Flynn, N *Contracting for Care* (Joseph Rowntree Foundation, 1992).

Coombs, M *Right to Challenge – the Oxfordshire Community Care Rights Project* (Joseph Rowntree Foundation, 1998).

Cooper, J and Vernon, S *Disability and the Law* (Jessica Kingsley, 1999).

Counsel and Care *More Power to our Elders* (1994).

Cox, B 'Community Care: Top-Up Funding: R v Avon CC ex parte Hazell' (*Legal Action*, October 1993).

Dean, H 'Social Care Provision: Problems of Redress' (*Legal Action*, December 1995), p 8.

Department of the Environment *Assistance with Minor Works to Dwellings* (DoE 4/90).

Department of the Environment *House Adaptations for People with Disabilities* (DoE 10/90).

Department of the Environment *Local Government and Housing Act 1989: House Renovation Grants* (DoE 12.90).

Department of the Environment *Local Government and Housing Act 1989: Parts VII and VIII* (DoE 5/91).

Department of the Environment and Department of Health *Housing and Community Care* (DoE 10/92, DoH LAC (92) 12).

Department of Health *Approvals and Directions for Arrangements from 1 April 1993 Made Under Schedule 8 to the National Health Service Act 1977 and Sections 21 and 29 of the National Assistance Act 1948* (DoH LAC (93) 19).

Department of Health *Community Care in the Next Decade and Beyond: Policy Guidance* (HMSO, 1990).

Department of Health *A Framework for Community Care Charters in England: Consultation Document* (HMSO, 1994).

Department of Health *Hospital Discharge Workbook* (HMSO, 1994).

Department of Health *Implementing Caring for People, Impressions of the First Year* (HMSO, 1994).

Department of Health *Long-Term Care for Elderly People: Purchasing, Providing and Quality* (HMSO, 1992).

Department of Health *Monitoring and Development: First Impressions, April–September 1993* (HMSO, 19984).

Department of Health *Partnership in Action – New Opportunities for Joint Working between Health and Social Services* (HMSO, 1998).

Department of Health *Patient's Charter* (HMSO, 1991).

Department of Health *Quality and Inspection* (HMSO, 1992).

Department of Health/Social Services Inspectorate *Houses Are For Living In* (HMSO, 1989).

Department of Social Security *The Way Ahead – Benefits for Disabled People* (Cmnd 917) (HMSO, 1990).

Department of Social Work and the Law School *Ethical Dilemmas and Administrative Justice* (University of Hull, 2000).

Diba, R *Meeting the Costs of Continuing Care: Public Views and Perceptions* (Joseph Rowntree Foundation, 1996).

Dimond, B 'How Far Can You Go?' (*Health Service Journal*, 14 April 1994).

Dimond, B *Legal Aspects of Care in the Community* (Macmillan, 1997).

Disability Alliance *Disability Rights Handbook 1995/6*.

Easterbrook, L *Funding Long-Term Care: Reshaping the Debate* (King's Fund, 2000).

Eastman, M *Old Age Abuse*, 2nd edn (Age Concern, 1994).

Eekelar, J and Pearl, D (eds) *An Ageing World: Dilemmas and Challenges for Law and Social Policy* (Oxford University Press, 1989).

Ellis, K *Squaring The Circle: User and Carer Participation in Needs Assessment* (Joseph Rowntree Foundation, 1993).

Exchange of Ageing *Law and Ethics: A Study of Legislation Affecting Older People in Developed and Developing Countries.*

Finch and Elam *Managing Money in Later Life* (DSS, 1995).

Fordham, M *Judicial Review Handbook* (Hart, 1997).

Fruin, T *Finding and Funding Residential Care* (Kogan Page, 1995).

Glendinning *The Costs of Informal Care* (1992).

Gordon, R 'Challenging Community Care Assessments' (*Legal Action*, August 1993), p 8.

Gordon, R *Community Care Assessments* (Longman, 1993).

Greengross, S *The Law and Vulnerable Elderly People* (Age Concern, 1986).

Griffiths, A, Grimes, R and Roberts, G *The Law and Elderly People* (1995).

Griffiths, R (Chairman) *Community Care: Agenda For Action* (1988).

Hancock, R *Charging for Care in Later Life* (Nuffield Community Care Studies Unit, University of Leicester, 1999).

Harding, T, Meredith, B, Wistow, G *Options for Long Term Care* (HMSO, 1996).

Hardy, B, Wistow, G, Leedham, I *An Analysis of a Sample of English Community Care Plans 1993/94* (Community Care Division, Nuffield Institute of Health, 1994).

Health Committee *Long-Term Care: Future Provision and Funding. Third Report*, Vol 1, HC 59–1 (Stationery Office, 1996).

Health Committee *The Relationship Between Health and Social Services. First Report*, Vol 1, HC 74–1 (Stationery Office, 1999).

Health Service Commisioner *Report on failure to provide long-term NHS care for a brain-damaged patient* (HMSO, 1994).

Health Service Commissioner for England and Wales and for Scotland *Annual Report for 1993–94 and 1994–95.*

Henwood, M *Community Care and Elderly People* (FPSC, 1990).

Henwood, M, Wistow, G *Hospital Discharge and Community Care: Early Days* (Nuffield Institute of Health Care Studies, 1994).

Henwood, M, Wistow, G *Monitoring Community Care: A Review* (Nuffield Institute of Health Care Studies, 1994).

Hills, J *The Future of Welfare* (Joseph Rowntree Foundation, 1993).

Hinton, C *Using Your Home as Capital* (Age Concern, 1994).

Housing Association Ombudsman Annual Report 1993–1994 (1995).

Johnson, E *Getting The Message: Users' and Carers' Experience of Community Care in Leeds* (Leeds CHC, 1995).

Jones, R *Encyclopedia of Social Services and Child Care Law* (Sweet & Maxwell, 1993).

Jones, R *Registered Homes Act Manual*, 2nd edn (Sweet & Maxwell, 1993).

Joseph Rowntree Foundation *The Cost of Care: The Impact of Charging Policy on the Lives of Disabled People* (Policy Press, 1996).

Joseph Rowntree Foundation *Housing Research Findings 123: Adaptations and Disability* (September 1994).

Joseph Rowntree Foundation *Housing Research Findings 135: Housing Management, Community Care and CCT* (February 1995).

Joseph Rowntree Foundation *Housing Summary 6: Financing User Choice in Housing and Community Care* (October 1994).

Kennedy, I and Grubb, A *Medical Law*, 3rd edn (Butterworths, 2000).

Laing, W *A Fair Price for Care?* (Joseph Rowntree Foundation, 1998).

Laing, W *Financing Long-Term Care* (Age Concern, 1994).

Law Commission *Mental Incapacity* (1995).

Law Commission *Mentally Incapacitated Adults and Decision Making: A New Jurisdiction* (1983).

Law Society *Gifts of Property: Implications for Future Liability to Pay for Long-Term Care: Guidelines for Solicitors* (1995).

Leat, D *Re-development of Community Care for the Independent Sector* (Policy Studies Institute, 1993).

Leathier, P and Mackintosh, S 'Adaptations for Disability' *Housing Research Findings* 123 (Joseph Rowntree Foundation, 1994).

Leeds Community Health Council *Getting the Message: Users' and Carers' Experience of Community Care in Leeds* (1995).

Letts, P *Managing Other People's Money* (Age Concern, 1990).

Longley, D *Public Law and Health Service Accountability* (Open University Press, 1993).

McCafferty *Living Independently: A Study of the Housing Needs of Elderly and Disabled People* (DoE, HMSO, 1994).

McDonald, A and Taylor, M *The Law and Elderly People* (Sweet & Maxwell, 1995).

McGlone, F *Disability and Dependency in Old Age* (Family Policy Studies Centre, 1992).

McGlone, F and Cronin, N *A Crisis in Care?* (Family Policy Studies Centre, 1994).

McKewan, E *Some Help with Care: Rights, Charging and Reality* (Age Concern, 1992).

Mandelstam, M *An A–Z of Community Care Law* (Jesica Kingsley, 1998).

Mandelstam, M *Community Care Practice and the Law* (Jessica Kingsley, 1999).

Mandelstam, M and Schwehr, B *Community Care Practice and the Law* (Jessica Kingsley, 1995).

Marks, L *Seamless Care or Patchwork Quilt: Discharging Patients from Acute Hospital Care* (King's Fund Institute Research Report, 1994).

Means, R and Smith, R *From Poor Law to Community Care* (Policy Press, 1998).

Meredith, B *The Community Care Handbook*, 2nd edn (Age Concern, 1995).

Mesher, J and Wood, P *Income Related Benefits: The Legislation* (Sweet & Maxwell, 1995/96).

Ministry of Housing and Local Government *Housing Standards and Costs: Accommodation Specially Designed for Old People* (MHLG 82/69, Welsh Office Circular 84/69).

National Audit Office *NHS Residential Health Care for Elderly People* (1996).

National Consumer Council *Charging Consumers for Social Services* (1995).

National House Building Council *Sheltered Housing Code of Practice* (NHBC, 1990).

National Institute for Social Work *The Kaleidoscope of Care: A Review of Research on Welfare Provision for Elderly People* (HMSO, 1990).

Neilson, W *Residential Care Fees: Defend the Assets* (Spinning Acorn, 2000).

Office of Fair Trading *Older People as Consumers in Care Homes* (1998).

Oldham *Moving in Old Age: New Directions in Housing Policies* (SPRU, HMSO, 1990).

Philpot, T (ed) *The Residential Opportunity?* (Reed Business Publishing, 1989).

Public Law Project *Challenging Community Care Decisions: A Briefing by the Public Law Project* (1994).

Richards, E *Paying for Long-Term Care* (IPPR, 1996).

Ridout, P *Registered Homes: A Legal Handbook* (Jordans, 1998).

Royal College of Nursing *Rationing by Stealth – A Review of the Legality of Health Authorities' Continuing Care Policies in England and Wales* (1999).

Royal College of Nursing *A Scandal Waiting to Happen? Elderly People and Nursing Care in Residential and Nursing Homes* (1992).

Royal Commission on Long Term Care *With Respect to Old Age: Long Term Care – Rights and Responsibilities*, CM 4192–I (Stationery Office, 1999).

Schorr, A *The Personal Social Services: an Outside View* (Joseph Rowntree Foundation, 1992).

Schwehr, B 'The Legal Relevance of Resources – or a Lack of Resources in Community Care' (1995) JSWFL 17.

Schwehr, B 'Rational Rationing of Community Care Resources' (1995) *Public Law* 374.

Smith, C, Preston-Shoot, M and Bradley, J *Community Care Reforms: The Views of Users and Carers* (University of Manchester, Department of Social Policy and Social Work, 1995).

Social Services Inspectorate *Caring for People: Progress on Implementation* (HMSO, 1993).

Social Services Inspectorate *Discretionary Charges for Adult Social Services* (HMSO, 1994).

Social Services Inspectorate *Inspection of Assessment and Care Management Arrangements in Social Services Departments: October 1993–March 1994* (HMSO, 1994).

Social Services Inspectorate *Inspection of Complaints Procedures in Local Authority Social Services Departments* (HMSO, 1993).

Social Services Inspectorate *Inspection of the Complaints Procedure: North York-shire* (HMSO, 1994).

Social Services Inspectorate *Inspection of the Complaints Procedure: North York-shire, July 1993* (HMSO, 1993).

Social Services Inspectorate *No Longer Afraid: The Safeguard of Older People in Domestic Settings* (HMSO, 1993).

Social Services Inspectorate *Partners in Caring* (4th Annual Report 1994/5) (HMSO, 1995).

Social Services Inspectorate *The Right to Complain: Practice Guidance on Complaints Procedures in Social Services Departments* (HMSO, 1991).

Social Services Inspectorate *Second Overview Report of the Complaints Procedure in Local Authority Social Services Departments* (HMSO, 1994).

Social Services Inspectorate/NHS Executive *Community Care Packages for Older People* (HMSO, 1994).

Titmuss, R *Commitment to Welfare* (Allen & Unwin, 1968).

Wagner, G (Chair) *Residential Care: A Positive Choice* (1988).

Warner, N *Community Care: Just a Fairy Tale?* (National Carers' Association, 1994).

White Paper *Caring for People: Community Care in the Next Decade and Beyond* (Cm 849, 1989).

Whiteford and Kennedy *Incomes and Living Standards of Older People* (DSS Research Report No 34, 1995).

Wistow, G *Inaugural Lecture* (University of Leeds, November 1994).

INDEX

References are to paragraph numbers.